THE HIKER'S BIBLE

Robert Elman

THE HIKER'S BIBLE

Doubleday & Company, Inc., Garden City, New York, 1973

ISBN: 0-385-04551-4
Library of Congress Catalog Card Number 74–175411

CONTENTS

Introduction

THE PLEASURES AND PITFALLS OF HIKING

The easiest and most natural of all outdoor activities, hiking and the allied adventure of camping are by far the most popular and fastest-growing recreational pursuits. The last official estimate by the Department of the Interior put the number of American camping enthusiasts at about fifty million; it's generally agreed that this figure (which excludes hikers who frequently go on rambling walks but do not camp out) is extremely conservative.

There are several reasons for hiking's ever-increasing popularity. First, because the romantic spirit of the adventurer lurks in the psyche of every human being, nothing is more fun than the exploring which is inherent even in a short stroll through a local park. Second, there is a feeling of pride associated with setting and achieving a goal, whether it's the summit of a distant mountain or a fishing hole at the end of a meager mile. Then there's the exhilarating sense of liberation upon escaping from the tensions, hustle, and crowding of business and modern urban society—getting back to and along with nature.

The small discoveries bring back a sense of wonder: a primrose opening or a bloodroot closing in the late afternoon, silver maple leaves turning up before a storm, a spittlebug frothing a plant stem to shield its eggs, or a spider engineering its web, a red-winged blackbird guarding its tiny territory from rivals perched on neighboring cattails. With the recent awakening of ecological concern has come a new interest in the outdoors. Hiking, a necessary adjunct of more specialized pastimes such as fishing and hunting, has now gained recognition as a sport in its own right.

But perhaps the greatest attraction of hiking is the apparent modesty of its demands. A healthy nine-year-old child of either sex can comfortably walk four miles—even with a light pack—and enjoy every step. That would be an hour-and-a-half hike, going along at perhaps three miles an hour or a trifle less, over reasonably level, unobstructed ground, and taking a five- or ten-minute rest stop every half-hour. With rest stops and time out for lunch—and without the encumbrance of a pack—a strong walker can cover 20 miles a day quite easily; after all, many housewives trudge almost half that distance without realizing it in the course of their daily chores.

Since hiking is intended to be a pleasure and not an endurance test, experienced walkers usually set an easy mileage limit, traveling no more than six hours in a day. Nevertheless, a skilled backpacker thinks nothing of making ten miles a day while toting a 35-pound load—or fifteen miles if the hiker is eager to reach a particular goal. Of course, a twelve- or fourteen-year-old youngster should have a lighter load—under 25 pounds. But that much weight is necessary only on week-long hikes, and the burden becomes lighter and lighter as food is consumed. A day's outing from home or a base camp requires little more burden than lunch, water, and snacks.

Hiking and camping are family occupations which can be enjoyed by everyone from children to the elderly if a sensible pace is maintained. Bill Merrill, a veteran forest ranger, tells of the time he was packing along California's John Muir Trail (a section of the famous Pacific Crest Trail), and when he reached Foresters Pass, at an elevation of 13,200 feet, he met two backpackers, each toting about 25 pounds. In the course of conversation, Merrill discovered that these two gentlemen were, respectively, seventy-five and eighty-two years old. While such heavy packs definitely are not recommended for elderly people, the incident demonstrates that hiking can be enjoyed by all age groups.

But this emphasis on ease presupposes a requisite degree of outdoor knowledge and proficiency as well as good muscular condition, good general health, and an observance of sensible rules. Hiking and camping can be difficult, even dangerous, if improperly done. The dangers include excessive fatigue, soreness, illness, injuries, exposure in inclement weather, and the possibility of getting lost—all of which can be avoided if you're in good condition, properly prepared, clothed and equipped, and know where, when, and how to go hiking. By covering all of these aspects of outdoor living, this book will help you maintain safety and comfort while increasing the joys of hiking—and it will also guide you to America's finest trails, trail systems, and hiking-camping areas.

If you're not an experienced hiker, you might as well start with the basic if startling assumption that you don't know how to walk. It isn't just a matter of putting one foot down in front of the other. There are techniques for walking, for climbing, for packing, even for resting, which will eat up miles without eating up your energy. Even if you are an experienced hiker, this book will endeavor to increase your knowledge of conditioning methods and camping procedures, the latest improvements in clothing and gear, and the tremendous new increase in trails, trail systems, organizations, services, facilities, and areas for hiking and camping.

Since sore feet and prickly heat or chilblains are not conducive to outdoor pleasure, let's start with clothing and related items of gear that are vital to the full enjoyment of hiking.

Chapter 1

CLOTHES MAKE THE HIKER

My preferences in outdoor gear will always be influenced by the recollection of one superb but blemished hiking experience. It was May, late May, and the crags we scanned weren't high enough to hold unmelted snow, yet my hiking companion pointed to a puzzling little white patch just below the rim of the nearest cliff. "It moved," Jack said as I raised my binoculars. "Must be a mountain goat."

"It's two," I said. "A nanny and her kid."

The mother was already shedding her winter coat. She was stained yellow here and there and as ragged as a bursting milkweed pod. Yet she and her stubby infant were beautiful in their serenity. We watched for several minutes, until the kid followed her over the summit and out of sight. Such encounters are among the headiest joys of back-country hiking, and we had our share that day near the coast of British Columbia: a blacktail doe bounding into a balsam thicket, a pair of Canada geese setting their wings to alight on a tidal flat, the darting flight of a ruby-throated hummingbird, the sun glowing through a prism of dew on elderberry petals.

But that day's most poignant memory is of pain. In a momentary lapse of common sense I had decided to wear my waterproof rubber boots. They were superb specimens of the modern cobbler's art—shin-high, resiliently cushioned, insulated for warmth in winter, yet roomy enough for the added coziness of two pairs of socks. Warmly recommended for short midwinter hikes, snowshoeing, ice fishing, hunting in frigid weather; but heatedly disdained for long, warm hikes. Laziness was my only excuse. I had worn them in order to avoid taking off and putting on my boots and socks for the fre-

quent stream crossings on this hike. (Despite manufacturers' claims, not many waterproof leather boots retain their touted waterproof feature permanently even if you spray them periodically with a commercial silicone waterproofing solution.)

As for avoiding the chore of removing the rubber boots for stream crossings, I was eventually delighted to take them off and soak my feet in cold creek water.

Our camp was eleven miles away, beyond the end of the winding gravel logging road we followed. There were stretches where we could walk along the turf at the side of the road, and that gave me some relief. But the last few zillion steps on shifting gravel were torture. Insulated rubber boots are hot and heavy, and they make the feet perspire (again, despite manufacturers' claims). To make matters worse, this pair was too roomy for the light socks I was wearing, and my feet slipped around in the approved manner for raising blisters fast. It was as if I wanted to prove that friction can set feet on fire.

My soft, ankle-supporting, Vibram-soled leather boots would have made that hike seem short but otherwise perfect. The right outfit, from head to foot, is that important.

Boots, Socks, Shoes, and Sneakers

It's fortunate that heavy, snug, knee-high boots have at last begun to go out of fashion, for in most cases fashion rather than practicality seems to dictate their construction. Many of the designers must be dedicated indoorsmen. On the other hand, a certain amount of ankle sup-

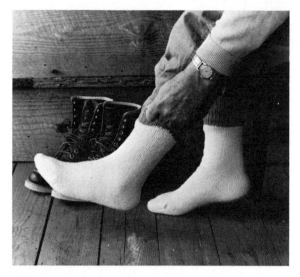

Hiker dons medium-length, pilè-lined L. L. Bean socks. Boots are well broken in and are roomy enough for very thick socks or two pairs of socks.

port is desirable for serious hiking, and low-cut, oxford-style shoes therefore have only limited uses. We won't overlook these uses, but let's begin with the requirements for the more versatile boots.

The most popular are those with five- to eight-inch tops. Even for walking in tangled brush or traversing difficult, rocky terrain, nothing higher than nine inches has any real benefit, and for conventional trail-walking five- or six-inch boots are the most comfortable of all. Many of the current models have scree-proof padded top edges—comfortable bindings that are *better* than high-tops for keeping out twigs, pebbles, leaves or other debris. Some also have stiffened or reinforced toes and heels, yet are reasonably light and have comfortably soft (often padded) inner surfaces. Some feature "speed lacing"—wide metal hooks, rings, or exterior tubular grommets instead of conventional eyelets for the laces. There are a few hikers who prefer eyelets because, theoretically, hooks might catch brush, but I've never found that to be a problem, so I believe the preference is a matter of personal taste.

Good ankle support can reduce fatigue and often prevent a bad twist or sprain. A five-inch height is sufficient for this support, particularly if the boot's ankle section is sturdily built. There are models with a light internal reinforcement

on the facing page—a good (though not essential) feature as long as it permits reasonable freedom of movement. A padded tongue can also help by making the ankle support snug without being too tight. Lacing boots too tightly will impede circulation. However, reasonably tight lacing is desirable—up to a certain point—with high-tops that don't give enough ankle support. To get this support where it's needed, without binding your legs excessively, pull the laces just taut enough to be snug but comfortable up to the top of your arch and tie them there in a square knot, then lace them more loosely the rest of the way up.

The best all-around hiking and camping boots are leather, with thickly lugged or cleated soles made of a composite such as Vibram. Leather heels and soles can be slippery enough to cause accidents. All-rubber heels and soles are better, but don't wear quite as well as Vibram. Hobnails

Mountain climber Mitch Michaud (*above*), using Himalayan backpack, is wearing mountain boots with scree-proof anklets. Other photo shows Raichle-Molitor rough-country boots (being worn) and mountain boots.

can be of help in high, snowy country, or on damp, mossy terrain but slip badly on smooth rock. Some mountain-climbing boots have special calks which are better than hobnails, but neither feature is needed on ordinary walking boots. Most of the modern mountain boots, by the way, are somewhat like ski boots—well reinforced and providing excellent traction, but too heavy and stiff for anything but their special purpose of climbing. Some lines of boots, such as the Raichle imports, include good compromise models for traversing very rough country.

Unless you have unusual foot problems or do a tremendous amount of walking on rough terrain, there's no need to spend $70 or $80 on custom-made boots. Prices of hiking boots range from about $18 to $60, with good five- or six-inch Vibram-soled leather models averaging from $20 to $25 or so.

In wet or boggy areas, the rubber-bottomed, leather-topped hunting boots made famous by L. L. Bean are excellent in either the six- or eight-inch height. Prices for lightweight models of this type begin at around $17. Such "shoe-paks" or "Sno-Paks" are also good choices for snowshoeing since hard-heeled boots can damage the webbing of snowshoes. But they don't give much ankle support or cushioning. You can make them more comfortable by inserting inner soles. Still, the best general-use hiking boot is the all-leather type, with or without an inner sole, but with an outer one of the cleated composition type. Good boots of this kind are available from many manufacturers and outfitters, including Bauer, Bean, Browning, Dunham's, Hinman, Sears, Vasque/Red Wing, and Wisconsin Shoe Company.

(*First row from left to right*): Eddie Bauer Voyageur hiking boot, Bean Mount Katahdin ladies' model, Browning ladies' Ridge Roamers, Dunham's Tyroleans. (*Second row from left to right*): Bob Hinman Rock Hikers, Sears Lightweight Hikers (with nylon uppers), Vasque/Red Wing Hiker II, and Wisconsin Alpine model. Note that all have padded scree-proof tops.

The limited uses of insulated rubber boots have already been mentioned. Pretty much the same observations apply to the nylon-and-rubber snowmobile boots with nylon zippers, which are an improvement over lacing in situations that don't call for firm arch support, but aren't designed for extended walking. Felt liners can be bought for these and other boots. In terms of warmth—for winter hiking or snowshoeing—the liners are superb. But after washing or when damp with perspiration, felt takes forever to dry out; if you use felt liners, be sure to pack an extra pair.

Insulated leather boots are wonderful for winter hiking, but even the best of them will overheat your feet and cause excessive perspiration during a summer hike. Such boots are also relatively expensive, so their purchase makes sense only if you plan to do a lot of cold-weather hiking or go on an extended winter camping expedition.

There are exceptions to the rule that allegedly waterproof boots are generally just water-repellent. Until very recently, the only waterproof boots I owned that lived up to the adjective were the nine-inch insulated hunting model marketed by Browning. Most of the older boots of this kind had imperfectly sealed seams, moccasin-style stitching around the uppers (an invitation to seepage) and soles stitched to the uppers in the conventional way, then "sealed" with cement. An impregnation of silicone compound was supposed to keep water out, but it just didn't suffice. The Browning boots, which cost a little over $40, have deeply cleated crepe soles sealed to the one-piece uppers by a hydrodynamic process, and the other seams are also well sealed. Lacing is done through large metal rings.

Now I've come across another exception to the not-really-waterproof rule, having acquired a pair of Dunham's Duraflex nine-inch leather boots—another insulated, waterproof hunting model. Instead of metal rings, these have delightfully oversized lacing eyelets that are just as quick to use. They cost about $40, but a version without insulation can be bought for just over half as much, and there are six-inch models which will appeal to the majority of hikers.

Since the waterproofing is guaranteed for the life of these boots (unless you cut or otherwise damage them), I tested them by leaving them

Author tests his waterproof Dunham's boots by weighting them with rocks and keeping them immersed to the ankles in water for three days. They haven't leaked yet.

immersed in water up to the ankles for several days. They didn't let in a drop. Just for insurance, I plan to treat them with occasional silicone applications, but they do live up to the ads. One secret of their success is that a silicone preparation is tanned right into the leather; another is that the seams are really sealed watertight, and added protection is furnished by a soft glove-leather lining. But the most important factor may be that the well-cleated soles are vulcanized to the uppers. It's likely that more and more makers will adopt vulcanized seals.

I'm not saying that the Dunhams and Brownings are the only truly waterproof leather boots—just that they're the only ones I can vouch for on the basis of personal experience. My shopping advice is to look for well-known brands and features like those I've described. Boots with one-piece uppers rather than a moccasin-style seam running around the top surface of the uppers will be most likely to keep your feet dry. The fewer seams there are, the fewer leaks you'll have. Leather boots advertised as waterproof should have sealed seams, and the leather should be impregnated with a silicone compound (though the solution is not always tanned into the leather). Eventually the waterproofing is likely to dissipate but can be renewed by an application of silicone solution, sold at camping-supply stores. If the leather is kept in good condition, leakage can be kept to a minimum, though the boots may not remain absolutely waterproof.

Leather care is important. Waterproof boots should get frequent and generous sprays of silicone. Non-waterproof boots should be treated with grease or oil—preferably both. On a vacation or long camping trip, pack a small can of ski-boot grease and rub some into the leather at least once a week. Upon returning home, rub in neat's-foot oil. Both the oil and the boot grease will soften the leather and lengthen its life.

Never dry either leather or rubber boots by putting them very close to extreme heat—a campfire, furnace, steam pipe, or radiator, for example—as this will make them stiff and brittle. Electric boot driers are available, and on an extended hike or camping trip it's a good idea to have an extra pair of boots so that wet ones can be allowed to dry naturally and slowly. (Even if you don't get your boots wet, changing to another pair can sometimes increase your foot comfort.) For home drying without a commercial drier, you can use a very small light bulb on an extension cord—just insert it into the boot. A note of caution: This works well with damp boots, but very wet ones can burst a hot bulb. Also, make sure the insulating layer on the extension cord is in perfect condition since water conducts electricity. If you're not in a hurry, artificial drying is unnecessary; just stuff the boots with rags or paper to help them keep their shape. If leather boots become stiff, use saddle soap to clean and soften them. And treat them with saddle soap or grease before storing them.

Footwear for hiking should be roomier than the shoes you normally wear. For one thing, your feet will expand during a long walk, especially under the weight of a pack. It's not a matter of swelling—an uncomfortable condition caused by improper footwear and/or overheating or over-exertion—but a normal spreading effect. For another thing, all boots, even insulated ones, should be large enough to be worn comfortably with two pairs of socks or one very fluffy pair. In very hot weather, most hikers—myself included—prefer to wear only one pair of socks, but in that case they should be thick, loosely knit cotton ones. These will provide absorption, cushioning, and a cooling insulation. In cooler weather, inner and outer socks are a better bet. The inner socks can be light, thin wool, cotton, silk, or one of these materials woven in combination with spun nylon, but they should never be made entirely of any non-absorbent synthetic material. They should not be loose, because friction against wrinkles will cause soreness or even blisters. The best material for the outer pair is wool, or, on warm days, thick cotton. Again, the objectives are padding, absorption, and insulation. There are special boot socks with fleeced cushion soles; when these are worn alone, without inner socks, many hikers prefer to turn them inside out so that the smooth surface is next to the skin.

More will be said about foot care in the chapter on basic hiking techniques, but the most important tips involve the choice of socks and boots: Soreness and blisters can be caused by socks that are darned, or have holes in them, or are too loose or too tight, or are wet, or are colored with dyes that run. A boot should be roomy enough around the toes and ball of the foot to allow for spread and just snug enough around the arch and heel to provide support and prevent friction. Looseness in these areas will cause your feet to slide about with every step, rubbing up blisters. Unless you're certain (from past experience) about a particular boot type and size, it's usually wise not to buy them until you've tried them on while wearing two pairs of socks. Most people are comfortable hiking in boots a half-size larger than their "city shoes."

If you find that you've bought too large a pair of boots, you may be able to correct the mistake by inserting mesh inner soles. These also add cushioning and insulation, help keep your socks dry, and permit air to circulate under your feet. Many hikers consider inner soles essential.

The same tips regarding size (and socks and inner soles) apply to oxfords or other low-cut hiking shoes, which are fine for walks of moderate length on dry, easily negotiated terrain, particularly with no pack or only a light pack. Low-cut shoes are, of course, cooler than boots. They're best for "car camping" and are also excellent for walking relatively manicured trails, dirt roadsides, and plains or meadows with low grass rather than brush, rubble, and the like. They're fine around camp, too, of course, as are moccasins, rubber-bottomed canvas tennis shoes, canvas sneakers, or leather-topped basketball sneakers.

Moccasins, sneakers, or tennis shoes are also very good choices for canoeing. Sneakers or tennis shoes are, in addition, fine for short hikes on easy terrain—especially in hot weather—or for a temporary, cooling change of footwear during a long hike. Even better for these purposes are the L. L. Bean "Maine Hiking Shoes" which cost about $10 and are quite similar to ankle-high sneakers. They're made of army duck, with cushioned, arch-supporting, corrugated rubber soles that have a high, vulcanized edge running around the sides of the uppers.

Some experienced outdoor enthusiasts pack sneakers for wear during lunch stops, long rest stops, or for wading across streams. Barefoot wading in an unfamiliar stream can be dangerous, especially if the water is too roiled or muddy for you to see the bottom.

Underclothing and Pajamas

I don't wear an undershirt in the summer, though most outdoorsmen insist that a very light one serves as absorbent, cooling insulation—and of course it can be taken off if it becomes uncomfortably damp. If you're on the side of the majority, the coolest types are pure cotton, cotton-and-synthetic-wash-and-wear combinations, and the string, or net, shirts. I can't seem to grasp the scientific basis of all-weather string underwear, but it does work. Somehow the netting traps a layer of air next to the skin, adding coolness in summer and warmth in winter. Good net underwear is supplied by Gerry and Orvis, among others.

Women seem to get along just fine in the summer without anything but a bra between skin and blouse. In this era of women's liberation, many a Ms. dispenses with the bra, too, but my wife's advice is to wear a light one for hiking comfort. I bow to her judgment in this area and can only pass on her advice.

Obviously, the lower undergarments should be light and loose—never binding or warm—for summer hiking. Recommended fabrics are the same

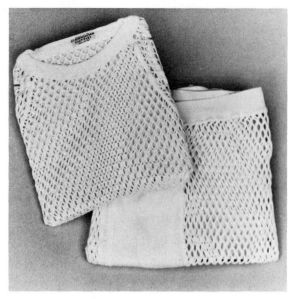

Net underwear like these Gerry garments work on "dead-air" principle to provide effective insulation.

as for the shirts. Men have the choice of boxer-type shorts or loose, light briefs. Women can wear the usual flimsy panty-type briefs in the summer, but in winter they will be well-advised to make warmth rather than femininity the prime consideration.

Cold-weather underclothing comes in sizes for both sexes—and for children, too. When it's moderately cold, conventional underwear will do nicely with warm outer clothing. When it gets a little colder, you may want to switch to long johns made of cotton, pure or combined with a synthetic, in a conventional weave or net construction. Some companies, such as Orvis, market solidly woven silk longs which are warm and absorbent without bulk and weight. Bear in mind that anything heavier than cotton flannel is rarely needed—and some people can't tolerate wool next to their skin.

In really frigid weather, net worn beneath loose cotton longs will let air (*warm* air) circulate cozily. A somewhat similar insulating effect is provided by "waffle-weave" cotton longs. And for the most extreme conditions there are two- and three-ply thermal longs, usually with a wool outer layer, cotton and/or other fabrics between the wool and your skin.

Quilted thermal underwear (most often nylon

filled with down or polyester foam or fiber) has lost some popularity lately, partly because of its bulk in comparison with other longs, partly because quilted thermal *outer*wear has replaced it, partly because a two-piece quilted polyester-insulated undersuit may cost as much as $40 and a down model as much as $60 or $65. A two-piece set of cotton-net or waffle-weave longs can be had for around $12, the three-layer type for around $15, and even silks for under $40. However, the quilted suits are great for hiking and camping under truly arctic conditions and for sedentary outdoor activities such as ice fishing or sitting in a wind-battered duck blind. For example, Refrigiwear and Utica Duxbak produce light, relatively thin polyester-filled suits that will keep you comfortable at temperatures down to 15 below, heavier models that remain effective at about 30 below. Eddie Bauer Expedition Outfitter offers down-filled models that have passed tests at 50 below.

For most winter hiking you won't need such extreme-weather underclothing, but it's wise to wear or pack a quilted thermal vest or jacket that can be put on between your shirt and outer jacket or parka. I have an old quilted Navy-surplus vest that cost me a couple of dollars;

Eddie Bauer Snowline Vest is one of those insulated with down. Insulated vests are also supplied by Alpine Designs, Comfy, Game Winner, Gerry, Hinman, and others.

when worn with long cotton underwear, a flannel shirt and a wool or quilted parka, it keeps me comfortable at temperatures down to zero—and it would be effective in still colder weather if it were one of the down-filled quilted vests whose prices start at around $20.

Relatively light quilted thermals have another use for which I recommend them highly: nightwear. They're great for lounging in a tent and unbeatable as winter pajamas. If you're using a heater or winter-weight insulated sleeping bag and the weather isn't absolutely awesome, you may actually find such pajamas *too* warm. In cool or moderately cold weather, clean cotton or silk longs, or a cotton-flannel sweat suit will be the best pajamas. If your feet tend to get cold easily, you can add a pair of fluffy socks or even down-filled boot socks. But don't get into the sack wearing socks you've been walking in; apart from the consideration of cleanliness, their fibers will have been compressed so that they won't trap and hold warm air.

On overnight hikes and camping trips in the summer, I can't see any sense in packing pajamas of any kind. Clean, light underwear is all I want between me and the sleeping bag.

Pants, Shirts, Sweaters, and Windbreakers

It would be interesting to know who invented trouser cuffs—and why. They're catchalls and catch-ons. A cuff snagged on a low branch or surfaced tree root can result in a bad fall. If your hiking slacks have cuffs, sew them closed or cut them off. Better still, wear cuffless pants. Bell-bottoms can be as annoying as cuffs for hiking. They tend to trail on the ground and get dirty. They also tend to snag exposed roots or anything else that's catchable.

Beltless pants are another poor choice. You want to have belt loops and a moderately wide, softly comfortable belt on which to hang small hiking accessories: a folding pocketknife, for instance, or a sheath knife or camping ax. You might want to hang a compass there, too (but away from any metal gadgets), or even a canteen if you don't want to sling a strap over your shoulder or lash it to a pack.

Very tight-fitting "western-style" jeans have two chief uses: to test the fortitude of cowboys and to test the efficacy of prickly-heat medications. They bind, they pull, they bunch, they make you perspire. As riding breeches they're fine, but not as walking pants. Reasonably loose jeans, on the other hand, are a good choice even if their legs are slightly tapered. Denims are tough enough to withstand hard wear and they improve with age, becoming lighter and losing any stiffness after a number of washings.

You want a fabric that will breathe but is closely woven to give some protection from thorns, insect bites or stings, poison ivy, oak, and sumac, etc. Good materials include denim, chino, drill, and poplin. Choose light slacks for warm-weather hiking. In the fall, medium-heavy twill, tightly woven gabardine, or corduroy is good. In the winter, wool is excellent if you aren't sensitive to it or are wearing long johns under it. For snowshoeing, cross-country skiing, or plain walking in extremely cold weather, there are also quilted thermal pants ranging in price from a little over $20 to more than $60 (depending on style, material, and type of insulation). For that matter, there are quilted thermal coveralls whose prices begin at around $65; less than that in children's sizes.

Personally, I don't like "walking shorts" even on hot summer days, because they furnish no leg protection. But many people go hiking, camping, and mountaineering in them. As with slacks, suitable materials include chino, poplin, drill, and so on. Bear in mind that a hot day may be followed by a chilly evening, and if you wear shorts it can be smart to pack along a pair of slacks.

When I plan to hike in real wilderness, especially on cool spring or fall days when I don't mind a little extra weight on my legs, I sometimes wear brush pants. Originally designed for hunters, they have reinforced facings on the legs—"double fronts"—which work more or less in the manner of cowboy chaps but aren't bulky or very heavy. These built-in facings shield you from thorns, brambles, scratchy brush, and so on. Utica Duxbak, Game Winner, 10-X, and other companies that make hunting apparel give you a wide selection of brush pants. The tougher the facings, the more expensive they are, but you don't need the heavy facings for a hike so you should be able to get a pair of brush pants for between $14 and $20.

Obviously, the foregoing observations apply to clothing for either sex. Some women like the leg freedom of skirts, and a skirt is all right for an easy walk over reasonably level terrain. But it just won't do for climbing, for pushing through tangled foliage, or for scrambling over obstacles.

Since your arms are as susceptible to scratches, sunburn, bites, and other irritations as your legs, short-sleeved shirts have limited use in hiking. They're fine under optimum conditions, but you can always roll up long sleeves. A shirt should be roomy enough for complete freedom of movement—particularly arm movement—and I like it to have pockets. Flap or zipper pockets are ideal for holding small items securely and conveniently. Almost any light, soft, absorbent, tough but cool material will do in spring, summer, or early fall. If your hike is to last more than a day, wash-and-wear materials are a tremendous convenience.

Depending on weather and your own preferences, you can wear a conventional shirt or a pull-over, sweat shirt, or even T-shirt. For a bit more warmth, I like cotton flannel or "chamois cloth." When it gets really cold, I often wear a wool shirt that has a lined collar to prevent neck irritation.

Summer temperatures can change abruptly. For evening wear and for hiking at high altitudes or during cool spells, a wool sweater, "shirt-jacket," or windbreaker is recommended. Sweaters have only one drawback—their lack of pockets. A windbreaker made of nylon or other tough fabric is excellent if it has enough pocket space. Some people prefer leather windbreakers, but they're rather heavy. A "bush jacket" with bellows pockets is wonderful when it's cool but not quite cool enough for a woolen shirt-jacket. And the latter is a blessing if you begin to shiver in the evening. Incidentally, a wonderful thing about wool is that it retains warmth when wet. In this respect, it's even better than down, which can become so matted and damp that it may lose some of its effectiveness after you've perspired for a couple of hours on a hard hike. This is why many experienced winter hikers wear a loose, down- or synthetic-insulated outer parka over a wool jacket or hip-length coat.

Jackets, Coats, and Parkas

In the fall, I like a light, short, quilted jacket

which permits freedom of movement and has pockets. If I'm chilly, I sometimes slip a loose bush jacket or cotton-duck hunting coat over it. Such a coat has plenty of conventional pocket space plus a roomy game pocket at the rear. Some models have a rubberized flap which zips, buttons, or snaps closed to form the game pocket; this outer flap can be let down like the "trap door" of old-fashioned long johns. When the flap is thus lowered, you can sit on it. This will help keep you dry if you sit on a damp log or stump or even in slushy snow.

For colder weather I prefer a well-lined, hip-length wool coat or mackinaw, or a quilted thermal parka with a hood. The hood should have a drawstring to keep it snug around the face and prevent it from catching cold winds. Some models also have drawstrings around the waist and/or bottom to hold in extra warmth. As mentioned above, wool and insulated apparel can be worn in combination, and there are insulated pants that can be worn with the other garments. It's a good idea to dress in layers that can be peeled off easily if the weather warms up a little.

In all cold-weather hiking jackets, coats, and parkas, elasticized inner wristlets and a collar that can be closed snugly are essential for retaining warmth and keeping out cold air.

Hats, Gloves, Mittens, and Handwarmers

Many hikers make it a rule to wear a light, visored cap or a wide-brimmed hat on sunny days. It's a good idea, especially if your face is easily sunburned. For most people, the visored cap is probably the better choice. A fully loaded pack frame can jostle a wide brim, and the wind can catch it and send your hat sailing, whereas a visored cap won't blow off as easily.

I've used the brim of a battered Stetson to scoop a drink from a spring, but I should have had a canteen with me, and I don't recommend drinking untreated water until you've boiled and/or chemically purified it. A better use for a hat or cap, when you come to water during a long, hot hike, is to moisten it and put it back on. The evaporating moisture cools your head delightfully.

In cold weather the best headgear is a visored cap or arctic cap with turn-down "storm flaps" to protect your ears and the back of your neck. For extreme conditions, an insulated cap can be combined with the use of a parka hood and perhaps a face-protecting wind mask or wind-mask cap. They're now being made of Orlon and other acrylic yarns which provide warmth without wool's scratchiness.

When it isn't cold enough for such clothing, but a cold rain is falling, you can protect your face and hands from chapping by thinly applying petroleum jelly—and there are also lip and hand balms that furnish good protection. Women whose hands chap easily can wear rubber dishwashing gloves, surgical gloves, or skin-diving gloves. In the north country, where black flies are a constant plague, you'll want to wear gloves and a headnet whether or not your skin is sensitive.

Gloves aren't just for warmth, and there's room in any pack for a light, thin, snug-fitting pair of golf or shooting gloves. They'll provide extra traction for removing stuck screw-off caps from jars or cans, and (after applying first aid) they'll help protect sore spots, cuts, blisters, chapping, or other irritations. Some people also wear them under mittens in very cold weather; when the mittens must be removed briefly to do some chore requiring dexterity, gloves prevent the hands from becoming excessively cold. Some mittens come with glove inserts, and there are models featuring a slit through which you can put your fingers when dexterity is needed. There are also several kinds of "one-finger" mittens which permit independent movement of the index finger.

Ordinary leather, wool, or acrylic gloves are usually sufficient on cool fall or early spring days. An excellent variation is the wool or acrylic glove with a removable leather shell. The next step up in warmth is the leather glove lined with fur, fleece, or pile. And the warmest of all is the insulated mitten, particularly with a glove worn inside of it.

Additional protection isn't needed under normal hiking conditions, but there are goose-down arctic muffs which have a neck loop so you can take both hands out. For camping in sub-zero weather, I suppose they are a help, but my preference for winter hiking is the so-called handwarmer which can warm you elsewhere, too. Probably the best known of these is the Jon-E warmer made by Aladdin Laboratories. It

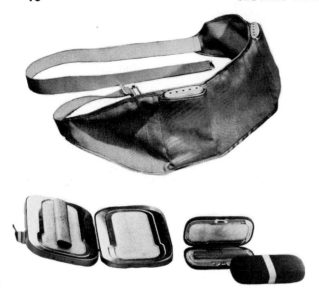

Hand- and body-warmers include Jon-E type with body belt (top) and White Stag Hotstik.

A recently introduced variation is the White Stag Warmer which uses Hotstik solid-fuel bars instead of liquid. It's made by Hirsch-Weis and, like the Jon-E, is available at camping and sporting-goods stores. You light a fuel stick with a match and put it into a fabric-covered metal case. It will continue to glow when the case is closed but won't flame or smoke. There's a hand size, which has an elastic safety band to prevent opening and which can be slipped into a pocket. It costs about $3.00; and a dozen fuel sticks for it cost about $1.25. A larger, body-warming size comes in a case that slips into a zippered pouch; it costs about $7.00, and you can get ten fuel sticks of this larger size for about $1.50. In the small size, one fuel stick provides heat for nine hours or so, the larger one for about twenty hours. Either can be extinguished in water. It emits a faint burning odor, but the smell doesn't seem to cling to clothes.

looks like a large cigarette lighter (and can be used for that purpose). You fill it with Jon-E fluid, which is much like lighter fluid and is available—as is the warmer itself—at camping and sporting-goods stores. After filling the device, you light a little wick and let it burn for about a minute to heat up the warming mechanism. Then you replace the metal cover on the gadget. The flame will go out, but by then a miniature flameless burner is working. You let it go on heating for about five minutes and then put it in a carrying bag that comes with it. Carry it in a pocket or wherever you choose. It will keep its heat all day unless you extinguish it. If your fingers get cold you can just wrap them around it, and you can light a cigarette through a hole in front of the little burner element.

The standard size costs under $5.00, and a giant one (which gives heat for two days without refilling) costs about a dollar more. For a couple of dollars you can get a body belt that will accommodate one size or the other. It has pockets for two warmers and is worn high over the hips so that the warmers are against the kidney area. This helps to keep your body comfortable, and you can always take a warmer out to heat up your hands.

Sunglasses

Winter or summer, if I don't wear sunglasses I pack a pair. Their value in the summer sun is obvious, but a lot of hikers don't realize that they can also guard against eyestrain and even snow blindness in the winter. My glasses have shatterproof prescription lenses and are fairly expensive, but sunglasses come in a wide variety of types and a wide price range. If you wear corrective glasses and don't want to spend the money for prescription lenses, you can get a clip-on or slipover type to use with your clear lenses.

Plastic-framed models to be worn with or without prescription glasses and featuring wide, "wrap-around" polarized lenses can be bought for as little as $5.00 or so. The Foster Grant Aqua-Mate sunglasses fit that description, come in several styles, and have the added advantage of floating. Polarized lenses are best for cutting glare, and floating sunglasses are obviously best when you go canoeing, boating, or fishing—activities that are often included on a long hike or camping trip. Several other companies, such as Bushnell and Mitchell, offer shatterproof lenses and metal as well as plastic frames. The prices range from about $8.00 to a little over $30 if you don't need corrective lenses.

Rainwear

For special activities, or in extremely wet climates, it may be worth while to spend $5.00 or $6.00 for a pair of rain chaps, or twice that for slipover rain pants. But the average hiker needs only a hooded rain shirt or jacket plus a hooded rain parka or a roomy poncho. The day of the expensive and heavy rubber types is gone and unlamented. Most of them are now made of nylon coated with neoprene, polyurethane, or a similar waterproof surface. They weigh practically nothing. A zipper-throated pull-over rain shirt, with drawstring hood and waist and elasticized cuffs, shouldn't cost more than about $15—well, maybe a little more if it also has pockets. A long zip-open parka with the same features might come to $20 or a trifle extra if you need a very large size. A good, big, hooded poncho—say 45×96 inches—can be bought for $10 to $15.

Each of these garments has special advantages. Even on a one-day hike, I often pack a rain shirt, just in case. It can be rolled up into a very small cylinder (like a rolled sleeping bag but with a diameter of only three inches or so). I tie it into a tight roll with the drawstrings, and then use the strings to hitch it to my belt at the rear. It's so light and small that I'm unaware of its presence until the need for it arises.

A rain parka can't be rolled quite that small, but it, too, can be carried at the rear of your belt, or rolled under or over your pack, or folded and put into the pack or between it and the pack frame, or rolled around a sleeping bag. It makes a small but serviceable ground cloth for emergency use, and in the rain it can keep you dry down to your knees. However, I recommend reserving it for wear around camp or for one-day hikes when you're pretty sure of wet weather but are determined not to cancel out.

When you're going to be on the trail or camping for several days or more, especially if you don't use a tent with a built-in ground cloth, a poncho is still supreme. It won't make quite as small a roll as a light parka, but some models fold into themselves—that is, they fold compactly into an integral pocket. A poncho gives full rain protection when worn with the snaps closed to form sleeves and with the hood up. When opened, it's a great waterproof ground cloth. It can also be draped over a pack and sleeping bag or other gear, and it can be tied or propped up at an angle to form a lean-to shelter against rain and wind.

Chapter 2

BASIC HIKING TECHNIQUES AND TIPS

The average human being stands and begins learning to walk during the first year of life, and most people walk several miles every day without realizing it. How strange, then, that nearly all of us walk incorrectly and know little or nothing about foot and leg care. If you're in reasonably good health, have a normal physique, and make use of the tips about to be set forth here, you should be able to complete the most arduous hikes without undue fatigue, muscle strain, or foot trouble.

Foot Care

With every step you take, minuscule particles of dust, fabric fibers, and other debris are ground against the skin of your feet. On some hiking trips, a complete daily bath is out of the question, but when possible, make it a point to bathe your feet (and legs) at least once a day, not only to keep them clean but to relax the muscles. Use a brush—a soft one if you have sensitive skin—to stimulate circulation.

Massage your feet and legs weekly, or at least occasionally, to improve muscle tone and circulation. Regular massaging with rubbing alcohol will help to toughen your feet. If you're not accustomed to long walks, you can toughen them further by massaging them frequently with salt or bathing them with epsom salts.

Keep your toenails fairly short but not uncomfortably so. If they're too long, the front edges will press against your socks and cause your toes to ache after a mile or two of hiking. Trim them almost straight across rather than in a toe-shaped curve, as this tends to prevent the corners from turning down and digging into the skin.

Before putting on your socks and boots, dust your feet (or the inside of your socks) with foot powder or talcum powder. If you're a tenderfoot, you can reduce the likelihood of blistering by rubbing a little moist soap onto the backs of your heels and inside the heels of your socks before powdering them.

Socks should not only be free of holes and darning lumps but extremely clean. On a hiking trip you should wash your feet at least every night, and change your socks at least every day. Even if socks have been worn for only a short time and don't seem soiled, they should be washed to restore their fluffiness; you want every bit of cushioning you can get.

If your feet ache at the end of the day, contrast baths—resting them in hot and then cold water—will bring relief. And during a rest stop at a stream or pond, you'll feel rejuvenated after soaking your feet for a few minutes in cold water. However, you shouldn't doff your footwear and plunge right in. Let your bare feet cool off before immersing them, because cold water on hot skin can bring up blisters on any sore or tender spots.

Dry your feet thoroughly by rubbing or by exposure to air before putting your socks and boots on again. A brisk rub with a towel has the advantage of flaking away any dead skin.

After a foot bath during a rest stop, the socks you put on should be as thoroughly dry as your feet. It's best to change into clean ones, but if you're conserving them, turn the socks inside out and dry them in the breeze—preferably in a sunny spot. Be careful not to let them wrinkle

"Shakedown hikes" or short conditioning walks are recommended to increase stamina and to check what each person ought to carry. Here, Mom totes full-sized backpack, teen-age daughter has light rucksack, and subteen son wears rolled rain parka (containing his lunch) at rear of belt.

when you put your boots on again.

If your boots begin to feel very tight, your feet are swelling, and in this event it's not always wise to take the boots off during a brief rest stop. If there's no cool water where you've halted, and you plan to be on the go again in just a few minutes, you may not be able to get your boots back on. During a stop of that kind, you'll probably be better off just to loosen the laces until they're comfortable. When there's no water handy at a rest stop, you can relieve aching or burning feet by lying on your back with your legs somewhat elevated and your feet resting on a log or pack.

The most frequent causes of swelling are overheating and ill-fitting or stiff boots. The best hiking socks are new ones, but the worst hiking boots are new ones. Break them in thoroughly before using them for long walks. The best way is to wear them for frequent conditioning walks—short ones at first—prior to a big hike. While conditioning yourself you'll also be conditioning the boots, which become more flexible and form themselves to your feet as they're used.

Never walk even a short way with a pebble, twig, or sand in a boot. If you don't stop to remove it, you may soon be limping. This is especially important when a backpack adds to the weight pressing on your feet.

If a callus or corn produces unpleasant pressure, cover it with a commercial pad before proceeding. If you feel a chafed spot developing, cover it immediately with an adhesive bandage to stop the friction before the irritated spot becomes a blister. Some hikers tape tender spots before starting out. Do the taping carefully to avoid the pressure of wrinkles or bulkiness.

After a blister has started to form, the tape will do more harm than good. Wash the spot carefully and prick the blister at the side to let it drain. Apply antiseptic, and *then* cover it with a bandage and put on clean socks. Change your boots, too, if you have an extra pair with you.

At the end of a day's hike, examine your feet, wash them, take care of any minor injuries, and then massage the leg and foot muscles to relieve any cramp and prevent them from tightening up.

The Hiker's Walk

A pamphlet distributed by Wolverine World Wide, a maker of good hiking shoes, notes that the human body is balanced on three points—the heel and the ball of the foot under the great toe and under the little toe. A 175-pound man hiking ten miles over level terrain "will bounce about 1,540 tons onto the soles of his feet at these three points." That's a lot of weight and a lot of bouncing, but the body can absorb it easily if the walk is correct.

The trouble is that almost everyone in Western civilization is taught to walk improperly. We all know that a pigeon-toed walk (with the toes pointing in) is unhealthy, but few realize that it's just as bad to walk with the toes pointed out very far. Toeing out is encouraged by just about every institution from Mother, kindergarten, and ballet class to the Army, yet toeing out puts a strain on the arch and shortens your stride. Your feet should be pointed straight ahead, because this forward-pointed stride, or so-called "Indian walk," is better-balanced, less fatiguing, and more efficient.

At first, you may have to practice it—concentrate on pointing your feet straight as you hike —but it's so comfortable and natural that you'll soon be doing it without thinking.

The average pace covers twenty-four to twenty-seven inches per step, though long-legged hikers may cover more ground, and shorter people (particularly women and youngsters) may take slightly smaller steps. The difference isn't great, but an average or short pacer can become weary keeping up with a long-legged loper. The youngest, smallest, or slowest walker may want to go first and set the pace.

The ground-eating trail pace of Indians and north woods guides is sometimes called a "swinging" gait, but the term can be confusing. It refers to the free and easy stride itself, accompanied by a slight, easy, natural swinging of the arms. The shoulders and hips should *not* swing. There should be no wasted or unbalancing movement. If you wish to develop great hiking stamina, begin—without a pack—by walking tall. The human being is the only species that normally walks erect. Perhaps it's silly to take any pride in that, but a proud carriage will help you do it properly, i.e., effortlessly.

A slight forward lean is of tremendous help when carrying a pack or when going uphill, but otherwise it's unneeded. The body weight should be balanced over the feet. Starting from the hip, swing one thigh forward with the knee relaxed and the toe pointing forward. Bring the foot down at a comfortable, natural distance ahead of the rear leg. The heel and toe touch ground almost together, but the heel comes down first. Try to come down lightly with the forward foot, in a smooth motion that reaches ahead and flows into the next motion of pushing up and off with your toes.

When you hit a rhythmical stride, keep going. Boys in their middle and upper teens have a tendency to walk at about four miles an hour —not to show off but because that's a natural speed for them. Youngsters with shorter legs, and adults who are unaccustomed to much walking, are apt to go a bit slower. The most common walking speed is about three miles an hour; with a backpack, two miles an hour is quite satisfactory; and when climbing steep terrain, a thousand feet an hour is a good rate of progress—a rate that will let you reach a crest or peak without being winded. These speeds are offered only as vague guides, however. Your lungs, legs, and body are unique, and you must develop your own stride, a pace that permits you to breathe naturally and reach your destination with enough energy left to pitch camp and enjoy yourself.

Avoid stepping on logs, rocks, or exposed roots. A small obstacle of that kind may slip or shift under your weight, twisting and perhaps spraining an ankle. Either hold aside any low branches so they won't whip back into the face of the hiker following you, or else maintain a safe spacing between members of the party.

Brief but frequent rest stops are recommended and can be used to ward off hunger as well as fatigue. In this case, family is sharing Trail Chef pineapple snacks.

Also be sure to call out a warning to those behind you if you spot a hole or other hazard.

When going uphill or downhill, shorten your pace slightly, for the sake of caution as well as to conserve energy. If a hill is quite steep, you can turn your foot slightly sideways as a brake and to get a firm purchase on the ground. A hiking staff can be a help in walking hilly or mountainous country. It gives you an extra point of balance and something to lean on when necessary, and it can help you push yourself upward or brake yourself when going downward. Some hikers drive a spike into one end of a broomstick, sapling pole, or whatever is being used as a staff. The spiked end of the wood can be wrapped with wire to impede splitting. The idea is to have something which can be driven into the ground for a firm hold, but I've never found any real need for a spike. As a rule, I don't even start out with a hiking staff but eventually, along the way, I pick up a fallen sapling

or branch for use as a staff. If it's too long, I break or whittle it to the desired length, at the same time trimming off any twigs or sharp protuberances.

Most hiking staffs are about shoulder-high or a little longer, but that isn't important as long as a staff is light, stiff, and of a maneuverable length. Grip it at whatever height suits you. If it's a sapling or branch with very rough bark and you don't want to bother peeling it, you can make your hold more comfortable by wrapping a handkerchief around the gripping area.

When going up a very steep hill, you may find the "lockstep" helpful: At the completion of each stride, straighten the lower, or rear, leg and rest on it for a moment. At the end of the next stride, repeat the pause, resting on your other leg. In this position, your bones support more weight than your muscles, so you won't tire as quickly as you will if you rest your weight on a bent leg. Occasionally, when going down a steep hill, you may want to use this trick in reverse, resting your weight momentarily on your straightened forward, or lower, leg.

Balance is obviously crucial when going uphill or downhill and is more difficult to maintain when wearing a pack. The only advice that can be given is to proceed cautiously, never rush, and do the natural thing—lean forward when going up, and slightly backward when going down (unless the weight of your pack is such that it might pull you backward off balance).

Most experienced hikers find that fairly brief but frequent rests are more invigorating than long but less frequent stops. The most common procedure is to stop for five minutes every half hour or every two miles. If the going is tough or the hike is long, you may want to lengthen these stops, resting for eight or ten minutes before pushing on, but too long a rest can sometimes stiffen muscles. Try to make the halts where there's something interesting to see or do, so that you'll move about at least a little after the first few minutes.

Your lunch break is one rest stop that must *not* be cut short. Although an occasional energy-giving snack along the way doesn't necessitate a stop, anything more substantial than a snack triggers a burning of energy during the first stage of digestion. Too much exertion immediately after eating can cause cramps. And even if it doesn't, exertion at this time wastes some of the fuel you've just taken in, thereby making you tire sooner than you would normally. After a meal, rest for fifteen minutes to half an hour before hitting the trail again. (Suggested snacks and lunch menus will be covered in the sections on trail and camp foods.)

Whether you space your rest stops on the basis of mileage or time segments, you should become reasonably adept at judging distances. This will help you not only in setting intermediate goals for rest stops but, later on, in giving or receiving directions, using landmarks for reading or making maps, locating campsites, gauging the length of time required to reach some goal (or gauging your ability to reach it), and locating caches of food or gear.

Many experienced hikers know how many steps they require to walk certain distances, such as fifty yards, half a mile, or a mile. Once they know this, they don't count off paces unless some special necessity arises—they don't have to, because they begin to know intuitively how far they've walked, and gauging distances also becomes intuitive. A mile consists of 5,280 feet, or

1,760 yards, or 63,360 inches. If you have a normal stride of, say, twenty-six inches, you'll cover a mile in a little more than 2,400 steps.

If you want to find out how long your stride is, you can simply take several paces from a marked starting point and then measure the distance you've covered. Incidentally, a handy measuring device for this as well as all sorts of trail uses is your belt, if you know its exact length and the distance between buckle holes.

Some hikers enjoy wearing a pedometer clipped to the belt, a belt loop, or side pocket. Good pedometers are adjustable (to compensate for differences in stride length) and they generally measure walking distances in quarter, half, and full miles. The indicator on the dial of a pedometer is connected to a small internal pendulum which swings with each step you take. Even good ones aren't precise since they record every leg movement—sitting down, rising, kneeling to tie a lace, etc.—but they're accurate enough to be useful, and they're fun if you're curious about distances traversed.

Since you have a normal walking speed as well as a normal length of stride, you can also judge distance by timing yourself with a watch. Do it at first over known distances to establish your average speed. Then you'll know that you generally cover a given distance in a given period—a mile in twenty minutes, for example.

New Haven pedometer, purchased from Orvis, hangs at author's belt as he measures hiking distance. Also on belt is small leather sheath containing sharp, sturdy folding knife made by Buck Knives—another handy hiking accessory.

Conditioning and Shakedown Hikes

Whether you're an old trail hand or a tyro, chances are that two weeks before a daylong hike or a longer hiking and camping trip is scheduled, you're sadly out of shape. If you're still in poor condition two weeks later, you may be in for a less than totally joyful experience. Actually, two weeks isn't nearly enough time to shape up, but it's better than nothing.

I know an outdoor photographer who is an avid mountaineer. For at least a month before leaving for the Appalachians, the Continental Divide, the Pacific Crest, Canada's Bruce Trail, or wherever, he and his son trot up and down the grandstand steps of the local high-school stadium for half an hour a day. I've read of another man, a city dweller who hardens himself for a knapsack trip by loading his pack with forty pounds of books and toting it up and down the stairs to his apartment twice a day. He lives on the seventh floor.

That sort of thing can be hazardous to anyone who is overweight, or has heart trouble, or any other physical disability of even a minor nature. If you're a hiker, it must be taken for granted that you have periodic medical examinations, follow your physician's advice, watch your weight, smoke as little as possible if you must smoke at all, eat sensibly and take regular, frequent exercise.

The exercise needn't be as strenuous as the examples just given, but it must amount to more than pushing yourself away from a table three times a day. If the distance to your place of business isn't too great, walk to and from work instead of riding. Even commuters can often walk to and from the station. Do your shopping on foot. Take time to walk an extra couple of blocks each day. If you like jogging, it's an excellent method of conditioning yourself. For those who don't feel up to steady jogging, the "Scout's pace" is wonderful exercise: Alternately dogtrot and then walk for a predetermined number of paces (usually from thirty to fifty). This is also a fine way to cover distance fast but without exhausting yourself when you're in a hurry to reach a campsite.

The best conditioning exercise for most people is a series of short hikes which serve as preludes to longer ones. Whether you live in the city or the country, you should have no difficulty thinking of pleasant two- to five-mile routes to interesting destinations. Try a walk of this kind on as many Saturdays or Sundays as possible, beginning with short distances and working up. After half a dozen such walks, most people are astounded to find that a ten-miler is a breeze.

On these conditioning walks, it's best to wear the same socks and boots you'll be wearing on the trail. And conditioning walks also provide an opportunity to break in new boots. Just bear in mind that your footwear is likely to be stiff at first and may be uncomfortable if you go more than a couple of miles the first two or three times out.

If you're planning an overnight or longer trek, it's a good idea to make your final conditioning walk a "shakedown hike"—a dress rehearsal. This can be especially important if you don't have much camping experience or if you're using new gear with which you're not yet very familiar. Wear and carry exactly what you'll be wearing and carrying on the big trip. (Sample packing lists will be offered in the section on packing.) Pick a reasonably close destination but one where you'll be able to unpack and practice pitching camp, cooking, washing, and so on. If this isn't possible, at least try a short hike with what you'll be wearing and carrying, then rehearse the camping procedures when you get home—in your back yard or on the living-room floor if necessary.

The importance of the shakedown will become painfully clear the first time you try to roll up a sleeping bag compactly, or operate a new camp stove, or erect a new tent. *Never* assume that the instructions packed with a tent will be clear. There is no doubt that the people employed to write those instructions must first pass a difficult course in doubletalk. Once you've deciphered the instruction sheet and have practiced putting up and taking down your tent a few times, you'll be able to do it in just a few minutes. Modern tents are wonderfully designed for fast, almost effortless management after you've mastered the step-by-step instructions.

Such problems are partly solved if you rent the gear you need instead of buying it. All kinds of backpacking and camping gear are now rented by many outfitters who also sell such equipment. The prices are reasonable, and renting has several advantages, particularly for inexperienced hikers. First, the supplier will be able to give you good advice about what kinds of gear—and how much of it—to take along on a given kind of trip. Second, he'll be able to explain or demonstrate the operation of any equipment that isn't accompanied by perfectly simple, clear instructions. Third, if you have only rare opportunities to go on long hikes, it may be more economical for you to rent some items than to buy them, and you'll also be saving storage space. Fourth, and perhaps most important, renting gives you an opportunity to try a particular style of tent, sleeping bag, pack, pack frame, or whatever. If you like it, you can buy the same kind; if not, you'll be forewarned to buy another kind.

Walking with a Pack

When you're wearing a pack, especially a large or heavy one, your walking technique requires a small modification. Lean slightly forward from the hips, so that the combined weight of your body and pack—rather than just your body—is balanced over your feet. If the bulk of your pack is sufficiently high, it will have the effect of pushing you forward. Let your arms hang or swing, and keep them relaxed. Try walking with a hiking staff, but continue its use only if it feels comfortable.

The newer pack frames come with well-contoured and well-padded shoulder straps and you can also attach a padded hip strap that helps to keep the weight desirably high while also relieving the shoulders of some of the burden. Nevertheless, you may find that the shoulder straps are digging in uncomfortably, in which case a small towel can be used as extra padding. Generally speaking, when you load a pack you should put more of the heavy items near the top than on the bottom. (See the section on backpacks for detailed suggestions regarding items to take along.) The idea is to distribute the weight up around your shoulders, where it will be most comfortable and least tiring. But bear in mind that this can easily be overdone, and a top-heavy pack can nudge you off balance, impede walking, and cause neck or shoulder strain.

Most hikers lash the rolled sleeping bag to the frame under the pack. The logic determining this placement seems to be that a sleeping bag is light for its bulk and therefore ought to be placed low. Also, you may want to unpack a number of other things before you need your sleeping bag. But some hikers prefer to lash the bag on top, and it doesn't make much difference as long as the weight is well distributed and you can get at items you may need along the trail. I have a pack with a very large top flap which I sometimes use to hold the bag in place on top. Occasionally I roll odds and ends such as toilet articles in the sleeping bag, lay the rolled bag on top of the open pack, pull the flap down over it, and secure it quickly by just hitching the two corner flap thongs through their rings.

While there are no hard and fast rules about loading a pack, it's obvious that any items you might need along the way should be stowed conveniently in the external pockets or up near the top opening. And anything with hard corners should be cushioned. Although modern pack frames are shaped to put a space between your back and the load, padding is especially important wherever a hard or angled surface might conceivably dig into you.

You can accustom yourself to wearing a pack by using one, even though it isn't really needed, on a number of short hikes. These walks can also serve as shakedowns, or rehearsals, during which you can perfect the best order of loading and unloading the pack contents. At the same time, you can get a better idea of which articles are really essential and which can be left out. On a one-day hike, the most you should *ever* have to carry is about twenty pounds, including food and cooking utensils; you can get along nicely with less than half of that—but since you won't be saddled with it day after day, you may well decide to take along various non-essential items. It's a matter of working out your own ratio of weight versus luxuries. On longer hikes, some men carry as much as forty or fifty pounds, and women often carry up to about thirty-five pounds, but the packs get steadily lighter as food is consumed.

A long walk with a really heavy pack can be a strain even with padded shoulder straps and a hip strap. On such occasions you may want to use a detachable tumpline—a wide strap that

Both hikers are wearing lightweight Sears packs, which are not overloaded, so they've decided not to unharness during brief rest stop. Man, carrying heavier load, rests bottom of pack frame and rolled sleeping bag on rocks behind him to take all weight off his back while he sits.

attaches near the upper corners of a pack or frame to form an adjustable loop. It goes over the top of your head or your upper forehead. This head strap lets your neck muscles do some of the work, shifting a good portion of the burden from the shoulder harness. A tumpline is needed only with extremely heavy loads or for occasional shoulder relief on a very long trek. It's actually a torment at first, but eases your work surprisingly once you get used to it. The Canadian voyageurs used tumplines to carry heavy bales of fur, but it is said that many of them drowned when they became entangled with a tumpline upon falling into the water. Practice releasing yourself from your pack quickly with any harness arrangement you plan to use. If you ever slip while crossing a stream, or lose your balance on a narrow bridge, you'll want to be able to release yourself instantly.

It's also important to experiment with all the strap adjustments until they're just right for your build and gait. They should not be bitingly tight, but they must be snug enough so the pack doesn't sway, tilt, or sag. This is just as important as getting the weight balanced inside the pack, because a swaying load can exhaust you even if it doesn't throw you off balance and cause a fall.

With practice, you'll be able to get in and out of harness quickly, but there's no denying that it's a bothersome chore. During short rest stops, many experienced hikers don't bother to doff their packs. You can get the weight off your body without actually removing it. Try sitting down with your back to a rock, log, or stump, for instance, and resting the pack frame on top of this support. Or sit or lean against a tree, with the weight of the pack shoved up against it. During longer stops, of course, you'll want to take the pack off, but for brief rests it isn't necessary if you take advantage of whatever support nature offers.

Guidelines for Trail Conservation

For the most part, America's backcountry is no longer a vast wilderness untouched by man. This is difficult to realize when you're far from any habitation, perhaps in an area where you would be lost without map and compass. Yet people have been there before you, and others will come after you. It's imperative to conserve the land and its resources, sometimes by practicing restraints that are not self-evident. The Appalachian Mountain Club has published a list of desirable restraints for trail users under the heading *Some Guidelines for Backcountry Campers*. On a long trip into a truly primitive region, some of the guidelines won't be applicable (for example, there are immense tracts where there aren't any of the designated camping areas or manmade shelters mentioned), but on the trails and trail systems maintained for hikers—not just the Appalachian Trail but others all across the country—these guidelines will go a long way toward protecting the environment:

CAMP IN DESIGNATED AREAS

The tremendous increase in backcountry campers necessitates controlled use. The woods cannot afford indiscriminate camping.

CARRY COMPLETE SHELTER

Shelters are often full. It is especially important that groups be prepared to camp at a shelter site outside the shelter . . . Boughs and branches should never be cut for shelter.

DO NOT DAMAGE GROUND COVER

If a provided shelter is full and a tent or other shelter must be pitched, pick a level site that is clear. Do not clear an area for shelter and do not trench around a tent. If a tent site is well chosen there should be no need for a ditch around it.

ALWAYS CARRY A PORTABLE STOVE

There is simply not enough wood left around most shelter sites for all campers to have a wood fire. Stoves must be used with care, but they are necessary.

USE THE WATER SUPPLY ONLY FOR DRINKING

The water supply, spring or stream, should not be used for any kind of washing . . . Leftover food should be carried out in a garbage bag . . . Wash with soap (not detergent). Dispose of soapy water away from any water supply.

USE PROVIDED SEWERAGE FACILITIES

They are provided for a reason. It is especially important that group leaders see that their whole group uses the facilities. If sewerage facilities are not provided, dig a trench with a stick . . . It need not be any deeper than one foot. When you break camp, cover the trench so that it cannot be found.

CARRY OUT MORE THAN YOU CARRIED IN

If all campers carry out extra trash we can keep the backcountry clean. Paper, plastic, cans and garbage should all be carried out. (There is no need to burn anything.) Every individual should have a refuse bag in his pack.

To these guidelines some qualifications should be added, for the advice regarding the use of a stove rather than a fire will be confusing to hikers who have ventured where campfires are permitted and expected. There are government and private lands where you'll be welcome but where a fire permit is required, so be sure to make inquiries before setting out. You may also have to comply with a few regulations. For example, the Forest Service expects people on extended trips to make campfires and imposes requirements to assure that they can do so properly and safely. When passing through a National Forest, therefore, mounted travelers or hikers leading pack animals must pack several fire tools: an ax with a handle at least twenty-six inches long; a long-handled shovel with a blade not less than eight inches wide; and a water container with a capacity of at least a gallon.

A fire should be kept as small as possible, and a container of water should be kept near it in case a fast dousing is needed. Food will cook better over glowing embers than over leaping flames, and a reflector will direct a fire's comforting warmth where desired without the danger of high flames. The ground under and around a fire for a distance of at least six feet on each side should be cleared of all brush, leaves, twigs, or anything else that might be ignited by a spark. There is no need to build a fire near a tent, sleeping bag, or gear; a reflector can radiate warmth beyond the range of leaping sparks. Before you leave a campsite (even for a brief period), make sure the fire is completely out; the safest way is to drown and stir it and drown it again.

Chapter 3

PLANNING A RAMBLE

The companionship of friends or family enhances the fun (and safety) of hiking, but it's harder to estimate the time required for a group to reach a given destination than to estimate the time needed for a solo walk to the same destination. This is another reason to begin with shakedown hikes. After a few trial excursions, you'll have a good picture of your group's speed, stamina, and preferences regarding places to go.

Those places are countless. Even in large, crowded cities there are green oases and unusual points of interest. The nation's largest city park, Fairmount in Philadelphia, contains over 300 miles of hiking and bridle paths. Another example that comes to mind is New York City's Central Park—840 acres in the middle of Manhattan. It stretches more than two miles from its southern to its northern end, and within its boundaries it would be easy to work out a circuitous route for a six- or eight-mile hike. In addition to parks, there are zoos and botanical gardens in many cities, and those with sufficient acreage are often ideal for half- or full-day hikes. There are also museums and historic sites that can be visited, but I recommend only short rambles in urban areas because walking on pavements is more tiring and less pleasing esthetically than cross-country walking.

For suburban families, an obvious and delightful compromise is a town-and-country ramble. A variation on this theme involves hopping into the family car (or a bus or train) and heading for the nearest green spot—a state park, perhaps, or a municipally maintained strip and pathway for hiking and picnicking. A town or suburban hike should be planned in advance if the area to be covered is unfamiliar. You can usually get a map and often some helpful advice from a local visitors' bureau or chamber of commerce.

Beyond city limits, the hiker's horizon really widens. In 1968 a Federal Law was enacted to create a National Trails System encompassing three types of trails: National Scenic Trails (major, long-distance routes); National Recreation Trails (shorter trails for hiking, nature study, riding, and other designated activities); and connecting, or side trails (for access and trail-to-trail connection). The Scenic Trails alone—those already established, those now being surveyed and marked, and those not yet officially designated but under study for future maintenance—total about 23,000 miles.

In addition, there are about 250 miles of the shorter Recreation Trails—twenty-nine of them, ranging in length from a quarter mile to thirty miles and mostly situated near urban population centers in nineteen states and the District of Columbia. In the National Parks there are nearly 12,000 miles of trails, of which more than half are well marked and maintained. In the National Forests there are at least 165,000 miles of trails. And these figures do not include vast tracts maintained by the Bureau of Land Management or the millions of acres of privately owned timberlands where considerate hikers are welcome. In addition, there are many thousands of miles of local, state, and regional trails. The last chapter of this book will be devoted to America's network of trails and suggestions for their use. Maps and information can be obtained from hiking clubs and conferences, state and federal agencies, campground operators, etc.; these sources will be listed.

A procedure that's becoming more and more popular is to set up a family headquarters at one of the many commercial or park-maintained campgrounds and set out from there on daily hikes. Today's campgrounds include facilities for

Rehearsals or shakedown hikes will enable hiking family to learn what gear may be needed on much longer hikes. In this instance, Harry V. Smith and family pack gear for extended campout at Highlands Hammock State Park in central Florida. (*Florida News Bureau Photo***)**

motorized campers and for those who travel by shanks' mare and backpack their shelters. Trail maps or maps of the vicinity are often available at campgrounds, but it's best to obtain and study your maps in advance. Besides, you may not want to restrict your hiking to mapped trails, parks, or other specially maintained areas.

Using Map and Compass

If you stick to a marked trail and have a map of it, you're fine. Otherwise, the first thing you need in planning a hike is a topographic map of the area you have in mind. Ordinary road maps are useless once you strike out cross country. Fortunately, the Geological Survey has thoroughly mapped just about every part of the United States. Sporting-goods stores, campground operators, and bookstores sometimes carry the Survey maps of local areas, but it's advisable to send for a map index of the state where you plan to hike. This index divides the state into small sections called quadrangles and lists maps for all quadrangles. The index is free, and the maps range in price from $.50 to $1.00. For a map index of any state east of the Mississippi River, write to the Washington Distribution Section, Geological Survey, Washington, D.C. 20242. For states west of the Mississippi, write to the Denver Distribution Section, Geological Survey, Federal Center, Denver, Colorado 80225. The maps themselves are available from the same sources.

You can get both large- and small-scale survey maps. To mark out a route through a sizable

Park walks and town-and-country rambles can be of almost any length and can be leisurely or invigorating. Here, Dad's pack consists of future hiker who weighs less than average backpacking load. (*Bureau of Outdoor Recreation Photo*)

Municipal, state, and federal agencies are building and marking thousands of nature trails which are ideal for conditioning walks. (*Bureau of Outdoor Recreation Photo*)

region, you may want a map on which one inch equals four miles, but chances are that you'll also want more detailed maps on which an inch equals two miles, or one mile, or (often most useful of all) 2,000 feet. Roads, foot trails, ranges, peaks, elevations, rivers, streams, and lakes are all marked clearly on the maps. Those depicting large areas will indicate divisions of land: six-mile-square townships and mile-square sections within those townships. Those depicting smaller areas at a scale of one inch to 2,000 feet will show the smallest details, right down to clearings and ditches—thus enabling you to determine exactly where you are if you know how to use a map and compass. Wooded areas are indicated in green, and brown contour lines are spaced at elevation intervals of twenty feet.

As a rule, maps issued by the Park Service, the Forest Service, trail conferences and clubs put more emphasis on trails, facilities, access points, waters, and outstanding landmarks than on detailed topography. Such maps are perfectly adequate where there are well-marked trails, but if you leave the trails it's best to have both types. Sources for trail maps as well as topographical ones will be listed.

All of the symbols on a Geological Survey map are easy to read, and the map's key will indicate its scale, date of publication (in case man or nature has made some recent alterations in topography), and declination. Simply stated, declination is the variation, or angle, between true north and magnetic north. This difference changes considerably from region to region on the North American continent. In central Maine, for instance, the declination is about 20° west; it's 10° or so east in central Texas and clear up through the eastern Dakotas, and almost 25° east at the northwestern tip of Washington. True and magnetic north coincide—producing a declination of zero—only along a narrow strip reaching from the easternmost point of the Georgia coast up through sections of the Carolinas, Tennessee, Kentucky, Ohio, Indiana, and then right through Lake Michigan. Since a compass needle points to magnetic rather than true north, it's necessary to orient your map and compass in order to get your bearings and find your way.

First, however—before you begin a hike—you should study the map of the area and mark the jump-off, or access point, from which you'll commence hiking. There's almost sure to be

Camping vehicle can be used as mobile family headquarters from which to set off on daily hikes. (Courtesy Winnebago)

some easily recognizable feature or landmark there, if only a trail marker, the entrance to a trail or the end of a road. Matching your location to a point on the map is the essential first step. Once you've done that, you should be able to find your way with no trouble and with no danger of getting lost even if you're not following a clearly blazed trail.

Mark your position on the map and then lay the map on level ground or on a stump or flat rock. Now place the compass on the map at that point so that its north and south markings line up with the map's north and south grid lines. Good topographical maps (including those printed by the Geological Survey) have a compass rose or arrow pointing to true north, and a shorter arrow angling out from it—forming a lopsided V—in the direction of magnetic north. Turn the map, with the compass on it, until the compass needle parallels the declination— that is, the short leg of the V. Map and compass are now oriented to your real position and you can proceed in the desired direction, as indicated by the map. (You'll check your direction of progress periodically if you're not on a marked trail or other path, but let's not get ahead of ourselves.)

Suppose your topographical map lacks the short declination arrow. In that case, place your compass on the map so that its north and south marks line up with the north-south grid lines, and turn the whole works until contour lines or symbols on the map are aligned in the same direction as visible landmarks. The declination is the angle now formed between the compass needle and its north mark. It's a good idea to draw this angle on the map for future reference. Of course, if you're using a compass that's adjusted for your area's declination, you simply place the compass on the map so that its north and south marks parallel the grid lines and turn map and compass until the needle points to the north mark.

You should never be hiking in an unfamiliar area—even a small one—without a compass. But in the event that your compass is lost or broken, you can still orient the map if you know your position and can identify a landmark or second point which is shown on the map. Just turn the map so that an imaginary line drawn from your position to that landmark on the map would, if extended, hit the actual landmark. You don't have to know your exact position if you can find two landmarks to work with. Just turn the map so that a line between those two points parallels an imaginary line between the actual landmarks, and the map will be oriented.

A good hiking compass should have an azimuth circle marked around its face or dial. The azimuth, or bearing, is the number of degrees (reading clockwise) from north, which is zero degrees. Since there are 360° in a circle, due east is a bearing of exactly 90°, south is 180° and west is 270°. When you come all the way around to 360°, you're at due north again, or 0°. A good compass also has a sighting line, pointer, or notch to let you sight it—aim it—at a distant landmark such as a mountain peak. Then you can read your bearing (your azimuth in degrees from north) from your position to that landmark. To keep yourself oriented, draw a matching line on your map and jot down its azimuth. That's the azimuth you'll want to follow to reach that landmark. Or perhaps you'll want to plot a course a certain number of degrees to the right or left of the landmark. The object is simply to mark your path both visually and on the map so that you won't become lost and can follow an imaginary

Small-scale map depicting stretch of Salmon River in Cascade Range is shown with Sportsman compass, which has declination adjustment, azimuth circle, and easy-to-use sight line. Map is marked with Ranger stations, trails, and terrain features.

trail if there's no real one, or, if there is a real one, know your location on it.

In addition to the magnetic needle, some compasses have an adjustable line-of-travel arrow which can be set to the desired azimuth. Once it's set, an occasional glance at it will let you maintain or instantly correct your course as long as you want to keep on the same bearing.

With the aid of a compass, a pair of landmarks can also enable you to confirm your position or mark it more precisely on an oriented map. First take a compass bearing on one of the land-

marks; that is, turn the compass until its sight line is aiming at the landmark. Now you have the angle from your position to one landmark and you can transpose it—draw a matching line—on the map. Repeat the procedure with the second landmark, and the two bearing lines will intersect on the map. The intersection is where you're standing.

If you haven't used a compass, all this may sound complicated. It isn't. Not once you've read the directions that come with a particular model of compass and practiced with it a little. When you're hiking, having marked your starting place and destination on the map, all you have to do is occasionally check your map, compass, and visible terrain features to remain on course. And a return hike along the same route will be all the easier because you've plotted the directions on the map.

Some compasses, like this one from Compass Instrument & Optical Co., have line-of-travel arrow which can be set to desired azimuth, and front and rear sights to help take bearing on distant landmarks.

Before starting on a long hike, incidentally, you should mount your maps by pasting them on sturdy cloth, and it's also advisable to carry them in a plastic envelope or other protective case. Otherwise, they may well disintegrate before the end of your trip.

Traveling Light—Gear for Short Hikes

In addition to the basic outdoor clothing, boots, rain shirt, sweater or jacket, cap, and sunglasses described in Chapter 1, there are a few essentials that you should have with you even if you plan to be home again by nightfall. To avoid forgetting something, many hikers make up gear and food lists, then check off the items before leaving home. In the section on backpacking, I'll provide suggested packing lists for longer hiking trips. For the moment, here's a list of items suggested for half- or one-day outings, with a few words of explanation or description accompanying each item.

Knife: Although a sheath knife or large folding model is useful on long camp-outs—and a hatchet or ax as well—a small folding knife is most appropriate for short hikes. It's useful for

dozens of jobs, from cutting luncheon meat to removing twigs from a fallen branch when you want a hiking staff. An excellent type is the Scout knife, a pocket model with several versatile blades including a can opener and screwdriver. This kind of knife has a shackle, or lanyard ring, by which it can be attached to a belt clip, but I don't like the bother of clipping and unclipping it. It's a pocketknife, and I carry it in the obvious place. Incidentally, there are fancy models that incorporate folding spoons and forks. These gadgets are strictly optional on a short hike—and on a real trip you'll have separate eating utensils.

Matches: If the weather is warm, and if you plan on having a sandwich lunch, and if you're absolutely certain of being home before dark, perhaps you can get along without matches. Those are too many ifs for me. I prefer to carry a waterproof container of wooden kitchen matches—the kind that can be struck against any rough surface. In case I need to light a fire in the rain, I like to dip the match heads in melted paraffin or paint them with nail polish. That way, the matches as well as the container will be waterproof. The coating won't impede lighting them. On the contrary, it will make them burn with a bigger flame. Wooden matches are best for starting campfires because they burn long enough to be an integral part of the tinder. You can buy a plastic or metal waterproof container for very little, and some types feature a small built-in compass. (I recommend it only as a spare compass; you should have a larger, more expensive compass for long hikes.) On occasion, I've used a metal film cannister as a waterproof match container—the 120 size, as 35mm cannisters are too small.

Candle and Fire Starter: A short candle makes a good emergency light and is also excellent for starting a fire when you can't find really dry tinder. As insurance, however, I also recommend carrying a fire starter. One of the best is the Metal Match Fire Kit introduced several years ago by Ute Mountain Corporation, and now sold by a number of outfitters, including Bean. Its basic element is an ingenious little metal stick, attached to a key chain to prevent loss.

To use it, you first pile up some fine tinder and very small, dry kindling twigs as you normally would to start a fire. Then, with a knife blade or any fairly sharp utensil, you scrape small particles off the metal match onto the tinder. You don't need many shavings, but keep them in a concentrated area for best results. Using the same knife blade, scrape the metal match with a fast, hard, downward stroke toward the tinder. You'll produce a little spray of sparks which will start your fire. A small Metal Match costs about $2.00, a large one about $2.50, and for about $3.00 you can get a kit including the Metal Match, an envelope of good tinder, a scraper for producing sparks, and a plastic pouch to hold the whole works. Other fire-starting preparations, including handy little "heat tablets," are available at some camping-supply outlets. They all seem to work well.

There are also three excellent kinds of home-made emergency fire starters. One consists of tightly rolled newspaper strips, tied into cylindrical shape, soaked in melted paraffin (which is inflammable—be careful when heating it) and cut into short sections—like tiny logs. The second consists of ordinary sawdust soaked in kerosene and kept in an airtight metal film container. If someone in your family is a hunter, an alternate container consists of a fired 16- or 20-gauge shotgun shell, which can be corked or slipped snugly into a fired 12-gauge shell; it won't usually leak, but tape should be used to keep it sealed. The third consists of ordinary fine steel wool, kept dry in any small airtight container. It works like fine, dry tinder, but is most effective in combination with a sprinkling of the saturated sawdust and a small, fluffy pile of natural tinder topped by kindling twigs.

Flashlight: A two-cell flashlight with fresh batteries (plus a pair of spare batteries) can be extremely important for emergency signaling as well as illumination. On longer trips you may prefer a larger flashlight or camp lantern, but a small one is fine for one-day or even overnight excursions.

Maps, Compass, Pencil, Paper: The importance and proper use of a topographical map and compass have already been covered. A pencil is needed to mark your map. I generally carry at least two conveniently stubby ones because I generally lose at least one along the way. I also carry a very small notebook or pieces of scrap paper, which are handy for jotting down notes about terrain or trail directions as well as observations of nature—and can be used as one more kind of emergency fire starter.

Canteen: Even if you know for sure that there's a safe water supply at your destination, you ought to have a full canteen in case you get thirsty en route, as you probably will. Both the aluminum and polyethylene canteens now available are light and very durable; take your choice. Of the two most common styles—bottle-shaped containers and flat, circular canteens—you can also take your choice. Some hikers prefer a flexible water bag; shape doesn't matter, as long as it can be slung or clipped in a convenient position and isn't awkwardly bulky. You need to concern yourself only with its capacity. I haven't much use for the little seven-ounce models, and

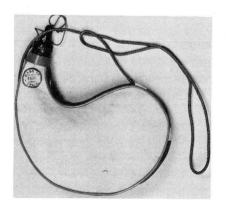

One- or two-quart canteen or flexible water bag is recommended. At left is Gloy's canteen, at right Compass Instrument's Spanish "bota."

I wouldn't tote one of the big four-quart "desert" canteens unless I planned a long trip in arid country. Water, after all, is heavy. For short hikes, a one-quart model will usually do nicely. On longer excursions you may prefer the two-quart type, but as a rule it isn't really essential.

Water Purifiers: If you start out with a full canteen and are headed toward safe drinking water, you won't have to worry about water purification on a short hike. However, it had better be mentioned here because it's a must on longer hikes or on short ones where you may have to drink stream or spring water. The safest way to purify water is to boil it for ten minutes. Boiled water tastes flat, but can be improved after it cools by pouring it from one container to another several times. It can also be improved by adding a little juice (or concentrated powder) of lemon or lime. For safe water in a hurry, you can use purifying tablets such as halazone, or a chemical purifying and filtering kit. Some hikers boil their water and then purify it as well, which is doubly safe.

Thirst Quenchers: If you're hiking where water is scarce, you'll want to conserve it. This can be partly accomplished by rinsing your mouth instead of swallowing big gulps (which can cause abdominal discomfort). But you should also have along some thirst quenchers. Believe it or not, sucking on a lemon or lime now and then will relieve thirst. So will munching on raisins or other dried fruit, which will act as an energy-booster at the same time. Make it a rule to have something of this sort in your pack or pocket. Sometimes the body doesn't really need more water, but the mouth becomes dry and causes a strong superficial thirst. It can usually be relieved by sucking on a washed pebble to get your salivary glands working.

Energy-Giving Snacks: Eating between meals is definitely recommended when you're on the trail. You'll burn up a lot of energy, and big heavy meals should be avoided even if you're very hungry because exertion after a big meal can cause severe digestive distress. In fact, it can put a strain on your digestive system and your heart. Snacking should not be overdone, either, but in moderation it can prevent both hunger and fatigue. Although candy bars, cookies, and crackers tend to produce thirst, they're good energy boosters and should cause no problem if

you also carry a full canteen and some thirst quenchers. "Tropical chocolate" and the high-nutrient candy rolls known as food sticks (available at some camping-supply dealers) are especially good in terms of energy value. Other recommended snacks include the dried fruits mentioned above, nuts, fruit pemmican, fresh fruit, hardtack, cheese, and wafers of various kinds.

Trail Lunch: In this age of sophisticated dehydration processes, freeze-dried foods, flavor-sealing packaging techniques, concentrated powders and mixes, and other wonders, there's no reason to eat poorly or monotonously on a hiking trip. Camp cooking and camp menus—including tips on what and how much to lug into the wilderness—deserve detailed treatment and will be covered in Chapter 8. But the less ambitious culinary planning for a daylong or shorter hike must be included here, because food may be the most important item packed for a ramble of that kind.

To begin with, it's smart to pack lunches in roomy plastic bags which can serve afterward as refuse bags. All refuse should be packed home for disposal. No garbage of any kind should be burned, buried, or left in any form in the woods. The population explosion has led to a hiking explosion, which, in turn, has led to a disgraceful litter explosion.

Chicken legs, thighs, and wings make a hardy lunch and they don't require much space. The same goes for a chicken sandwich—two if you're a big eater. Or a sandwich of meat. Or cheese. Or fish. Or frankfurters, or cold cuts. I like lettuce with my sandwiches, but to keep it crisp and prevent it from making the bread soggy, I pack it in a separate plastic bag and add it at eating time. The same goes for sliced cucumbers and tomatoes. Such refinements as mustard or mayonnaise needn't be sacrificed for fear of making the bread soggy, either; they, too, can be packed separately in small sealed plastic packets or tight-lidded containers. Potato chips are apt to be crushed if they're crammed into a small pack, but potato *sticks* are a nice extra treat. Fresh fruit makes a great dessert. If my pack is going to be full and I'm worried about crushing soft fruits such as grapes or plums, I simply take hard ones like apples or pears.

Hot meals will be treated in the chapter on

On short hike from base camp, members of Trail Riders of the Canadian Rockies take time out for lunch of easily packed and quickly prepared trail foods. *(Canadian Government Travel Bureau Photo)*

more ambitious culinary endeavors, but when hiking at high altitudes or during a cool season, you may want to pack along a vacuum bottle filled with hot soup, coffee, or tea. Be sure to choose an unbreakable vacuum bottle for trail use. In hot weather, you may want to take a vacuum bottle of cold fruit juice, iced coffee, iced tea, or some other beverage. You can carry milk that way, too, although it doesn't keep as well as most drinks. Before a hot-weather hike, I sometimes freeze a can of fruit juice or lemonade and take that along instead of a vacuum bottle. By about noon it has usually thawed and provides a refreshingly cool drink. After consuming the juice, I flatten the can and put it in the garbage bag. On the return hike, it's lighter and less bulky than a vacuum bottle.

Essentials for Cleanliness: Although soap is an obvious must for anything longer than a one-day hike, I usually do without it on short rambles. Instead I pocket a few of the small, premoistened paper washing napkins which are sold at drug and variety stores in individual sealed packets. I also take an absorbent towel in case I need it for padding or for drying off after cooling my feet, face, or hands in a stream. And I take a generous supply of facial tissues, which also serve well as toilet tissue.

Essentials for Repairs: I don't take along a sewing kit on one-day outings, but it's a good idea to pocket at least a couple of safety pins, and many hikers would feel insecure without a needle and thread. On longer trips, I do recommend a sewing kit, of course, and it should include a large, strong needle, a stout thimble, and heavy-duty thread for possible use on canvas or leather. I also recommend a kit for repairing rubber or other waterproof material. The traditional kit consists of rubber patches, a scraper to rough up the surface for better adhesion, and a tube of waterproof cement. However, the simplest and most compact kit consists of nothing more than a little Wader Repair Stick of the sort that Orvis sells to countless fly fishermen at less than $2.00 a stick. To make repairs, just heat the end of the stick with a match flame and apply a dab of the resulting goo to the rip.

Essentials for Comfort and Safety: There's no such thing as skin which is impervious to sunburn. And sometimes, when there's a little haze or the sun just doesn't seem very bright, the beneficial rays are being filtered out while the harmful rays come right through and cook you. Always carry and use an anti-sunburn lotion on spring, summer, and fall hikes—and on sunny winter days, for that matter. On cold, windy, or rainy days, carry a skin balm to prevent chapping. And, except in winter, carry a small plastic bottle of insect repellent. If an outing is to be so short that you feel safe without a first-aid kit, you should nevertheless pocket or pack a few small items to take care of any mishaps: medicated adhesive bandage strips (for possible blisters as well as cuts and abrasions); a blister-piercing needle if you don't pack a sewing kit; a small bottle or tube of antiseptic; tweezers for removing thorns or slivers; an elastic bandage for the relief of sprains; and some aspirin tablets. The towel previously mentioned for padding and drying can also serve as a tourniquet or small sling if the need should arise. You or a member of your family may want to add other items to this list on the basis of individual health needs—allergies, asthma, a delicate digestive tract, etc. In very hot, arid regions, you may also want to pack salt tablets, but they must be used sparingly; follow the directions on the label precisely. On longer hikes, you'll want to have vitamins and any other health supports your doctor recommends. A more complete first-aid kit, and other equipment and precautions for health maintenance on longer trips, will be described in the next chapter.

Optional Hiking Gear: Your own needs and preferences (and willingness to play the beast of burden) will determine to some extent what you pocket or pack on any hike, long or short. You'll

Small rips in rubberized gear can be fixed quickly by heating end of Orvis Wader Repair Stick and dabbing it on torn spot.

still be traveling fairly light if you take all the items I've listed for short hikes, but you may well strike some of them from your personal packing list. Conversely, the items I'm about to mention as optional accessories may strike you as musts. If you're inexperienced, pack the items that seem most important to you and start with short enough rambles so that learning by experience will be painless. After a few such hikes, you may add items to your list or delete some.

I feel that a pair of binoculars verges on being essential but doesn't quite make it. Though field glasses can be used for picking out distant terrain features, the mapped landmarks in most areas are prominent enough to need no magnification. What I like field glasses for is to get a closer look at scenery, plants, birds, and animals. Not essential, perhaps, but binoculars certainly add to the enjoyment of hiking. Most outdoor enthusiasts prefer fairly wide-angle binoculars in the six- to eight-power class (those marked "7×35mm" are just about ideal); greater magnification is unnecessary and cannot be achieved without shrinking the field of view perceived through the lenses. The price range of "good enough" binoculars is tremendous—from $35 or so to a couple of hundred. You don't need expensive ones for hiking. Pick a fairly light, compact, strongly built model that focuses easily for you, feels comfortable in use, and has a neck strap.

Some people prefer a small telescope to binoculars; this is fine if you get one with a belt sheath so you can keep it handy.

I'm tempted to list a camera as essential, too. It may not seem so when you start out, but when you want to record a once-in-a-lifetime sight, or still later when you're reminiscing, you may well reconsider. If you do pack a camera, you'll need lens caps and a case to protect it from dust, rain,

hard knocks, etc. And you'd better pack nearly twice as many rolls of film as you think you'll need.

Finally, I recommend pocketing or packing a small field guide to whatever interests you most —trees, wildflowers, animals, birds, insects, etc. It won't add much weight or take much space, and it will certainly increase hiking's greatest pleasure: the sense of discovery and recognition.

Some hikers consider binoculars essential. Here, backpacker views panorama from high Alaskan peak. (Leonard Lee Rue Photo)

Chapter 4

SAFETY, HEALTH, AND COMFORT

Accident statistics indicate that people are safer on the trail or in a wilderness camp than they are on city streets or at home. Unfortunately, this isn't very comforting in view of the high accident statistics for homes and streets. But regardless of where mishaps occur, they can usually be prevented by a little forethought.

Take the matter of ropes, which are a common cause of injury among hikers and campers. In the dark you can break your neck by walking into a camp clothesline, or take a bad fall by tripping over a low-strung tent rope. Some modern tents are designed to remain stable without any need for ropes except in high winds, and there are others that employ only short guy ropes, but I wouldn't choose a tent just on that basis, because ropes of one sort or another are a camping necessity. It makes more sense to abide by an important rule of camping safety: hang light-colored "warning objects" or reflector tapes from tent ropes, clotheslines, lines for hanging gear, or any other ropes that are strung up. Occasionally accidents happen during daylight as well as at night, and some hikers prefer never to leave a line up if it's not actually in use.

Strips of reflector tape can also be used to mark other objects or places of potential danger, including tent entrances and gear, as well as to mark a path to a camp latrine or any area that might be traversed at night and to blaze a trail during short exploratory hikes from a gathering point or base camp. Of course, these safety precautions are not a license to leave tape scattered in the woods. When you've broken camp and begun the return trip, the wilderness should look as it did when you arrived.

Safety and comfort are factors to consider in the actual selection of a campsite, too. Look for a reasonably clear, level spot with good drainage. If you do so, there will be no need to dig a drainage trench around your tent. (With a tent that has a built-in waterproof ground cloth, you'll seldom need a trench even on poorly drained ground.) On the rare occasions when a trench is necessary, a small one will do—perhaps five or six inches deep and a few inches wide. Try to fill it in again and leave no trace when you break camp. In addition to level, well-drained ground,

Lines strung from trees or—as in this picture— those hanging from tents should be marked with light-colored objects or strips of reflector tape if they're not taken down at night. (*Bill Browning/Montana Chamber of Commerce Photo*)

desirable features include a nearby source of water and fallen wood. (Living trees make the worst firewood, so there is rarely any excuse for killing them.) Don't pitch camp right at the water's edge, however, or in a gully or canyon. An unexpected heavy rain can then turn your camp into a swamp, and a flash flood can be really dangerous. As a general rule, high promontories should also be avoided because they tend to be too windy.

A good position for a tent is with its rear to a hill or some woods, which will serve as a windbreak. In most areas, facing a tent to the southeast will enhance your protection from strong winds and will give you morning sun and after-

Backpacker has selected good campsite at Buck Creek Pass in Glacier Peak Wilderness, Baker National Forest, Washington. Tent has been pitched in lee of mountain on reasonably level clearing. (Forest Service Photo by Jim Hughes)

noon shade. Finding a windbreak and facing the tent away from prevailing winds can be important in cold weather. In hot weather, on the other hand, you may want to catch the breeze, and you will want to locate it in a spot that's shady most of the time.

I don't like to pitch camp right under trees because they're lightning attractors—another reason to find a small clearing. But don't carry this too far. If you're the tallest object in an open field during a lightning storm, you're no safer than if you're huddled under a tall tree. In the event that a severe lightning storm catches you on open terrain, get low to the ground—prone if need be—wet perhaps, but safe. For the same reason, don't take refuge in an isolated shed or shack unless you know it's been lightning-proofed. Stay away from wire fences, too. Safe refuges include metal-topped automobiles and any sturdy human habitation with ventilator pipes, rain spouts, or lead-in electrical wiring. (But don't stand by a fireplace, as lightning sometimes skitters down a chimney.)

If a lightning storm catches you in the woods, almost any tall trees can be dangerous, but oaks are probably the worst offenders. Strangely, the beech is one species that seems to repel lightning. Beeches are very rarely struck, and birches are almost as safe, so these two species give some measure of protection in the woods. Better still is a cave, or a sheltered spot under an embankment or cliff. If you're swimming, canoeing, or boating when a storm hits, get ashore fast and stay low to the ground as you scurry for shelter.

Forecasting Weather

Printed and broadcast weather reports aren't going to help you much on a long wilderness hiking trip, when sudden and localized weather phenomena can take you by surprise. However, you can learn to predict changes with a reasonable degree of accuracy. The formations and colors of clouds are the most reliable indicators in nature. For $.25, you can obtain a booklet entitled *Clouds* from the Superintendent of Documents, U. S. Government Printing Office, Washington, D.C. 20402. If you study the illustrations in this booklet and practice matching them with the clouds you see, you can become reasonably proficient at predicting rain and wind conditions.

With or without the aid of that booklet, you can base your forecasts on a number of general rules. If rain starts quite soon after heavy clouds gather, the storm will probably be brief, but if it's preceded by a long cloud build-up you can figure on a long rain. More often than not, winds from the northwest, west, and southwest bring pleasant weather in the United States and Canada, while bad weather is more probable with winds from the northeast, east, or southeast. A cloudy sky, with the wind shifting from southwest to southeast, usually indicates an oncoming squall. Heavy, clammy-feeling still air can be the calm before the storm during the tornado season in areas subject to twisters. However, a virtual lack of breeze—as when campfire smoke rises straight up—usually means there will be no change in the weather for at least a few hours. If a morning rain is accompanied by a wind blowing from some point between northeast and south which then begins to shift westward, the weather will probably clear quickly.

As for colors, a dull "Indian red" sky at sunrise or sunset usually means rain will arrive, possibly with high winds, within twenty-four hours, but a pale rosy sky at sunrise or sunset means good weather. A faint lavender near the horizon at either of those periods, with clear blue above the clouds, also means fair weather. An amber tinge or a sunrise above a great bank of clouds warns of wind but probably no rain. Pale yellow does signal rain, though—within the day.

The rippled clouds of a "mackerel sky" mean wind (which is what causes the rippling), sometimes foretelling a gale. A darkening mackerel sky means a storm is on the way. So does a halo around the sun, or around the moon. A sunset gathering of high, dark thunderheads—alto-cumulus clouds—against glaring white sunlight is a pretty reliable sign of heavy rain the next day. But fluffy little white cumulus clouds herald good weather. So do wispy cirrus clouds. So do combination cirro-cumulus clouds—unless the wind is from a point between northeast and southwest, in which case a short, late-afternoon shower is likely. High, filmy cirrus clouds, shapeless or lengthening into streamers, signal an overcast day but no rain for forty-eight hours or more if the wind is from north or northeast; if it's from

southeast to southwest, the same formations signal rain that day or the next.

Dark stratus cloud cover—a blanketing effect —usually means rain is coming, and the high, dark, ragged cumulus gatherings known as nimbus clouds usually herald showers or a thunderstorm. However, if the wind shifts to the west or northwest, the rain will soon end and the temperature will drop. An even more certain indicator is a quickly changing procession of cloud formations; that's a sign that the only dry place will soon be the inside of your tent.

Dew (or frost) on the grass in the morning usually means you'll have a clear day, but if no dew or frost has formed you'll probably have rain before night. A rainbow in the evening is also a sign of fair weather the next day, though

If sky is clear and breeze so gentle that smoke rises almost straight up, weather probably won't change for remainder of day. (L. R. Wallack Photo)

Darkening "mackerel sky" usually means windy storm is approaching, and halo around sun or moon indicates same forecast. (Dave Elman Photo)

a morning rainbow often signals a later rain. During the day, a rainbow seen upwind foretells rain, one seen downwind foretells clearing. Some plants also furnish subtle indicators—the downward curling of rhododendron leaves when the temperature begins to drop, the upward turning of silver maple leaves before a storm.

The behavior of insects and animals also portends weather changes. Insects can sense changes in barometric pressure. Before a storm they fly low—staying close to protective foliage and ground cover. Naturally, insectivorous birds follow their prey. When swallows are soaring high, so are tiny, invisible insects, and the weather will remain fair. But when they skim low consistently, a storm is brewing. The only frequent exception to this rule is a low evening flight of swallows over water, when they may be feeding on a hatch of aquatic flies. Deer furnish a similar clue. They bed during the day in concealed spots on relatively high ground, but they'll head for thick cover on somewhat lower ground if rough weather is approaching.

People who spend a great deal of time in the outdoors begin to "feel" weather changes, antic-

ipating them as if instinctively. In reality, they're taking note of all these weather indicators and others without thinking about it.

Safety in the Heat

There are parts of the country where the weather forecast for a summer hike will be automatic: hot and dry. There's a venerable but mistaken belief that only light meals—salads and the like—should be eaten by hikers in a hot climate. Actually, it's best to eat normal amounts, including more high-protein foods than usual but avoiding sweets or any food or beverage with a high sugar content. During the daytime, alcoholic drinks should also be avoided. Do drink plenty of water but drink it slowly—especially if it's cold.

Another mistaken but widespread belief is that it's dangerous to exercise in hot weather. Mild exercise is good for you, because sweating is good for you. Just don't overdo it. Have salt tablets with you but, as I have already warned in the preceding chapter, take them very sparingly and only as directed on the label. Wear light, loose clothing. Try to stay in the shade as much as possible, and keep a hat on your head.

The fear of exercise in hot weather has arisen because too much exertion can cause heat exhaustion. The symptoms of this dangerous condition are a weak pulse, excessive sweating, pronounced paleness, and slow, shallow breathing. Strange as it may seem, the victim should be wrapped in a blanket, and a hot-water bottle or heated rocks will also help, as will rubbing to stimulate circulation. A person suffering from heat exhaustion should be kept out of the sun and should sip small amounts of a stimulant—coffee, tea, or liquor.

Sunstroke, the result of overexposure to strong sun, is quite different. Symptoms include a flushing of face and body, with the skin becoming hot and dry. Often the pupils of the eyes become enlarged and sometimes the victim loses consciousness (which does not usually happen in cases of heat exhaustion). If the victim is conscious, he should be given a cool drink to sip slowly, but *no* stimulants. He should be placed in a cool area, and ice or cold-water packs should

In hot, sunny weather, shading your tent can be important for safety as well as comfort. (*Florida News Bureau*)

be applied to his face, neck, arms, and shoulders. If at all possible, get him to a doctor.

Sunburn can usually be prevented by the use of a long-visored cap or wide-brimmed hat, sunglasses, long-sleeved shirt, and long trousers, plus liberal applications of anti-sunburn lotion and the realization that too much exposure can produce a bad burn even on a cool day. Be particularly careful about sun reflected from water, as that will burn you faster than direct rays. Treatment for a mild burn is simply the gentle application of a balm or salve, but severe cases require medical attention.

Safety in the Cold

Chapter 1 contained advice about insulated clothing for cold-weather hiking, but some other precautions should be added here. The first concerns another widely held but mistaken belief—the notion of rubbing snow on frostbite. Don't do it! Don't apply anything cold to frostbitten skin, and don't massage or rub it vigorously. There is little or no circulation in the grayish-white frostbitten area, as it is a spot of literally frozen tissue. Rubbing can bruise and tear the tissue and may even cause gangrene. Exposure to sudden or strong heat can also be damaging, and will be painful.

Frostbite most often strikes the face, ears, hands or feet—areas that are subjected to the greatest cold and/or have the lowest circulation. Insufficiently insulated clothing is often to blame, and fatigue or poor health will make a person more susceptible. A high wind speeds up the freezing effect, so try to avoid exposing your skin to it. This danger is why mittens and a face mask are so important for winter hiking in very cold climates.

The treatment for frostbite is gradual thawing. Apply warmth to the area as quickly as possible. It may help to cup your hand over it, or breathe on it, or place a warm arm or clothing over the spot. Get indoors, if possible, or into the warmth of a tent. Wet a handkerchief or rag with warm water and apply it gently. After you're thawed, you may suffer no ill effects at all from a mild frostbite, but it's best to have a doctor examine the spot when you reach home.

Chilblains is a milder affliction resulting from exposure to cold. It's a local disturbance of the circulation, causing the area to turn purplish. Symptoms also include burning and itching. In this case, too, the treatment is to warm up.

Always carry waterproof matches and fire-starting material in waterproof containers on a winter hike. As a rule, you should keep your head covered, for this helps to regulate your circulation—forcing unneeded heat down from your head to your extremities. But you can become uncomfortably warm during a strenuous hike even on a cold day; in that event, cool off by uncovering your head for a while.

Drink plenty of liquids, whether or not you realize you're perspiring. It's doubtful that you'll need to conserve water on a winter hike—certainly not if there's snow to be melted for drinking—but you will want to conserve perspiration. When you're active, your system uses three or four quarts of liquid a day, and you require at least two quarts a day to be certain of survival. Without sufficient liquid, lethal dehydration can set in after just a few hours.

Jumping about isn't a very good way to warm up if you're trying to conserve energy. A better method is to flex and unflex muscles, straining one muscle against another in the isometric manner to accelerate your metabolism and produce internal heat.

One of the dangers of winter hiking is the possibility of breaking through treacherous ice. Unless you're absolutely certain that ice is safe, stay off it. If you ever do break through and get your trousers wet (you certainly won't be venturing on ice over water more than leg-deep), you may want to pack snow on the wet areas to freeze them before the water can soak through to your underclothes. Then head for a campfire, tent, or other warm shelter as fast as possible, change your clothes and warm up.

Another danger is hypothermia, a deadly lowering of body temperature until your system no longer produces heat and energy. This is the condition that precedes freezing to death. With

Camping spots like this one at Arches National Monument in Utah are hot and arid in summer. Hikers should pack water, salt tablets, and high-protein foods. Canyonlands National Park provides area with 84 miles of trails through desert country where, in spite of green oases, spring or autumn hiking is best. (*Utah Travel Council Photo*)

Near Buck Creek Pass in Washington's Cascade Range, two hikers on Pacific Crest Trail quickly pitch protective tent at start of sudden late-summer snowstorm. In high country of Pacific Northwest and other regions, abrupt weather changes are normal. Essentials may include insulated clothing, heater, and fire-starting material. (Forest Service Photo by Jim Hughes)

proper clothing, shelter, equipment, and procedures, it will never happen; but the symptoms and treatment should be described as an added form of insurance. A victim of hypothermia begins to shiver uncontrollably, feels drowsy and confused, and begins to stumble or move awkwardly because muscle control wanes. As the condition progresses, the victim loses interest in food and water. At the very first symptoms, something warming should be ingested—if only heated water—and the victim should be further warmed by clothing, a fire, a heated tent or shelter, whatever means is available. Then, whether hungry or not, the victim should force himself to eat six or eight ounces of some high-energy emergency ration such as glucose or a food stick. The onset of hypothermia is dangerous, but warmth will quickly cause it to subside.

Maintaining warmth can in itself be dangerous if you don't observe safety precautions. Basic fire-making precautions were offered in Chapter 2. To these should be added a warning for those who—like me—prefer to build a fire in a stone ring or fireplace. Stones reflect and hold heat, and flat-surfaced ones provide platforms on which to set pots, pans, and other utensils. They also provide support for a grille. A well-built fireplace is almost as handy as the range in your kitchen. But don't use stones taken from a stream or swamp until they've had plenty of time to dry out; or at least don't let them get very hot. They may be porous enough to hold water, which can make them crack or even explode.

An even better reflector than rocks, and one that also can serve as a windbreak, emergency tent-type shelter, ground cloth, or insulating blanket, is the metalized plastic sheet produced by Thermos and known as the Space Blanket. This foil-like blanket is shiny enough so it can also serve as an emergency SOS reflector if a lost party is trying to attract searching aircraft. A large blanket of this kind (56×84 inches) costs about $8.00, weighs only twelve ounces, and folds up to about the size of a cigarette package. It's safe to use around a fire, but flying sparks can burn tiny holes in the metalized surface, eventually reducing its efficiency, so you'll want to string and anchor it at a reasonable distance upwind of the fire.

Neither a fire nor any ordinary portable stove should ever be used inside a shelter. There are wood-burning camp stoves (such as the famous sheepherder stove, a favorite among western hunting guides) which utilize a stovepipe and can be set up inside large, straight-walled tents equipped with a metal- or asbestos-ringed vent. But these are for use in big base camps that are kept in operation for long periods. Heavy equipment of this kind, generally packed in by horse or bush plane, is not for the hiker. Genuinely portable stoves—fueled by gasoline, kerosene, or propane and designed for backpackers—are safe only when used outdoors. They will be covered in Chapter 8.

However, there are several types of heaters for use inside well-ventilated tents. The older models, fueled by white gasoline or naphtha, are not to my liking because they require priming and preheating. Since this initial operation produces a high flame, such a heater must be started outdoors and can only be brought inside the tent after about ten minutes, when the flame has died down. Another disadvantage is that this type is not as precisely adjustable as

Foil-like Space Blankets are here being used as windbreaks, ground cloths, and insulating blankets. If weather turns severe, they can also be used as warming reflectors with fire or portable heater. In addition, their shiny surface can provide SOS reflector.

the newer designs. But like the others, it's available in models built on a catalytic principle—that is, it's flameless once it's properly started.

A second type is fueled by alcohol, is wickless (the fuel being held by absorbent material in a reservoir and heater head—something like the packing in a cigarette lighter), and has the advantage of not producing a high flame when first lit. It, too, is catalytic—flameless once started.

Most models are non-adjustable, but they come in several sizes, ranging from a little eight-inch-high, two-pound model rated at 3,000 BTU

up to a nine-inch-high, six-pound heater that puts out 7,000 BTU. Prices range from about $16 to more than $35, depending on features and size. Most of these heaters are more or less drum-shaped and have a detachable lid and a handle like that on a tea kettle. A couple of the Thermos models, though non-adjustable, can serve as efficient hot plates when the lid is left on. The adjustable Gloy's Heat-Pal models can be turned up high enough for cooking; they are not truly flameless, as the absorbent pad releases little flames like those on a gas range. But with the lid on, the tiny fire is completely shielded.

A third type is the very small heater employing an infrared element backed by a reflector, fronted by a protective grid, and fueled by butane or propane. Small models employing a disposable butane cartridge are offered by Primus

Some heaters which are safe and efficient: Thermos catalytic Safety Heater works on alcohol, white gasoline, or special Thermos fuel. When lidded, it can be used as hot plate. The Garcia Gaz butane heater (*above*) weighs less than one pound with fuel. The Paulin propane model can be turned face-up for use as portable stove. The very compact BernzOmatic catalytic propane heater utilizes circular head.

and Garcia Gaz for about $11 to $14. They're fine if you must have a light, tiny heater on a backpacking trip, but not as powerful as the infrared propane-cylinder models which are slightly larger and are supplied by such firms as Primus and Paulin. Primus makes one that's adjustable from 1,000 to 5,000 BTU, and Paulin makes several models, including a couple that can be turned up to 7,000 BTU and positioned

Catalytic propane heater such as Coleman model pictured here is excellent for warming up in morning, while preparing breakfast.

and consisting of a stand for the fuel cylinder and a circular head like that of the equally small infrared heaters.

Regardless of shape, propane "cats" use a special catalyst pad which is completely flameless, cannot flare up, and is well shielded by a grid. Some models not only have an on-off indicator but an automatic shut-off valve to stop the fuel flow immediately if the "cat" should, for some reason, go out or fail to light.

Rectangular propane heaters are a little larger and heavier than the others, with some models over eight inches thick, more than a foot square and weighing fourteen pounds. But they can be started indoors, they consume very little oxygen and they emit almost no carbon monoxide—additional reasons for considering them safest.

Nonetheless, *all heaters should be used only where there is good ventilation.* And I agree emphatically with the well-known outdoor writer Bill Riviere, who stated in *The Camper's Bible* that he doesn't like the idea of an unattended heater of any kind in the confines of a tent and therefore has "never felt completely safe sleeping in a heated tent." He uses a heater only in the morning and evening, or when lounging in camp on a cold day. For nighttime warmth, he relies on a suitable sleeping bag.

Even the use of a sleeping bag requires one safety precaution—especially in winter, when you're likely to use a heavy, thickly insulated model, perhaps snuggling all the way inside whether it's the rectangular type or a "mummy" bag. Forgetting this precaution can be fatal: *Do not get into a sleeping bag that has been dry-cleaned until you have thoroughly aired it.* Some cleaning agents contain carbon tetrachloride, which can kill if it's inhaled for a long period. There's a possibility of never awakening after breathing those fumes while asleep, yet the carbon tet is easily, harmlessly dissipated by a good airing. Some dry cleaners employ other chemicals which are harmless both to the sleeping bag and its user, so you might inquire about the cleaning agent beforehand, but I prefer to play it safe and air away all fumes. Many sleeping bags, including water-repellent and well-insulated ones, are now washable, but many others require dry cleaning. Be sure to read the directions and labels when buying a bag; washing a non-washable one can ruin it.

face-up for use as a single-burner stove. Prices range from about $20 to $30. When used carefully, these units are safe enough, but you can obviously burn yourself or ignite something against an infrared burner. I would use them only outside a tent—for warming up in the morning or evening, or for cooking.

The safest type of all, in my opinion, is the catalytic propane heater pioneered by Coleman. BernzOmatic, Coleman, Primus, Trailblazer, and Zebco/Traveler offer fully adjustable models fueled by disposable cylinders or a refillable tank. With some of these "cats," the volume of radiant warmth can be turned up to 10,000 BTU. Prices average between about $35 and $50. A heater of this kind stands upright, like the conventional electric heaters used in homes. Most are rectangular, but BernzOmatic makes a very compact model costing not much more than $20

Preventing Strays

Group and family hikes have become increasingly popular in recent years. This is a laudable trend, not just because hiking is all the more enjoyable with friends or family, but because it's safer. Forest Service booklet PA-887, entitled *Outdoor Safety Tips,* contains the following advice: "Travel alone *only* if you are an experienced woodsman. On the trail, keep your group together; don't let anyone lag behind. Make camp before dark. Traveling in darkness or during a storm may lead to tragedy."

This pocket-sized booklet, written for visitors to the National Forests, has 13 pages of other good tips on safety, first aid, survival techniques, etc. It's available for $.15 from the Superintendent of Documents, U. S. Government Printing Office, Washington, D.C. 20402, and I recommend getting it. But I think a couple more tips should be added regarding how to prevent party members from straying and perhaps getting lost.

More and more hiking families—especially those with young children—are adopting the rule that everyone on an outing must have a loud, police-type whistle. It can be kept on a lanyard, clipped to a belt, or pocketed, as long as care is taken not to drop or mislay it. If everyone is equipped with a whistle, all the members of the group can maintain contact with one another. The children will have to be taught not to blow their whistles needlessly, but then some discipline is important anyway, for hiking safety.

The sound of a whistle carries farther than the human voice and requires less effort than shouting. A whistle code should be worked out, and each group member should know the meanings of all signals. Keep them simple, and don't use three blasts for anything except "Help!" or "I'm lost." Three whistles, three gunshots, three smudge fires—three of any signal is the traditional, universally recognized SOS. Any stranger within earshot is apt to respond to three blasts (for which you might be very thankful), so use that signal for its intended purpose. Work out other signals for "Chow's on," "Come see what I've found," "Wait for me," "I'm coming," "Everybody out of the water," etc. Keep the signals simple to prevent confusion.

In addition to these precautions, train yourself and everyone in your family to watch the trail, be observant, note streams, hills, mountains, the lay of the land—memorize the route. Never rely on guesswork when you can consult your map and compass to check position and destination. Before setting out, leave word with someone about where you're going and when you expect to return. And always allow more time than you think you'll need to reach your campsite.

Getting Unlost

Everyone in your group should be thoroughly instructed about what to do if some day, despite all the precautions, a hiker gets lost. The first and most important thing to do (and the hardest thing to teach people) is to sit down and rest. Being really lost is less common than thinking you're lost. After giving yourself time to rest and calm down, you'll have less trouble finding your way.

Try to recall how you got where you are. You'll probably remember enough of the mountains, trails, streams, and other points of reference to figure out your location or retrace your steps to a known trail or previous location from which you know the way. If you're still stumped, climb a tree or other elevation and search for recognizable landmarks. But don't do any hazardous climbing, as this is the worst time to sustain an injury. From a tree or elevation, if you can spot no recognizable landmark you may see something just as good or better—a road, trail, building, smoke from a habitation, or other sign of civilization. Or a telephone line or power line. Or perhaps a waterway.

By now you may be unlost. If not, calmly think about whether the situation is a genuine emergency or just an inconvenience. If, for instance, you're pretty sure that other people are going to be coming along within a reasonable time, it's a silly gamble to do anything but wait. If you can't find your way to your original destination but can find your way to civilization, head for civilization and don't turn the inconvenience into an emergency.

Assuming that none of this reasoning has solved the problem, you must decide whether to push on or stay put and wait for help. The Forest Service booklet of safety tips lists the following conditions as reasons for staying put:

if you're injured or nearing exhaustion;

if the terrain is rugged;

if nightfall or bad weather is imminent;

if shelter is available;

if you know someone will be looking for you soon.

The advice is excellent, as are the conditions listed by the booklet as reasons for pushing on:

if you're still strong enough;

if it's still daylight and the weather is good;

and if there's a reasonable chance for you to get your bearings.

In the event that you decide to stay put, the first thing to do is to find or make the best possible shelter. You can live for more than a week without food and for several days without water, but several hours of severe weather can be lethal. You want to get out of the wind—off any exposed ridge or open flat. You'll be more protected on the lee side of a mountain, hill, or cliff. Even a thicket of trees or large boulders can serve as a windbreak. You may find a natural shelter in a cave or rock formation, under a blowdown, or behind big logs in a woods. (But if it's winter, make sure your fire won't be smothered by snow dropping from overhead branches.) Don't take shelter in a ravine bottom even for the sake of avoiding the wind; a flash flood caused by a sudden storm could drown you.

A natural shelter can almost invariably be improved, and if you find no shelter at all you can make one. Prop sapling poles against trees to make the framework of a lean-to, and then thatch it with evergreens or other branches and foliage. (The possibility of needing to build an emergency shelter is one more reason why a knife is essential hiking gear.) If you can't build a lean-to from available materials, you should at least be able to stick boughs and foliage into the ground or snow to form a windbreak.

Gather firewood next. If the forest is wet, you can get dry enough wood by splitting dead branches or other pieces that have fallen but have been caught by tangles well off the ground. Lacking any tinder, small, dry shavings from the center of such pieces will get you started. You should, of course, have a fire starter and/or a candle with you, as well as waterproof matches. Be careful to conserve your matches. When the small twigs and branches are burning well, add larger pieces to make a long-lasting fire.

Your heating fire can be turned into a signal fire. If the weather is warm or it's early in the day and you don't need a fire for warmth, you'll want to build a signal fire the moment you've arranged your shelter. Under some circumstances you may want two fires—one near your shelter, with a reflector propped up to direct warmth, and another with green branches or damp leaves to send up lots of smoke as a signal. But don't waste matches or firewood.

A smoky signal fire can guide searchers, and three of them in a line, with enough space between them to send up three separate plumes of smoke, will provide an SOS signal. In a large clearing, you may also be able to write out a large X or SOS, visible from the air, by arranging logs, rocks, gear, etc., or tramping letters in snow.

Hikers who venture into wilderness areas are well advised to include distress flares in their gear. Some types send up long-lasting, colored smoke signals and can be used to broadcast the fact that you're lost as well as your position. Others feature bright illumination or smoke which doesn't last long, but when you spot a plane searching the area, they're excellent for getting the pilot's attention and showing your position. A military-type pocket mirror (or any bright object) can also be used to flash an SOS. A flashing mirror can be seen from a surprising altitude and distance.

If you're in dry country and low on water, you'll want to look for a spring while awaiting help. Hollows on the sides of mountains are good bets, and the presence of certain trees shows that water is close at hand. Look for willows, cottonwoods, sycamores, box elders, alders, birches, eastern hemlocks.

Food is not as great a problem since, if you have none in your pack, you can get along without it for quite some time. In some areas, of course, you'll be able to catch fish or kill small animals or birds. If not, watch what the birds and animals eat because in most cases the fruits and nuts they favor are also edible for humans. Do *not* eat mushrooms (unless you're a genuine expert at recognizing the safe varieties); do not eat holly berries, either, or unknown roots and greens.

Wild onions and sassafras roots are safe, nourishing, and tasty. Edible nuts include pecan, beech, pinyon, hickory, and walnut. Acorns are also palatable if you first boil them well. Good edible fruits include blueberries, raspberries, huckleberries, currants, wild grapes, blackberries, cherries, chokecherries, pawpaws, and rose hips. Persimmons can be added to the list if they're fully ripened.

If, on the basis of all the applicable considerations, you decide to push on instead of waiting for help, the foregoing tips on fire, food, and water may be all the more important. Go slowly, heading first for a high, clear point from which you can view the land and plan your route. Mark your trail occasionally with directional pointers fashioned from rocks or branches. The pointers may help to guide a search party, or they may be useful if you should decide to backtrack.

If you don't manage to get back on the trail, follow a waterway downstream; it will usually lead to a trail, road, or transmission line. And, of course, transmission lines themselves are among the homeward-pointing signs to look for. Telephone poles and high-tension towers are often marked with consecutive numbers, and a countdown is likely to lead to a settlement. In any event, the lines will at least give you a path leading eventually to a road or other access point.

First-Aid Kit

Opinions differ widely regarding the ideal contents for a first-aid kit. Certain items will depend on your individual needs or those of family members. Someone with sinus trouble will certainly want to include a suitable medication though it wouldn't ordinarily be listed, and someone with tooth trouble might pack toothache drops or ointment. If any fishing is to be done during the trip, the kit should also contain a small pair of needle-nosed wire-cutting pliers in case it's ever necessary to remove a fishhook. The container should be sturdy (metal or plastic) and should latch closed securely. Generally speaking, it should contain the following basic items:

adhesive bandage strips (some with medicated pads) in small, medium, and large sizes;

three-inch-square gauze bandage pads in individual sealed envelopes;

one roll of inch-wide gauze bandage and one roll of two-inch gauze;

ten-yard roll of inch-wide adhesive tape (it can easily be ripped lengthwise when you want narrower strips);

sterile cotton;

safety pins;

small scissors (fly-tying scissors are better-honed than the manicure style and have larger finger holes; they're excellent for cutting tape or bandage and small enough to fit in a compact kit);

tweezers for removing slivers or thorns;

small magnifying glass (not only helpful in removing splinters, but an emergency device that can be flashed in the sun like a mirror to signal for aid, and can be held over tinder, with the sunlight focused through it to a pinpoint, to start a fire);

oral thermometer in breakproof case;

aspirin or other analgesic tablets;

salt tablets;

water-purifying tablets;

liquid antiseptic such as iodine or merthiolate;

anti-infective ointment or powder (such as sulfa or an antibiotic for open wounds);

spirits of ammonia (good for insect bites as well as shock treatment);

poison-ivy lotion (plus anti-bacterial cleanser or piece of laundry soap and rubbing alcohol to be used as soon as possible after contact with poison ivy, as described in next chapter);

Unguentine or similar unguent for burns;

boric-acid powder (for burns as well as eye irritations);

ophthalmic ointment;

lip or skin balm;

laxative and anti-diarrhetic (such as Kao-pectate);

tablets, powder, or liquid for indigestion.

I haven't listed a tourniquet or sling, as these things can always be improvised from towels, clothing, gear, etc. Needles (sterilized with a match flame) are often best for removing slivers, but they're included in your sewing kit. Incidentally, if you must remove a sliver from a child's skin, you can lessen the pain by chilling the area first with a cold compress or piece of ice, which works like a local anesthetic. For soothing insect bites or stings, you can use witch hazel or ordinary mouthwash, but a poison-ivy lotion such as calamine works even better. Another balm for stings and itches is a paste of baking soda and water; you'll have baking soda with your cooking gear, anyway, and it's also good for an upset stomach or to remove odors from pots, utensils, vacuum bottles, insulated coolers, and the like. (The odors are killed by a simple soaking in a water and baking-soda solution.)

Some first-aid kits also contain a few wooden tongue depressors (which can serve a secondary purpose as small splints) and some sterile cotton swabs. While I wouldn't add these to my own list of essentials, I'd certainly add a first-aid manual.

Another optional item is a surgical hemostat. Unlike pliers, this type of clamp locks closed, and it's great for removing porcupine quills. Because the quills are barbed, removal is painful—but absolutely necessary to prevent them from working farther and farther in. Snipping a bit off the quill ends will partially collapse them and make removal easier.

It's rare for people to be pincushioned by a porcupine, because it's easy to avoid close contact, but if you take a dog on a hiking trip the hemostat may well be wanted. You may have to tie the dog down before you remove the quills. It's much easier with a helper. One person straddles the dog and holds him still. A stick can be inserted in the dog's mouth sideways—in retrieving position—and pulling back on the stick's ends will help hold the animal's head still. An-

other technique is to tie a noose around the dog's body just in front of the hind legs, attach a rope from it to a tree limb and thereby hold his hind legs a few inches off the ground so he can't struggle so much while you work. Begin by removing the quills from the most dangerous areas—around the eyes, mouth, and nose. When a quill has penetrated the lip or tongue, it may be easier on the dog to push it on through the thin tissue than to pull it out. Pulling is more difficult and painful because of the barbs.

A snake-bite kit should also be included in first-aid equipment for wilderness hikes almost anywhere in this country. Chapter 5 will cover this subject in detail, together with protection from other seriously troublesome animals, insects, and plants.

Burns and Cuts

You're not likely to burn yourself if you heed the fire precautions that have been offered, and if you keep a water bucket, spade, and padded pot holder by your fire or stove. The pain of minor burns and scalds can be relieved by soaking the spot in cold water. If a blister rises, puncture it with a sterilized needle, apply an unguent, and bandage it loosely.

Severe, extensive burns are fortunately rare. They should not be treated with an unguent or any ointment, nor should absorbent cotton ever be applied to an open burn. If possible, clean the wound with distilled water. On the trail you would probably have to make do with drinking water (which has either been obtained from a safe source or has been boiled and cooled). Aside from contamination of the wound, shock is the major peril. A shock victim should be made to lie down, with the legs slightly elevated above the body. Clothing should be loosened. The patient should be kept warm, but no blanket should cover a burn as it may shed lint. Stimulants such as tea or coffee (not alcohol) should be given if the patient is conscious. A whiff of spirits of ammonia may help clear the victim's head. Never give an unconscious person food or drink. Get to a doctor—or get a doctor to the patient if the latter can't be moved—as fast as possible.

A few precautions can prevent serious cuts.

Some campsites, like this one provided by Weyerhaeuser Company on its timberlands, are equipped with chopping blocks. It's dangerous to stand logs on rocks or ground for splitting. If ax is left unsheathed, imbed its head securely in wood as shown here.

When using an ax to cut a fallen log, stand with your feet apart and well away from the wood being cut. When limbing a fallen tree, chop in the direction in which the branches grew—that is, from a point that would have been below the upward-slanting limbs, not above, when the tree was standing. When bending a sapling to make cutting easier, keep the hand that does the bending far from the chopping area. When splitting a log or other wood, never stand it on a rock or the ground. Use a stump as a chopping block, or lay the piece to be split lengthwise and propped up slightly in the crotch of a fallen tree or log. Then chop downward, not with a sweep back toward you. Never leave an unsheathed ax lying about; sheathe it, pack it, or, with a chopping stroke, imbed its blade edge firmly in a log or wood block. The rules for using a knife are even simpler—don't leave a sheath model unsheathed when not in use, don't leave a folding model open, and never whittle or cut in such a way that the blade can move toward your hand or body. The cutting direction is away from yourself, as when striking a match, and the hand that holds the work stays behind the knife, not in front of it.

Having taken all these precautions, it's still best to know what to do in case of a knife or ax wound. If the cut is minor, let it bleed for a few moments to clean out the wound. Then apply slight pressure just above it to stop the bleeding while you put on antiseptic, antibiotic, and a bandage.

For severe bleeding, more drastic first-aid is needed. First cover the wound with a clean cloth and apply direct pressure, using your fingers or the heel of your hand to deter the bleeding. When it stops, use the antiseptic, antibiotic, and bandage. Use a tourniquet only as a last resort. It is tied above the wound, kept tight for only a few minutes, then loosened. Repeat if necessary. If the wound is a puncture, it should also be treated with hot soaks for two days to reduce the possibility of inflammation and infection. But regardless of the type of wound, if it's severe the victim must be taken to a doctor as quickly as possible.

Artificial Respiration

You'll probably never have to restore a person's breathing, but you'd better know how. Apart from drowning and asphyxiation, various severe injuries can cause breathing to stop—and the first thing to do is start it again by mouth-to-mouth artificial respiration. Open the victim's mouth and make sure nothing is blocking the air passages. With the victim lying supine (unless water must be pumped out by rolling), pinch the victim's nostrils, put your open mouth to his and blow until his chest rises, then release. Repeat this twelve times per minute with an adult, twenty times per minute (and shallower puffs) for a child. Don't quit. Keep it up until normal breathing resumes.

Chapter 5

TROUBLESOME PLANTS, INSECTS, AND ANIMALS

A variety of plants will produce a mild, localized skin irritation, but severe skin trouble is commonly caused by only three species—poison ivy, poison oak, and poison sumac. In all three, the toxic agent is urushiol, a virulent substance present throughout the plants (in stems and roots as well as leaves). You can contract the irritation by touching a dog, person, or object previously brushed by one of the plants. The reason poison ivy patches are seldom burned is that even the smoke carries enough urushiol to be dangerous if inhaled.

But as virulent as the substance is, you'll rarely have any trouble if you simply avoid contact with these plants. Learning to identify them is the best means of prevention.

Poison Ivy

Poison ivy is characterized by sets of three pointed oval leaves growing from single stems. Usually the leaves have irregular indentations or serrations on one or both edges but are not as definitely saw-toothed as some triple-leafed plants. As a rule, they have a glossy or waxy-looking upper surface so there is little danger of confusing them with the rough triple leaves of many harmless plants such as wild raspberries and strawberries. The leaves are green, sometimes with a red tinge. When the plants are fruiting, they bear clusters of small white berries.

Poison ivy most frequently occurs as a ground vine or a tree-climbing vine, often with fuzzy fibers or clinging tendrils on the stems, but there is also a small shrub form which is common.

Poison Oak

Poison oak is actually just a subspecies of poison ivy, less common but perhaps more bothersome because the leaves can be mistaken for those of a harmless oak seedling. They are often slightly longer than poison ivy leaves, and the indentations along the edges have evolved into oaklike lobes. The color has more variation and may be more deceptive—green, green tinged with red, or autumnal shades of brown, orange, and red which also resemble oaks. The stems, too, are smoother and more oaklike. Of course, a real oak seedling has no berry clusters, but it's easy to be fooled by poison oak that isn't in the fruiting stage. If you're not certain about a plant, don't touch it.

Poison Sumac

Poison sumac is the least common of the three offenders and is fairly easy to recognize. It occurs as a tall shrub or small tree. Each set of leaves (actually leaflets growing on a central axis) is composed of seven to eleven bright green, pointed oval leaves arranged oppositely in pairs except for a terminal one that forms the stem tip. The leaves are smooth-edged, relatively long and narrow, and not as sharply pointed as non-poisonous sumac—but there are surer means of identification.

True sumac bears tight clusters of red berries, whereas poison sumac bears loose clusters of smaller, greenish-white berries. And whether or not the plants are at the fruiting stage, there's another mark of identity: the axis, or stem, of the leaf-sets on true sumac is green, whereas the leaves of the poisonous variety sprout from a conspicuously red stem.

There are other harmful plants—particularly certain mushrooms and berries—but they're dangerous only if eaten. A good rule is not to eat anything you're not sure of, and not to touch anything that might be poison ivy, oak, or sumac. The texture, size, and configuration of leaves varies surprisingly from region to region,

but a good guide to identification of the three irritant plants is Department of Agriculture Bulletin No. 1972, available from the Superintendent of Documents, U. S. Government Printing Office, Washington, D.C. 20402.

Treatment of Skin Irritations

If you believe you've touched one of the poisonous plants, or at the onset of suspicious itching, the best remedy is to scrub as soon as possible with strong laundry soap and water or with an anti-bacterial cleanser, then gently pat on some rubbing alcohol. (The soap or cleanser and the alcohol are among the items recommended for a first-aid kit in Chapter 4.) Unfortunately, if this is done more than about ten minutes after contact, it often fails as a preventive though it may keep the affliction milder than it would otherwise be. Personally, without even waiting to see if itching developed, I would follow the scrubbing and alcohol treatment with an application of calamine lotion. I would try not to scratch, as this deepens and spreads the allergic reaction, and I would wash off the lotion with a mild boric-acid solution two or three times a day and put on a fresh application, continuing this until absolutely sure the symptoms were gone. The same treatment will also soothe irritations or scratches caused by nettles, thorns, and other unfriendly vegetation.

A few (very few) individuals seem to be almost immune to poison ivy, while a great many people are peculiarly sensitive to it. The superstition that immunity can be achieved by eating poison ivy has probably led to more than one death. It acts as a violent irritant internally as well as externally, and the treatment of an internal infection is extremely difficult.

But if experience has taught you that you're very sensitive to the urushiol plants, you *can* be immunized (though immunity may not be permanent). Inoculations are given for this purpose, and immunity can also be built up by means of oral tablets which must be taken for a period of time before exposure to the plants. Anyone who is especially sensitive to plant irritations—or to insect stings—should consult a doctor about getting a desensitizing treatment before going afield during the warm growing seasons.

Wasp

Black Widow Spider

Leech

Hornet or Yellow Jacket

Leaf-cutting bee

Bumblebee

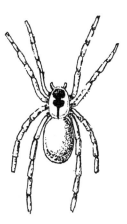

Fiddler or Brown Recluse Spider

Dangerous Insects and Arachnids

The miseries of an allergy to pollen and other airborne substances have been well publicized. Allergies to insect stings can be severe enough to be dangerous, even though most people suffer no more than brief pain and lingering discomfort when stung. Most of the pain and swelling is caused by a venom which is contained in a tiny sac attached to the stinger of a bee, wasp, or hornet. Wasp and hornet stings can be especially painful, yet the aftereffect of a bee sting sometimes lasts longer because a worker honeybee—unlike most stinging insects—leaves its barbed stinger, sac and all, in the puncture.

You should immediately examine a bee sting, with a magnifying glass if necessary, to see if a stinger has been left in your skin. If so, pull it out with a pair of tweezers or a knife blade, taking care not to squeeze the tiny poison sac on the end. Then suck at the stung area to get out the poison—any traces that enter your system won't harm you. To alleviate the pain, apply an ice pack, cold water, or even plain old cool mud.

You can shorten the period of discomfort, or at least make it milder, by taking an antihistamine tablet. Calamine lotion will also have a soothing effect. Better still is an anesthetic ointment such as Nupercainal or the calamine-antihistamine preparation known as Caladryl. Bactine will also

Tarantula

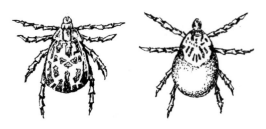

Rocky Mountain Wood Tick

American Dog Tick

Scorpion

Lone Star Tick

help, as will the disposable moist towelettes sold at drug and camp-supply stores.

The best treatment is prevention, of course, and this can be achieved by using insect repellent and by leaving stinging insects alone. Poking at a hornets' nest or beehive—or disturbing stinging insects in any other way—is not conducive to campsite tranquillity.

Ticks are another matter. The combination of odor, warmth, and movement seems to attract the nasty little vampires, prompting them to drop onto an animal (human or otherwise) and dig right in. Though ticks are disease carriers, it's fairly rare for people these days to contract a serious illness from a tick bite. There's greater danger of a localized but severe infection. The only preventive is insect repellent, which usually keeps ticks off, but not always. To enhance the repellent effect, apply oil of peppermint to your sleeve and trouser cuffs. Some repellent preparations, such as G-96 Ticks Away, are specially formulated to be effective against ticks and chiggers.

At first you may not feel a tick that has attached itself to you, but the faster you rid yourself of the creature, the less chance there is of

infection. When hiking or camping in any region where ticks are prevalent (and that means most regions), a careful daily examination of your entire body is in order.

If you see or feel the intruder immediately, you can brush it off and kill it. But they dig in quickly, and once a tick does that, brushing or pulling it off will leave its head imbedded and that causes infections. Furthermore, rupturing the creature's body while it's on you may release infectious fluid into the bite. Instead, apply rubbing alcohol, nail polish, petroleum jelly, grease, or oil to its body. A tick absorbs oxygen through its body, and covering it with one of these substances will make it drop off. When it does, kill it.

A match flame or cigarette will also make a tick drop off, but you'll have to hold the heat close enough to burn yourself slightly, so that's recommended only if you have nothing else with you for the purpose. As soon as the tick is removed, apply a generous amount of antiseptic or more alcohol to the bite.

(Heat will also detach a leech. Fortunately, these pests aren't as common as they used to be, but there are still regions where they're annoying. I'm told that it was once a source of pride among young boys to dig them out at the suction disc with a knife point. Having given up my youth and some of my pride, I'd prefer a match flame. Small leeches can be pulled off manually, of course, and some will let go if doused with salt.)

Unlike ticks, most spiders are not only harmless but downright beneficial, for they prey on pestiferous insects. There are a few spiders that can hurt as much as a wasp if they bite—which they do only in self-defense—but in the United States the only seriously poisonous species are the black widow and the fiddler, or brown recluse, spider. The black widow has a black or brownish-gray body with a red hourglass marking on its belly. It is found mostly in the South but is said to be spreading its range. The brown recluse has a fiddle-shaped marking on its back, which explains its alias. It's found mostly in the South and Midwest. Contrary to popular belief, the tarantulas of the Southwest are much less venomous, and they're so lethargic that they seldom attack.

The fiddler's venom is probably more toxic than the black widow's, yet its bite is sometimes so nearly painless that it isn't noticed. Pain may not begin for two to eight hours and may be followed by swelling, blistering, and ulceration. Fiddlers try to avoid humans but seek dark hiding places such as shoes, blankets, sleeping bags. Gear should therefore be inspected and shaken out.

Fortunately, scorpions are rare except in the Southwest. Most of these arachnids, which look like miniature lobsters with their tails curved up over their backs, have a sting about as dangerous and painful as that of a wasp. But there are a couple of more venomous species, and at least one that can occasionally be lethal.

In any region where there's the possibility of an unpleasant encounter with a scorpion or spider, don't walk about barefooted, and don't put on shoes or any other clothing until you've examined them for intruders. Shake out your sleeping bag vigorously and thoroughly, then roll it extra-tight to prevent intrusions. Before getting into it, shake it out again and inspect it. The sting of a scorpion or the bite of a venomous spider should be treated in the same manner as the bite of a poisonous snake, a first-aid procedure that will be covered below.

Avoiding Snake Bite

I've seen a map of the United States imprinted with the ranges of about twenty different poisonous snakes, but a close scrutiny showed that most of them were merely regional subspecies of the rattler. In reality, there are only five venomous reptiles in North America—four snakes and the Gila monster, or beaded lizard. The Gila is a big lizard, sometimes attaining a length of two feet, but it moves so slowly that a bite is an extremely rare occurrence. Moreover, its range is limited to the southwestern deserts, chiefly in Arizona and Mexico. The Gila's venom-injecting mechanism is poorly developed but the venom itself is very toxic, so a bite should be treated promptly and in the same manner as that of a poisonous snake.

The four poisonous snakes are the rattler, the copperhead, the cottonmouth (also called the water moccasin), and the coral snake (also called the harlequin snake).

Although northern Maine has no poisonous snakes of any kind, rattlers of one variety or another are found throughout most of the United States. The thirteen subspecies range in size from the little ground rattler (also called pigmy rattler) of the South, which may be less than two feet long when fully mature, to the eastern diamondback (also called Florida rattler) which averages five feet and is sometimes larger. Coloration varies, too, but in general is rather dull—a tan, gray, brown, reddish, yellow or yellowish-green background with darker splotches, diamonds, or bands. The timber rattler has a black phase which is so dark that it might be mistaken for a harmless species.

Obviously, color is a poor means of identification. However, the rattle, a segmented horny structure terminating the tail, is almost always present. When you hear or see a rattle, beware.

Gila Monster

Rattlers and other pit vipers are also characterized by wide, wedge-shaped heads and a heat-sensitive pit (which helps direct a strike) located between eye and nostril.

Personally, I wouldn't get close enough to check for the presence of pits. When in doubt, I avoid any snake that might possibly be poisonous. I don't kill a snake unless I'm certain it's a venomous species, because some rodent-controlling and very beneficial species resemble the poisonous ones. Killing one that is definitely poisonous is neither difficult nor dangerous but does call for caution. Stay farther away than the length of the snake's body and you can't be struck. From that distance, you can kill it with a heavy rock or club.

The copperhead ranges from Texas and Oklahoma eastward to the coast and northward (though in sharply reduced numbers) to lower New England. Whereas various types of rattlers favor a rather wide assortment of habitat, the copperhead is very much an upland snake, most often found on dry ledges, holes in cliffs, and other generally rocky areas. It looks like a small, rattleless rattler, rarely exceeding three feet in length, with a coppery head and hourglass-shaped body patches. It, too, is a pit viper, as is the cottonmouth.

The latter, also known as the water moccasin, is a water and swamp snake of heavier build and more vicious temperament. It may grow to a length of almost five feet, though the average is a little over three feet. Within its range—the deep South and the lower Mississippi Valley—it might be encountered wherever it can prey on fish and frogs. The white interior of its mouth is certainly not a practical means of identification at a safe distance, and its dark, almost black body is only vaguely marked. In cottonmouth country, I'd refrain from wading in unfamiliar swamps and I'd give a wide berth to any snake I saw in, on, or at the edge of the water.

Poisonous snakes found in the United States: the Diamondback Rattlesnake, the Copperhead, the Water Moccasin or Cottonmouth, and the Coral or Harlequin Snake. If in doubt about species, don't approach closely; snake can't strike farther than its own body's length.

There are two varieties of coral snakes, which are closely related to cobras. The western coral snake, found only in Arizona and Mexico, is a small reptile, averaging a foot and a half in length when mature. The common coral snake is twice as long and ranges from Florida, Georgia, and the Carolinas westward through the Gulf States into Arkansas and Texas. Apart from size, the two coral snakes are very much alike, gaudily beautiful. The forward part of the head is black, the body ringed with bands of yellow, red, and black.

Unfortunately there is a strong resemblance to the scarlet snake and the scarlet king snake, harmless and beneficial reptiles which are endangered because they're so frequently mistaken for coral snakes. Before killing what appears to be a coral snake, notice whether its black bands are bordered on both sides by yellow. If so, kill it. But if, instead, its yellow bands are bordered by black rings, it's harmless and should not be molested.

Coral snakes are shy, burrowing creatures that feed on other snakes and on lizards. They spend so much time underground that they're seldom encountered.

Most venomous snakes like crevices, holes, and burrows, so the first rule for avoiding trouble is to refrain from reaching into these places. Don't reach up onto a ledge or down into a bush, either, if you can't see where you're putting your hand. Look before you sit. Be careful when stepping over a log, because a snake may be coiled or stretched under or along it.

One reason for the rarity of snake bite is that rattlers and copperheads do most of their feeding at night. If you pitch camp while there's still daylight, and if your tent has a built-in ground cloth and zippered screening, there's little chance of contact unless you go barefooted or poke around after dark.

There are knee-high snakeproof boots, made of thick, very tough leather. I can understand their use in very heavily infested regions, but the fact is that a snake can't strike very far upward, above its own level, and ordinary leather boots are usually enough protection, particularly if they're roomy enough to accommodate two pairs of socks when desired. The fangs of a snake are not, after all, very long.

Safety in snake country only requires a bit of caution. You're too big to be attractive as prey, and a snake will strike at you only if it believes it's being attacked. So don't crash along in a great hurry. Look where you place your feet and hands. On warm days, watch out for cool, shaded pockets where a snake might rest, and on cool days watch out for warm rocks and ledges where a snake might sun itself.

Pictured with canteen and Sierra Club-style drinking cups is Cutter snake-bite kit. It includes suction cups, sharp blade, antiseptic, and tourniquet—plus all-important instructions.

Treating Snake Bite

Despite these precautions, your first-aid equipment in snake country should include a snake-bite kit such as the type marketed by Cutter Laboratories. It includes three suction cups (two of which fit together to form the container for the other components) plus first-aid instructions, a sharp blade, a vial of antiseptic, and a cord-type tourniquet which can be manipulated with one hand.

The instructions that come with the snake-bite kit should be memorized and should be kept inside the kit as extra insurance. In case you decide to put together your own snake-bite kit, you can memorize and follow these instructions:

Immediately tie a tourniquet about three inches above the bite—that is, between the punctures and your heart. It should be only moderately tight, not so tight as to retard the return of blood in the veins, and it should be loosened for one minute in every ten or three minutes in every twenty. Next, with a sharp, sterile blade (razor blade, very sharp knife, or the little scalpel that comes with a snake-bite kit) cut a short incision a quarter of an inch deep across each of the two fang punctures. Now apply a suction cup over the wounds. Depending on the location of the punctures, it's possible that you may need to use more than one suction cup.

If you don't have a suction cup, you can suck out the venom, spitting frequently. Minute amounts taken into the system orally won't hurt you, but do this only if you have no cuts on your lips or in your mouth. Otherwise, the best you can do is keep the wound bleeding freely and squeeze manually to get the venom out.

The purpose of the tourniquet is to retard the spread of venom through the circulatory system. For the same reason, the victim must be kept as quiet as possible. Activity will speed up circulation, as will hysteria. If you're bitten when alone and you have no first-aid equipment, walk slowly toward help. If you have companions but no equipment, your friends must carry you to a vehicle and get you to a physician at once. An ice pack, applied at or near the wound, is another aid in retarding the spread of venom.

Never give alcohol to a snake-bite victim. In fact, it's best to give no stimulants of any kind for at least a couple of hours. After that, strong hot coffee will be beneficial if it doesn't have a nauseating effect.

The bite of a coral snake is an exception to a couple of the rules, because the venom is of a different type. In this case, the tourniquet is unnecessary and stimulants may be given. But watch for any sign of paralysis, which may stop the victim's breathing. Should this happen, artificial respiration must be administered immediately.

Regardless of the type of snake that inflicts the bite, a victim should be taken to a physician as soon as possible.

Other Troublesome Creatures

Most wild animals are more inclined to flee than to attack, but you can lose a finger by reaching for a snapping turtle. The species may be easily distinguished from harmless turtles by its long, ridged tail; its rough shell with a saw-toothed rear edge; its pronounced beak; big, powerful jaws, and long neck. The snapper is definitely not recommended as a camp pet.

Fastidious housekeeping is the best way to avoid attracting undesirable wildlife to a campsite. For example, a snapping turtle may occasionally be attracted to a camp near water if a catch of fish is left in the open. Food odors also attract insects, including several of the stinging varieties. Utensils should be washed as soon as possible after use, and foods should be stored in sealed containers.

If flies, yellow jackets, or other flying pests begin to hover about at mealtime, undeterred by repellent, set a separate "table" for them at a considerable distance from your eating area. A piece of fish usually works well, as do bread, cake, and sticky sweets such as jam. You can attach this bait to a piece of string and hang it from a tree limb so that the insects will swarm about it—well away from where you're dining. Or you can hang up a commercial insect trap. It will be more effective if you notice the direction from which most of the insects are approaching, and place the bait to intercept them before they come near.

By making sure that no food odors linger on your tent, bedroll, sleeping clothes, or any gear in the sleeping area, you can reduce the chance of a more menacing invasion by a skunk or bear. The kitchen and sleeping quarters should therefore be well separated, and it merits repeating that food should be stowed in sealed containers. Cans or other emptied containers should be washed. Edible leftovers can be buried (they'll decompose and will not harm the environment), or you can pack them out with you in tightly sealed plastic bags. No garbage should be left exposed, and none should be left behind.

Bears normally avoid contact with man, but their natural fear can be overcome by the aroma of food. That's what brings on a camp raid. Bears are very intelligent, always unpredictable, and always potentially dangerous. Normal camp activity generally keeps them away if they aren't tempted by food. If you do see one, stay calm and retreat quietly. Never approach a bear. There's no way of telling whether it's irritable,

Yellowstone grizzly prowls about dumping site. Most dumps are now being cleaned up, not just for esthetic reasons but because bears are dangerous when accustomed to humans and attracted to food odors. (*Fish and Wildlife Service Photo by E. P. Haddor*)

If skunks come prowling about camp, attracted by food scents, observe them quietly. Don't frighten them by giving chase or throwing things, and they probably won't bother you. If you do have trouble, follow deodorizing instructions in text.

and it may have cubs hiding nearby—in which case it's particularly dangerous.

It is said that a sprinkling of camphor balls or flakes will keep skunks (and probably some other unwanted wildlife) away from a campsite, but I don't feel such precautions are required. If the smell of food does attract one, the best procedure is just to keep your distance and leave it alone. If you don't bother it, it generally won't bother you. But if you inadvertently frighten a skunk, you can have big trouble. The most effective deodorizing treatment is to scrub yourself with carbolic soap and water, or wash with gasoline and then with soap and water. Wash your eyes with a mild boric-acid solution or another ophthalmic solution.

Except in the case of a really severe spraying, scrubbing with ordinary tomato juice will deskunk you, but you have to use plenty, rubbing it vigorously into your skin and hair. The scalp will be the most stubborn problem, and you may have to get a very short haircut if the aftereffects linger. Tomato juice will also remove odor from clothing; soak it for at least six hours, or wash it in ammonia or chloride of lime, then rinse it thoroughly and hang it in the breeze. Incidentally, the same deodorizing methods that work on people will also work on dogs.

Chapter 6

SELECTING AND USING BACKPACKS

On a short hike, when you're toting little besides lunch, you'll get along beautifully with a small rucksack (sometimes called a "day pack") or one of the small belt or shoulder bags that hang at the hip. My daughter uses a little Stromeyer rucksack that rides high on her back—or on mine, occasionally—and is light, roomy, tough and has a big outside pocket. It's so light, in fact, that her younger brother borrows it. Like most of the small European models, it's reinforced canvas with padded leather shoulder straps. When lightly loaded, it's so comfortable that a hiker might forget he's in harness. With the straps adjusted snugly enough to keep it riding high, it's also reasonably comfortable when crammed full, but the straps of all such packs tend to dig in a little with a maximum load. The straps of almost any rucksack can be improved by cementing foam-rubber strips to them. These padding strips can be purchased very cheaply at many sporting-goods stores.

The basic American style of rucksack is quite similar. It's the Yukon pack or standard Boy Scout knapsack—a canvas box with shoulder straps and external bellows pockets for easy access to items needed along the trail. The straps may be web rather than leather, but they can be foam-padded in the same way. Several sizes are available, and the range of quality can be judged by the fact that prices begin at about $5.00 and climb to more than $20. Some are made of nylon, which is excellent. Some have no outside pockets, which is all right with a very small model that permits you to reach anything you might need. However, the very smallest of these have such limited usefulness that I can't see much point in getting one. I'd say the minimum would be eleven or twelve inches wide,

fourteen or fifteen inches high, and five inches deep. Many packs of that size weigh less than a pound.

A larger type which looks rather similar but is not recommended for hiking is the Duluth pack. It's nothing but a huge flat pocket of heavy-duty duck, with a flap closing, shoulder straps, and a tumpline. It's great for storing things in a camp and even greater for stowing gear on a canoe trip—the tumpline helps on short portages with heavy loads. But it's far from comfortable on a long walk, and its tremendous capacity has now been outdone by pack-frame models.

Another great pack for canoeing and for storing things at camp (particularly breakable things and hard, sharp-cornered containers) is the Adirondack pack basket. It's a rigid, open-topped basket—sometimes with a canvas flap cover attached—made of woven ash or willow strips. It's practically indestructible but lacks the capacity of the large pack-frame sacks and is heavier and far less comfortable for long hikes.

Some of the modern rucksacks are wedge-shaped—narrow at the top, wide at the bottom—to provide more freedom of shoulder movement. This is fine if the bag has sufficient total capacity for your needs. Some models of either wedge or rectangular shape have a built-in or detachable triangular aluminum frame with a leather, web, or nylon strap forming the bottom of the triangle. This type is often called a ski pack or Norwegian-frame pack. It's very comfortable, and in versions with an extendable main compartment and oversized flap for overloads, it's extremely versatile. The strap rides across the small of your back so that the pack itself doesn't touch you. The shoulder straps are adjustable,

Waving at occupants of caboose on St. J & LC line during Vermont hike, author's daughter wears Camp Trails backpack borrowed from her father, and author's son wears featherweight Stromeyer rucksack borrowed from his sister.

and some of the newer versions make provision for a hip belt—like that on the bigger H-frame backpacks—to take much of the load off the shoulders.

Pack Frames

This brings us to the large, rigid-frame backpacks which are most versatile and easily best for any hike of more than a day's duration. The detachable tubular frame is usually made of light, tough, aircraft-type aluminum, though a few are made of magnesium (which is even lighter) or steel (which is slightly heavier). As viewed from the rear, the frame is more or less rectangular, sometimes narrowing slightly at the top. In most cases it's an H-shape, but with three or four crossbars instead of one. (Gerry calls its very fine model a K-frame, but it, too, looks like an H with extra crossbars.)

The vertical legs of some models, including the White Stag brand made by Hirsch-Weis, several of the Himalayan frames, Eddie Bauer's line, most of the Sears Hillary line, and the recently introduced Alpine Designs adjustable frame, are made from one piece of tubing bent to form an inverted U and strengthened by additional crossbars. The U conformation adds strength but also adds a tiny bit more weight. Of course, the more crossbars there are, the stronger but heavier the frame will be. The fact is that all of the popular aluminum frames are delightfully light and plenty strong for normal loads, regardless of configuration.

There are large, extra-strong frames such as the Astral Cruiser and the Freighter, both made by Camp Trails. The former is rated for loads up to ninety pounds and the latter, which has a folding extension shelf at the bottom for cumbersome items such as an outboard motor, can

Adirondack pack basket is good for short hikes, canoe trips, and stowing breakables at camp, though not capacious or comfortable enough for long hikes. Here, Adirondack outdoorsmen have used one to tote lunch up Mount Jo, near Lake Placid, New York.

handle even heavier burdens. These are wonderful for long canoe trips, for hauling heavy gear into base camps, and similar special purposes, but I hope I'll never have to take full advantage of such a frame. At the other end of the scale are very light, relatively small frames made by this and other companies for youngsters and slightly built women.

An advantage of the inverted U—aside from strength—is that its top slides up into an open pocket of fabric across the entire width òf the bag. This method of attachment keeps the bag rigidly in place and puts slightly less strain on the fabric than the conventional H-frame, which slides up into fabric sockets. However, I've never heard any complaints about an H-frame, and it has an advantage of its own—detachable upper extensions for some models to accommodate extra-big loads.

All of the good frames have one feature in common: a very slight S-curve when viewed from the side and two or more backbands of padded nylon, nylon mesh, or similar material. The modern frames are so cleverly designed that the pack rides close to your back (as it should, to prevent back and shoulder strain), but only the soft backbands actually ride *against* your back. Air circulates between your body and the high-riding pack, and nothing hard or heavy presses into you.

Some frames have a bottom shelf that bends

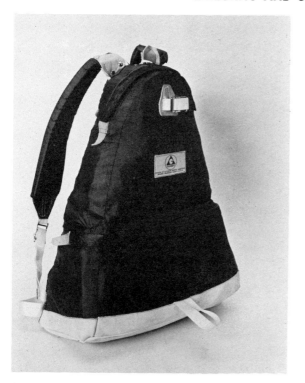

Gerry Climbing Pack is wedge-shaped type sometimes called "ski pack." Roomy enough for hikes of moderate length, it's designed for freedom of arm and shoulder movement.

This is Gerry's K-frame, with hip belt, padded shoulder straps, and nylon-mesh backbands.

out to the rear. This adds a tiny bit of weight and takes a little extra space when you want to store a frame. However, it provides a rigid base that makes it easier to stand your pack upright on the ground. Most packs are designed so that they don't extend all the way to the bottom of the frame. And most backpack manufacturers offer separate cylindrical "stuff bags," which can be quickly lashed to the frame under the pack itself. You can carry your sleeping bag in the stuff bag, and/or you can fill it with miscellaneous items. With a frame featuring the bottom shelf, nothing in the stuff bag can be broken or crushed against the ground when you set the pack down—another advantage.

The shelf design is no longer popular, probably because of the added bulk and weight, but I have a Camp Trails model of this configuration that serves me beautifully. The Precise Imports Crestline pack can also be bought with this type of frame, and it, too, strikes me as well designed. There must be a substantial number of other hikers who agree, because several manufacturers

now sell detachable bottom shelves—tubular aluminum bent into a frame-wide U shape—as accessories.

Some of the features I've been describing are primarily a matter of personal preference, but certain other features are almost mandatory. In most cases, the lower backband should be adjustable so that it can be placed to ride low on your hips—below the kidneys. One company, Trailwise, offers a single full-length backband that distributes the weight evenly and does away with this necessity, while another maker, Kelty, offers an optional foam pad for the lower band and this, too, is comfortable. It's also desirable to have backbands that are adjustable for tension. Depending on the load, you may want to increase or decrease tension for the greatest comfort.

The ends of the vertical legs of an H-frame should be capped with friction-tight plastic or rubber cups. This is primarily for safety, as you don't want the edges of the aluminum tubes exposed; they would be formidable gouges. The

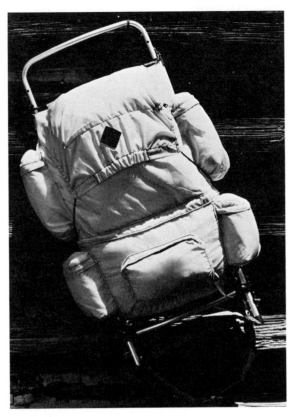

Alpine Designs frame is U-type and is adjust-able. Sack is nylon Expedition model with six outside pockets and double-partitioned main compartment.

Precise Imports distributes Crestline pack with bottom shelf formed by tubular aluminum frame. It provides stability when you stand it on ground and protects breakable items.

use of the caps also transforms the tubes into fine waterproof containers for an emergency match supply.

Some of the better frames come in several sizes, and the manufacturers have charts show-ing which size is recommended for a person of a given height and build. Unless you're quite small or unusually tall, chances are you'll be comfortable with any of the medium versions, which are generally about fifteen inches in width and about twenty-seven to thirty inches or so in height. If in doubt, the best thing to do is try on a frame—with some weight in the pack—and see if it's comfortable.

The best shoulder straps are of padded ny-lon, and they must be adjustable. Some hikers think of the padded hip belt as an optional lux-ury, but they'd change their minds instantly if they compared the feel of a fully loaded pack with and without one. It really does take a great deal of the burden off the shoulders and put it

where it's barely noticeable. I wouldn't buy a frame without an attachment for the hip belt.

Prices for frames run from less than $10 (for a small model, suitable for a youngster) to more than $30 (for a heavy-duty model). If a frame seems strong and comfortable and has the fea-tures I've described as important, the only other essential criterion is weight. With a waterproof nylon or canvas-duck pack bag, the whole unit shouldn't weigh much over four pounds—less if it isn't one of the large models. Some of the smaller ones weigh less than three, but you can't have great capacity without a little extra weight.

Frame-Type Bags

Either nylon or canvas is fine for the bag. Ny-lon is a shade stronger and lighter than canvas but is also more expensive. I don't have any strong preference as long as the bag is lock-

Orvis backpack-and-frame combination is shown with padded hip belt, which author considers essential for relieving shoulders of weight.

but separate cavities, each accessible from the outside without disturbing anything in the other cavities. More about these in a moment.

Most of the medium to large single- and double-compartment bags have three or more outside pockets. Three good-sized ones are generally sufficient, but some hikers prefer more. Some bags also have a spreader at the top to hold the compartment open for easy loading or unloading; this is far from essential but is a nice feature when well designed.

I believe it was Gerry that pioneered the compartmentalized sack, which is divided into four or five horizontal, bag-wide compartments, each separately accessible through a zippered opening that goes clear across the bag. It's an ingenious design that does away with the need for outside pockets since you can easily get at any item you want, from top to bottom, without disturbing the other contents. More or less similar construction is now featured in some sacks made by Alpine Designs and other makers. Compartmentalization is also an aid in distributing weight to your liking, and the bottom compartment is invariably large enough to hold a rolled sleeping bag—in many instances with a foam mattress pad and even a pillow.

However, it hardly needs to be pointed out that the separate compartments won't accommodate large pieces of gear as handily as one big sack. For cool-weather, high-country, or long hiking trips, I find it easier to stow bulky insulated clothing, a tent, etc., in a single- or double-compartment bag. Yet for shorter trips or when

stitched for durability. I rather like a bag whose flaps simply tie closed with long nylon cords; there are no fancy fasteners or buckles to bend or break, and the cords are long enough to tie closed when a compartment is overloaded. Besides, a cord can always be put to some other use in an emergency and is easily replaced.

Until fairly recently, most of the frame-attached bags simply consisted of a large top-opening sack with a few outside bellows pockets. Interesting variations on this theme have lately been appearing. For example, a number of models are now divided into an upper and lower compartment, and some of these are convertible —permitting you to open or close a partition to form two compartments or one larger one. Furthermore, there are one- and two-compartment packs that can be secured to a frame or harnessed without one for use as a large rucksack. Finally, there are the so-called compartmentalized packs which usually have four or five large

Gerry's compartmentalized and contoured Vagabond Pack is shown with mess kit, insulated sleeping bag, foam pad, and stuff bag—total weight eight pounds.

traveling fairly light in warm weather, the compartmentalized bag can't be beat if it has easy-
working, heavy-duty zippers. Either type can be
attached (by sockets or flaps and clevis pins)
to a standard frame produced by the same manufacturers.

I'm not necessarily suggesting that you get
both kinds of sack. The compartmentalized kind
is usually nylon and costs from around $24 or so
to more than $30. Top-loading canvas sacks
range from a little less than $15 for a small
model to more than $20, and the nylon top load-
ers range from around $20 to more than twice
that. You'll probably choose one type or another
on the basis of what kind of hiking trip you'll
most often take.

Not long ago, the Mountaineer Corporation
introduced a compartmentalized bag that
switches from zippered compartments to a single,
unpartitioned cavity and has snap-on outside
pockets. And all of the manufacturers I've mentioned supply double-compartment toploaders.

If you hike with your family, a fine idea is for
members of the group to choose a couple of different sack designs. This increases the convenience in terms of accessibility of frequently
needed trail items, flexibility of loading, and an
equitable sharing of the total load of equipment.

For use with one- and two-cavity sacks, a stuff
bag is all but essential. It fits on the frame right
under the sack, holds all sorts of things in addition to a sleeping bag, weighs practically nothing, and is usually purchased as an optional accessory for $6.00 or less. (There are even some
small ones for around $2.00.)

Hoisting Your Pack

There's a definite knack to harnessing up with
a fully loaded frame-type backpack. A rig that
weighs four pounds or so empty can furnish an
unpleasant surprise the first time you heft it after
loading up twenty pounds of gear for a four-day
trip.

Begin by trying on the *empty* pack and ad-
justing the shoulder straps for a comfortable
fit with the top of the frame riding fairly high—
about on a level with the tops of your ears,
higher if it's a large frame for heavy loads. It
may need further adjustment when you put it
on loaded, but a preliminary fitting will make
that easier.

Without heaving pack onto high stump or boulder to facilitate harnessing, average rig can
easily be shouldered in two-stage lift from
ground. First, face frame and slip hands under
shoulder straps, with palms up, and hoist pack

to one knee. Next, swing it high onto your back
so one strap glides over your elbow onto your
shoulder. Still holding rig high, you can then slip
other arm through strap and buckle hip belt in
properly high position.

After loading the pack and lashing all externally carried gear in place, stand facing the back
of the frame (the strap side, not the pack side).
You're now ready to make a two-stage hoist that
will be moderately easy and will avoid strained
muscles, charley horse, or hernia.

If you're left-handed, reverse the following

directions. Assuming you're right-handed, brace the bottom left corner or leg of the frame against your left toes. With your palms up and thumbs out, bring your hands up under the shoulder straps and cradle them, ready to lift. Don't try to cross the straps. Your left hand is under the strap that will end up on your right shoulder when you swing the rig around onto your back. That's as it should be.

Now bend your knees slightly and heave the pack up with one motion, *only far enough to rest its bottom on your left knee or thigh.* Pause for an instant to set yourself for the second stage of the hoist if the pack is heavy. Now heave it up along your left side and swing it around to your back, at the same time swinging your left hand back behind your head and raising that elbow. You'll find that you can now slip the left strap over your raised left elbow onto your forearm. Support the weight for a moment with the left arm, let go of the strap with the right hand, and reach up and back on your right side to lift the pack higher still. You'll then be able to slip your right arm under the right shoulder strap, lean forward a little, and slip both arms all the way through the harness so that the straps are on your shoulders.

During this procedure, the hip strap will, of course, be dangling loose from the bottom of the rig. At this point your hands are free again so you can reach down and grab it. As you buckle it in front, hunch a little and you'll be able to adjust it so that a good portion of the weight rides on your hips. Now—if necessary—make a final adjustment of the shoulder straps.

Advanced backpackers make a fetish of going light. They'll even save fractions of ounces by transferring foods from cardboard packages to plastic bags; using small, light diapers for towels; and carrying few or no eating utensils; the minimum of cooking equipment; a light plastic tarp for a tent; and even a minimum of underwear and socks (if they can face extra-frequent washing), or depending on scouring pads with built-in soap to save the weight of conventional soap. Extremists boast that they rarely carry more than twenty pounds on week-long hiking trips.

Nonetheless, the time may come when you have to hoist a heavier-than-usual pack onto your back, and even the method just cited can then be awkward. Don't strain. That can be dangerous when you're far from a vehicle, home, or doctor. Instead of heaving the pack to your shoulders, prop it up on a ledge, rock, or other elevation so that you can slip into the harness instead of lifting.

What to Pack

According to literature prepared by the National Sporting Goods Association, the following lightweight "his" and "hers" packing lists will make a very comfortable weekend hiking and camping outfit:

HIS		HERS	
Pack and frame	2 lbs.	Pack and frame	2 lbs.
Sleeping bag and pad	5½ lbs.	Sleeping bag and pad	5½ lbs.
Tent (including poles and fly)	4½ lbs.		
Food	4 lbs.		
Poncho and sweater	2 lbs.	Poncho and sweater	2 lbs.

Cooking			Cooking	
utensils, etc.	1¼ lbs.		utensils, etc.	2 lbs.
			Stove	1 lb.
Personal items,			Personal items,	
first-aid, etc.	1 lb.		first-aid, etc.	2 lbs.
Total weight:	20¼ lbs.		*Total weight:*	14½ lbs.

That's a good basic list, but the weights must be regarded as variable and approximate. Most pack-and-frame combinations weigh a little over three pounds, not two. Most tents weigh over five (and only the small backpacking models are that light). But even if you add six pounds to account for variables plus a change of clothing, the load can be split so that "his" burden is at most twenty-three pounds and hers is at most seventeen. And it's not difficult to go lighter.

The Sierra Club's authoritative booklet, *Knapsacking Equipment,* offers the following ultralight yet practical gear list (exclusive of food or cooking equipment):

Down-insulated mummy or semi- mummy sleeping bag	4 lbs.
Light plastic ground cloth	8 oz.
Light plastic 9′ × 12′ tarp (for use as tent shelter)	1 lb. 4 oz.
Plastic poncho	14 oz.
Ensolite sleeping pad (⅜″ thick, ¾ length)	14 oz.
Down jacket (or wool shirt or sweater, in addition to clothing being worn)	1 lb. 2 oz.
Nylon parka	12 oz.
Extra underwear and socks	12 oz.
Plastic lunch sack with spoon and cup (wide-diameter cup which also serves as plate or bowl)	4 oz.
Soap, small towel, toothpaste, tooth- brush, other toilet articles	8 oz.
Total weight:	10 lbs. 14 oz.

That's an impressively light and compact list, even if you add the luxury of a portable cooking stove, windscreen, and fuel—a total of perhaps six pounds but split between two hikers so that each adds only three pounds to his pack. If it's a long trip you may be carrying fifteen pounds of food, and you'll still be toting less than thirty pounds. Remember that less than twelve pounds of food will do nicely for a week-long hike.

Every authority seems to have his own ideas about what's essential or at least desirable, but the similarities in their lists are revealing, while the differences may give you ideas of your own. You can use one of the following lists as is, modify it, or choose some items from one list, some from another. Here's one that was described in *Outdoor Life* magazine enumerating the supplies taken by veteran backpackers Mike and Mary Hayden on a 3½-day fishing and photography trip in California's Sierra country:

HERS

Medium-size rucksack	3 lbs.	8 oz.
Food (for two)	16 lbs.	6 oz.
Full canteen	1 lb.	
Canvas water bucket		6 oz.
First-aid kit (including insect repellent and snake-bite kit—plus compass)		13 oz.
Toilet tissue (1½ rolls)		12 oz.
Garden trowel (good for digging latrine or "cat hole," or rain trench if necessary)		8 oz.
Washing kit (including soap and towel)	1 lb.	
Spare clothing (including shirt, socks, sweater, and waterproof parka)	2 lbs.	2 oz.
Cooking kit (including nesting pots, plastic cups, utensils and plates)	3 lbs.	6 oz.
Total weight:	29 lbs.	13 oz.

HIS

Extra-large pack and frame	5 lbs.	
Sleeping bags (two) in stuff bag	8 lbs.	4 oz.
Vinyl-coated ground cloth	1 lb.	12 oz.
Tarp tent (11′ × 11′)	2 lbs.	5 oz.
Nylon rope (100′)	1 lb.	
Folding lantern and six candles		10 oz.
Grill with cover		4 oz.
Repair and sewing kit (including items relating to fishing tackle and photography)	1 lb.	4 oz.
Chess set		10 oz.
Maps, fire permit, fishing license, notebook and pencils		6 oz.
Field guides (including flowers, trees, wildlife, and geology)	1 lb.	
Pocket radio		7 oz.

Spare clothing (including sweater, shirt, waterproof parka, wool socks, two sets of woolen long johns)	4 lbs.	12 oz.
Fishing tackle	6 lbs.	7 oz.
Camera and photo supplies	10 lbs.	
Total weight:	44 lbs.	1 oz.

Note that Mike Hayden would have been lugging about 27½ pounds without his extensive camera equipment and fishing tackle. The nylon rope is an excellent idea, though most backpackers don't carry quite so much of it. Moreover, the Haydens were in real wilderness country, and were not attempting to travel fast or go extra-light; their food was determined on the basis of having enough not for 3½ days but for *a full week—plus short rations for another two days!*

Gerry Cunningham, of the Gerry pack-manufacturing firm, put together this one-man list for a weekend outfit:

Pack and frame	2 lbs.	
Sleeping pad and ½-length foam pad	5 lbs.	7 oz.
Small backpacking tent	1 lb.	10 oz.
Cooking gear, miscellany and poncho	2 lbs.	1 oz.
2 lunches, 1 supper, 1 breakfast	2 lbs.	
Total weight:	13 lbs.	2 oz.

For a father-and-son weekend outfit, Gerry doubled the food carried by the father—another two pounds added to the list above, for a total of just over 15 pounds. The son would carry a light pack and frame, sleeping bag, foam pad, cooking utensils, miscellany, and poncho—a little under nine pounds altogether. The same list can be adapted to a husband-and-wife weekend by substituting a slightly larger, heavier tent and assuming that the wife will carry a few extra toiletries and miscellaneous items. The husband (who packs the tent) will then be carrying less than 18½ pounds, and the wife will have to tote less than 9½ pounds.

The Sears Hillary catalogue, which includes a number of hiking tips, offers a list for the average hiker on a longer backpacking trip:

Pack and frame	4 lbs.	
Down sleeping bag	4 lbs.	

Nylon tent	7 lbs.	8 oz.
Canteen	1 lb.	
Stuff bag		6 oz.
Short foam pad	1 lb.	4 oz.
1 compass		4 oz.
Knife		8 oz.
Flashlight		8 oz.
Nylon cord (40′)		6 oz.
Maps		6 oz.
First-aid kit		6 oz.
Cooking grill	1 lb.	8 oz.
Mess kit	1 lb.	3 oz.
Fork-and-spoon kit		6 oz.
Can opener		1 oz.
Dishcloth		2 oz.
Plastic bags		2 oz.
Nylon poncho	1 lb.	
Extra set of underwear		12 oz.
2 extra pairs of light socks		4 oz.
2 extra pairs of heavy socks		8 oz.
Toilet kit (including towel, soap, shaving equipment, insect repellent, mirror, toilet tissue, etc.)	1 lb.	12 oz.
Total weight:	28 lbs.	2 oz.

If you were to add a one-pound trail ax, a stove weighing about 1¼ pounds, a nylon tent fly, a set of thermal underwear, a jacket and even a pair of walking shorts, the burden would still only come to 35 pounds, and eight pounds of food would bring it to 43. That's going reasonably light without roughing it.

Forest Ranger and outdoor author Bill Merrill has pointed out that a hiker who sets out on a weekend trip with about 17½ pounds (a couple of pounds less if there's a companion to share the burden of "community property") will make the return hike lugging about five pounds less, because five pounds of food and fuel will have been consumed. He figures that two people setting off together on a two-week pack trip will get along fine if each totes just under 40 pounds. The load gets lighter and lighter, until each is carrying less than 17 pounds when they've started the return trek.

Some hikers add a light plastic tarp to go over the pack (and perhaps over the hiker, too) in an unexpected downpour. It adds only a few ounces more, but I just keep my ground cloth handy for such purposes.

How to Pack

A number of backpack manufacturers offer suggestions about the best way to load a pack for optimum weight distribution as well as convenience in reaching frequently needed equipment. These suggestions vary slightly, since they're based on different backpack designs. Moreover, your own preferences and the season and area of your hike will influence what you pack and where you pack it. Still, it's helpful to have some guidelines.

A chart distributed by Himalayan Back Packs recommends the following placement of gear in a large frame-type with two main compartments:

Stuff Bag Under Lower Compartment: sleeping bag.

Lower Compartment: air mattress or sleeping pad, tarp or ground cloth, small standard tent or tube tent, forty feet of nylon cord, extra socks, windbreaker jacket, extra clothing.

Upper Compartment: cooking kit, backpacker grill, stove (if needed), bags of food, extra bags, tent (if too large or heavy for bottom compartment).

Back Pocket: plastic bowl, plastic or metal cup, pot tongs, tablespoon, waterproof matches, sunglasses, lunch, and trail snacks.

Left Side Pocket: toilet kit (toothbrush, toothpowder or toothpaste, soap, etc.), paper towels, toilet tissue, scouring pad, flashlight, extra bulb and batteries, poncho.

Right Side Pocket: first-aid kit, sunburn cream, insect repellent, Chap Stick, water-purification tablets, matches in waterproof case, candle, canteen.

Flap Pocket: maps, fire permit, fishing or hunting license, notebook, pencil, identification.

A chart distributed by Camp Trails shows the following distribution for a two-compartment pack:

Stuff Bag Under Lower Compartment: sleeping bag, air pillow (if desired), foam pad (if small enough; otherwise, it can be carried on top of pack or under flap).

Lower Compartment: hat or cap, underwear, trousers, windbreaker, socks, handkerchiefs, shirts, gloves, rain gear, swim suit, bandana, wash basin, pajamas or long johns, wool shirt or down jacket and hood.

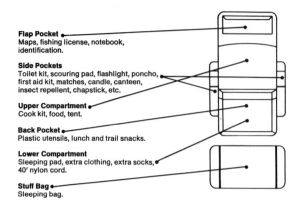

Flap Pocket
Maps, fishing license, notebook, identification.

Side Pockets
Toilet kit, scouring pad, flashlight, poncho, first aid kit, matches, candle, canteen, insect repellent, chapstick, etc.

Upper Compartment
Cook kit, food, tent.

Back Pocket
Plastic utensils, lunch and trail snacks.

Lower Compartment
Sleeping pad, extra clothing, extra socks, 40' nylon cord.

Stuff Bag
Sleeping bag.

Sears, Roebuck's catalogue of Sears Hillary back-packing gear includes this guide to convenient loading of double-compartment packs.

Upper Compartment: cooking kit, pot tongs, grill, GI can opener, food, condiment kit (salt, pepper, milk, sugar, coffee, cocoa, tea, cooking oil, flavorings), stove, water bag, tent or tarp, tube tent or ground cloth, air mattress (if desired).

Back Pocket: plastic bowl, matches, extra glasses, sunglasses, plastic bags, toilet kit, toilet tissue, dishcloth, paper towels or diapers, cup, lunch, trail snacks, rubber bands, tablespoon, juice crystals, thirty feet of nylon cord.

Left Side Pockets: sunburn cream, Chap Stick, medications, water purifier, insect repellent, repair kits, flashlight, extra bulb and batteries, canteen, stove fuel, rain gear.

Right Side Pockets: first-aid kit, snake-bite kit, safety pins, survival items (survival booklet, signal mirror, whistle, compass, candle, flint stick, notebook, and pen, etc.), windbreak, foil for stove, other items of same type as in left pockets.

Flap Pocket: maps, fire permit, fishing or hunting license, notebook, pen, information on personal medical or allergenic restrictions, identification.

It's worth noting that a chart in the Sears Hillary catalogue is in close agreement with the Himalayan and Camp Trails suggestions given above. In altering arrangements to suit yourself, just remember to pack heavy items high and close to your back, trail items in the handiest pockets. When using a compartmentalized, zippered pack, Gerry Cunningham suggests stowing the sleeping bag and foam pad, as well as other bulky but light equipment, in the bottom compartment; the middle compartments are for food, a rolled poncho and personal items such as a sweater and spare socks in plastic bags; and the top compartment is for a rolled tent, tent poles, camera, take-down fishing rod, reel, first-aid kit, flashlight, cooking kit, and the other gear that has been listed.

Chapter 7

SLEEPING BAGS, TENTS, AND TOOLS

I've slept outdoors on many summer nights in north-central Vermont, using a Comfy-Seattle-brand rectangular sleeping bag with a water-repellent nylon-and-cotton cover, a cotton-flannel lining, and about three pounds of Dacron-fiber insulation. The total weight is about six pounds. If my recollection is correct, it cost me less than $30, and I got it because I was reluctant to pay the price of a down-filled bag. I've been comfortable in it even on those rare occasions when the dew frosted. It has a detachable flannel liner—like an inner blanket—but I can remember only two nights when I snapped that in. Like many such bags, it has a canopy, or head flap, that can be propped up to keep wind and dew off my head on gloriously clear nights when I use no tent. The bag rolls up into this canopy, which has long drawstrings and forms its own stuff bag.

I've used that same Comfy-Seattle sleeping bag on cool fall nights on a prairie near Buffalo, Wyoming, east of the Bighorn Mountains, so I can vouch for the effectiveness of synthetic insulation in average hiking weather. But high elevations and winter hikes are another matter, of course.

The time came when I wanted to join some friends on an early spring hike in Canada and, just to play it safe, I borrowed a friend's old army-surplus down mummy bag. It had a couple of pounds of down in it and a total weight of a little over four pounds, which was a great attraction because we were going to be lugging a lot of weight on a long hike. Camping at high altitude one cold and windy night, I learned to appreciate goose-down insulation. Its ratio of warmth to weight has never been equaled and perhaps never will be.

That warmth/weight ratio is the main consideration in choosing a sleeping bag. So far I've mentioned only one brand, but there are literally dozens and most of them are quite good. You're not likely to get a lemon if you look for the features I'll describe and choose an appropriate design and recommended type and weight of insulation for a given temperature range.

The price range is nothing short of amazing. For example, Bob Hinman, a well-known Illinois outfitter, advertises a backpacking mummy bag that costs about $40 and weighs well under three pounds even though it's comfortably long and wide and is filled with two pounds of duck down. It rolls up to about the size of an oatmeal box. Although duck down is not as good as goose down (despite some manufacturers' claims that eider is best), this bag provides comfort when the temperature is in the twenties. The same outfitter offers an extremely comfortable "barrel-shaped" rectangular bag made by the famous Scottish manufacturer, Thomas Black & Sons; with about 1½ pounds of goose down and a total weight of 4½ pounds, it costs about $60, and with 2½ pounds of goose down, it costs close to $80. The lighter weight is sufficient for temperatures in the teens and the heavier will do when the mercury shrivels to zero. For sub-zero use, an optional inner bag (priced at about $40 to $50) can be inserted into the outer one, and two of the outer ones can also be zipped together to form a husband-and-wife double.

Another typical example of the wide price range is furnished by the Alaska Sleeping Bag Company, which supplies fine, lightweight mummy or semimummy (tapered but wider) bags with less than two pounds of goose down

—suggested for temperatures in the 20s or higher—at less than $70. But Alaska also has a rectangular arctic model with six pounds of goose down and a price of about $200. Why? Because prime, virgin, northern goose down is expensive, because such a bag has extra cold-weather features and the finest possible construction, and because this one has been comfort-tested to 60° below zero. For polar expeditions it would be supreme, though I think the average hiker can manage without it.

Eddie Bauer, Stag, Alpine Designs, Woods Bag & Canvas Company, Don Gleason, Coleman, Gerry, Himalayan, Thermos, Orvis, Sears, and a number of other suppliers feature various styles and types; the average price for a down-filled bag is between $60 and $80, though some cost as little as $50 and some as much as $100. Some companies, such as Trailblazer, also offer light, rectangular, acrylic-filled bags for less than $20. Naturally, the least expensive models are also least warm and least durable, but they serve well on summer nights in regions of mild climate.

Coleman's Dacron-filled rectangular sleeping bags come in standard or extra-large sizes and are washable. Same firm also makes down-filled bags in both rectangular and mummy style.

Synthetic-Insulated Bags

Several synthetics provide satisfactory insulation for mild-weather bags, but Dacron fiber seems to be the most popular. Generally speaking, bags so insulated are of rectangular construction. If you get such a bag, read the label carefully, bearing in mind that you'll need at least two pounds of Dacron to keep you warm in areas where the temperature dips below the mid-30s. Also bear in mind that, as a rule, women and children require more warmth than men, and more warmth means more weight to carry.

Many synthetic-insulated bags are washable (cleaning instructions should come with the bag). A removable washable liner is an excellent feature for extra warmth, but this, too, can increase your pack weight. The best material for the removable liner is soft, strong flannel. The permanent liner may be nylon or flannel. Nylon is the best material for the shell, but high-quality cotton (sometimes labeled "Egyptian cotton") or another material will do nicely if it's water-repellent—not water*proof* as it must breathe—and woven tightly enough to be durable and

wind resistant. Some bags are still being made with cotton insulation, but this will serve only in very warm weather. A synthetic-filled bag that's comfortable at 35° F. will also be comfortable at 60° if it has a full-length zipper or Velcro closure strip so that you can open it to let air in.

Synthetic-filled bags are much less expensive than the down-filled models, but you'll be warmer with two pounds of prime down than with three pounds of synthetic. I therefore recommend the synthetic-filled type only for mild weather and short hikes or hikes with otherwise light packs.

Down-Insulated Bags

There are federal and state laws requiring that down insulation be labeled correctly, so you know you're getting top quality when you buy a bag that's marked "100% prime northern goose down." That's the best there is. The color of good down varies and it doesn't matter. Anyway, you're not likely to see the down if you get a bag made of tightly woven and stitched material, which will be wind resistant, water repellent, fast drying—and won't leak its insulation. Again, nylon is usually considered best for the outer shell, though Egyptian cotton, "balloon cloth,"

To increase warmth of sleeping bag by about 25 per cent, you can get removable inner bag like this Eddie Bauer 16-ounce model, filled with prime northern goose down.

or a nylon-cotton combination will also do nicely.

The liner is most often nylon. In addition, many makers offer removable inner liners made of broadcloth, cotton or wool flannel, or nylon fleece. Or you can achieve an even greater degree of extra warmth by inserting a relatively thin down-filled inner bag of the sort already described. (Of course, you can just tuck an ordinary blanket inside, too, but that's heavy and bulky for backpacking.)

Aside from the amount and quality of the down, the most important warmth-giving factor in the use of this insulation is the method of keeping it in place. Its distribution must be securely maintained so that it won't shift about when your body weight compresses it, when you toss and turn or climb in or out, when you roll and unroll it, etc. Inner-tube construction is the answer to this problem, and the down-filled tubes may be horizontal or chevron-shaped. The tubes in some of the lightest and least expensive bags are "sewn through"—that is, they're formed by stitching the lining to the shell. But when this is done, the rows of stitching form cold spots between the tubes, thus reducing the bag's efficiency. Bags advertised as having "box-tube" construction are better; in these, the tubes are formed by walls sewn between the inner lining and outer shell. For some reason, walls that are angled instead of vertical seem to be most efficient, and manufacturers often emphasize such angling as "slanted-gusset" or "slant-wall" construction. Still another method is the "V tube,"

which is probably even warmer but adds a tiny bit to the weight and sometimes more than a tiny bit to the price.

A variation on the V tube is a trusslike diaphragm arrangement between the inner and outer fabrics. This permits a lengthening of the tubes without undue shifting of insulation. It's probably not quite as efficient as the slanted gusset or the V, but has been showing up on some excellent, moderately priced bags.

For really extreme weather, some bags feature a baffle system or laminated overlapping tubes. A good baffle is simply a wrap-around double layer of slanted-gusset tubing, so arranged that there aren't any thin spots. A good laminated overlapping system consists of two separate layers of wrap-around tubes held in their own *interior* sewn-through quilting; each thin spot on one layer is positioned against a thick spot on the other layer, so there are no cold areas—and there is a "dead-air" space between layers which enhances the insulating effect. Such construction is apt to be expensive but is extremely warm. A few models achieve the same goal by a lamination of one more or less standard sewn-through bag inside another.

It should be emphasized that such sophisticated and expensive heat-retaining designs are not necessary for most hiking in the United States. They are recommended, however, for winter hikes, high-altitude camping, and outings in the Far North.

Zippers and Other Closures

It should also be emphasized that many hikers deprive themselves of the delicious warmth of a less expensive box-tube or slant-wall down bag on the erroneous theory that down will be uncomfortable in mild weather. As a rule—except in a few parts of this country—nights are cool enough so that a light down bag with a full-length zipper is comfortable. If you get too warm, you can unzip it and toss the top down part-way or all the way off, just as you'd throw off a blanket.

Some bags have a two-way zipper, which is the most flexible of all for controlling your ventilation. The zipper should be a large, easy-to-manipulate, heavy-duty one—and that last term refers to strength, not weight. Nylon zippers are now as popular as metal; they never rust, never need lubrication, are very reliable, and don't "freeze up" and stick in cold weather. Personally, I've never had a metal one stick, but I've heard the complaint.

Since a zipper can't very well be airtight, it should be backed by a fairly wide weather strip. This often takes the form of a down-filled flap, but I don't think that's essential in a bag for the average mild-weather hiker.

A few of the recently introduced down bags have replaced the zipper with Velcro fastening strips which close tight when pressed together. These seem to work quite well. The only closure system to avoid like the plague (and it's rarely seen any more even on the lightest warm-weather bags) is the line of snap fasteners. They're hard to work, they pop open when they shouldn't, and they leave wide, drafty gaps.

Many bags—of both the mummy shape and the rectangular variety—have zippers that extend only part-way down. I strongly prefer a full-length zipper, not only for ease of entry and exit but to get ventilation on a warm night and to facilitate airing out the bag. On rectangular models, I particularly like the kind of zipper that goes all the way down and then across the bottom so that I can open the bag out like a blanket. A few of the mummy models have no zipper at all but only a drawstring at the top opening, which hoods your head. I suppose the lack of a zipper might be an advantage in terrifically cold weather, if you don't freeze before you struggle into the infernal cocoon. There are those who advocate a side zipper on a mummy bag and those who advocate a front zipper; I can't see that it makes the slightest difference as long as there is a zipper *somewhere*.

Cleaning Methods

Some hikers have steered away from down bags because of the supposed necessity of dry-cleaning them. However, many of the newer ones are washable with warm water and soap. A few can even be washed with mild detergent (though detergents have to be destructively strong to get things any cleaner than good old-fashioned soap, regardless of advertising claims).

As for bags insulated with synthetics, some of them are machine washable, and I've even washed my down bag in a machine without any ill effects that I can detect. Most bags have a label attached, stating what material is used for the cover, lining, and insulation, and usually it will also recommend a cleaning procedure. Leave the label on as a reminder, particularly if the bag must be dry-cleaned. A dry cleaner can do a better job and avoid damaging the bag if he knows what the material is.

As stated earlier, a dry-cleaned bag should be thoroughly aired out before use, to dissipate any toxic chemical fumes. Frequent and thorough airing also keeps the insulation fluffy (it won't insulate when matted) and keeps it smelling and looking good. For greatest efficiency, a sleeping bag should be clean and dry, and should be shaken out and fluffed like a pillow.

Sometimes after airing a sleeping bag I drop an extra bar of soap—wrapped in a plastic bag or inside a clean sock—down into the bag. The soap gives it a good, clean aroma. Pine- or balsam-scented soap is particularly nice for this purpose.

Bag Contours and Sizes

In warm weather I prefer the old-fashioned rectangular sleeping bag. I kick and toss and stretch in my sleep, and a rectangular bag gives me room to do so without getting all tangled up. It also permits the greatest air flow when you open the zipper in warm weather, and it can be opened flat (if it has a full-length, run-around zipper) to facilitate a thorough airing or washing.

Both rectangular and mummy bags are available in several sizes. There are rectangular ones over seven feet long for tall people, and even longer in the mummy style since the top is supposed to go around your head. There are also wide models for the portly, small ones for children, and double or zip-together rectangular models for couples. If you hike with your spouse, remember that one big sleeping bag is lighter than two small ones; it can be carried in one pack, saving weight and room in the other pack for additional supplies. A standard-size square-cut bag will usually measure something like 33 inches wide and 76 inches long.

Bauer full-mummy bag (pictured with insulated mittens and Primus stove that works on white gas, naphtha, or Coleman fuel). Filled with 100 per cent prime northern goose down.

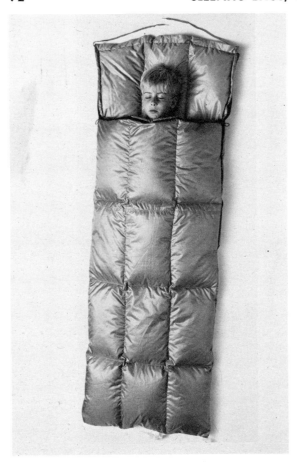

Down-filled Junior Camper from Eddie Bauer has pillow section whose corners can be tied below youngster's chin to form extra-warm hood.

Many rectangular bags have a canopy extension, and I consider this a desirable feature. But some are intended only for use inside a tent and they lack the extension. If a bag doesn't have a canopy with drawstrings, it should be equipped with roll-up ties for easy carrying and/or a stuff bag in which it can be packed.

Much as I like the rectangular style, I have to admit that a mummy bag is cozier in cold weather. A rectangular bag has to be substantially heavier for equal warmth. The name "mummy bag" is an accurate description of the form-fitting style but perhaps has an unpleasant connotation for some people, and this may be why it failed to gain complete acceptance for a while. Now, however, it's becoming more popular among backpackers than the rectangular style.

There are so many variations that it's hard to say what a "standard" mummy bag is, but the slim-contoured type that really hugs the body is—in medium size—a little more than two feet wide at the top and tapers to less than half that width at the bottom. At the very top, a "full-mummy" bag narrows again and usually has an elasticized or drawstring opening (in addition to the side or front zipper), so that you have a face-wide breathing hole but can sleep with your head warmly wrapped. Instead of or in addition to this top arrangement, some models have a detachable insulated hood.

There are slightly modified mummy bags, tapering from thirty inches or so at the shoulders to about twenty inches at the foot. The extra bulk means that it has to be a tiny bit heavier than a real form-fitter of equal warmth. But if you're uncomfortable—as I am—with your legs crammed together down to the toes, this type may be for you. I like even more room, and it can now be had in tapered bags whose tailoring is about midway between that of the mummy and the rectangle. A standard tapered bag is around thirty-three inches wide at the top and two feet wide where your two feet go. The bottom layer of some tapered models—the part that goes under your head—is longer than the covering layer, so that you have a pillowing effect, and it can easily be pulled around the back and sides of your head if you don't use a hood.

Still another variation is a full mummy or semimummy that flares out at the foot so that the over-all bulk is still less than that of a tapered or rectangular bag but your feet don't feel cramped.

Air Mattresses and Foam Pads

A one-half- or three-quarter-length foam pad makes a slightly bulkier roll than a deflated air mattress of the same length, but weighs less than a pound, whereas the air mattress will generally weigh almost two pounds. I don't generally bother with either, because I can soften a sleeping area sufficiently with leaves, or pine needles, or with a bed of dead evergreen boughs, needles, leaves, and ferns. When I plan to remain at a campsite for several days, I make a fairly deep, elaborate bed of these materials, held together by a frame of dead sapling poles or logs—one at the top, one at the bottom, one at each side. Two of the four can be notched for a mortised effect if they're thick and you want a deep bed that won't disintegrate.

But cushioning is only half the purpose of a mattress or pad. The other half (or perhaps two thirds) is insulation. The down or synthetic insulation in your sleeping bag becomes compressed with your weight, and the part of it that's underneath you is then nearly useless. Someone ought to design a bag with down or synthetic insulation on top and a foam pad built in underneath. At any rate, you may welcome a mattress or pad on a cold night.

Some sleeping bags have a long pocket into which a pad or air mattress can be slipped. The whole works—bag, pad, and all—can often be packed inside a stuff bag of adequate size. But if the pad or mattress is too bulky, it will have to be rolled (or folded) and packed separately.

If the pad isn't inside a bag pocket, it should be placed between the bag and a ground cloth or tarp. In damp areas, moisture sometimes condenses on a tarp, making the bottom of a sleeping bag damp and clammy if it's in direct contact. Keeping the bag up off the tarp is one more advantage of a pad or mattress—in addition to cushioning and insulation.

With or without this cushioning, you'll increase your sleeping comfort if you can find a clear sleeping spot with a slight hollow (just a slight one) for your hips. After all, there isn't much give to a thin pad and there's no give at all to the hard ground. Lumps, bumps, or bulges beneath your back will be uncomfortable. You'll also increase your comfort by rolling up some soft clothing for a pillow. I have a light quilted windbreaker which is ideal for the purpose when rolled and put into a stuff bag.

An air mattress is softer than a pad but poorer insulation. The best mattresses are rubberized nylon, which outlasts plastic. A rubber plug-and-stem valve is better than the metal type—easier to inflate and not subject to freezing up. Good mattresses of backpacking size are available for about $8.00 to $15, while good pads can be purchased for less than $10.

Polyurethane sleeping mats are softer than foam or ensolite pads but are relatively heavy and bulky. A foam or ensolite pad three feet long is really all you need. The foam type is generally about 1½ inches thick and is covered with nylon. The ensolite (or "closed-cell") pad needn't be covered as it won't absorb moisture. Since it doesn't compress very much, it usually isn't much over half an inch thick.

Ground Cloths, Tarps, and Tube Tents

Unless you'll be sleeping in a tent that has a sewn-in ground cloth, you should have a waterproof ground covering; it should measure at least four by seven feet, and the ideal size is about seven by nine. If two people are to share it,

Author's canopied Comfy sleeping bag is set for sleeping outside tent on bed of evergreen boughs and ferns held in frame of notched logs.

something a little larger is needed. Coated nylon makes an excellent ground cloth; it costs from about $10 up, depending on size. Rubberized cloth is cheaper but heavy. Plastic film is very light and very cheap, so a good many hikers prefer it, but it doesn't wear as well or dry as fast as coated nylon.

Whatever material you select, a generously proportioned ground cloth can also serve as a windbreak or emergency tent, and will make a good rain cover for your sleeping bag or any other gear carried atop a pack.

If you're not packing a tent, you should have a tarp in addition to the ground cloth. In case the weather turns really wet, you'll want a shield above as well as under you. For this purpose, plastic film is fine, and a seven-by-nine sheet is more than adequate for a shelter tarp. Some hikers buy a nine-by-twelve sheet (a standard size that shouldn't cost much over $5.00) and cut a four-foot strip from it for a ground cloth, then use the remaining eight-by-nine sheet as a shelter tarp.

Another approach is to buy or make a plastic tube tent, which will cost little more and will do away with the need for a ground cloth and/ or separate tarp. Many camping suppliers sell them ready-made. To fashion your own, start with a large sheet of plastic and seal two opposite edges together to form a tube. The sealing is done by placing the edges between strips of aluminum foil and pressing with a warm iron.

In use, the tube becomes a triangle, with two sloping walls like those of a pup tent and with the base of the triangle forming the floor—that is, a ground cloth under your sleeping bag. To set it up, just stretch a taut line through the tube and tie the ends to trees or poles to support it. This is one of the many uses for the nylon cord that I recommended packing. Your sleeping bag, placed lengthwise on the bottom, anchors the shelter, which should be several feet longer than the bag itself if it's to keep you dry.

Clothespins, which are handy gadgets for a lot of camp uses, will keep the top of a tube tent more securely positioned over the line that holds it up. All you need is one clothespin at each end.

For backpacking with a minimum of weight in mild weather, that's quite enough shelter. But if, like me, you prefer a little luxury when

possible, you can dispense with the ground cloth, tarp, or tube tent and pack a more sophisticated tent plus a poncho (which can serve as an emergency windbreak, shelter, or ground cloth).

Tents

Other hikers sneer when they see my Eureka two-man tent, and I'll admit it does weigh eleven pounds, but when I don't have to pack it far and I'm going to be camping for several days it's a nice luxury. With an external skeleton of short aluminum tension poles, it goes up in about four minutes, never leaks a drop of water, has a rain fly and zippered insect netting plus storm flaps at the entrance, and a built-in heavy-duty ground cloth. I seldom bother with· guy ropes because nothing less than a hurricane is likely to budge it when anchoring stakes are put through the corner grommets.

Still, I wouldn't dream of taking it on a really long hike when I could have an equally roomy one such as the Hinman Two-Man Backpacker Tent, which weighs less than four pounds—including all poles and stakes—and rolls to the size of a cereal box. That particular model has foot-high vertical walls (a fairly unusual feature on a light backpacking model) under a sloping

Author and his daughter rig aluminum supports of two-man Eureka tent.

roof that peaks at three feet four inches. It's four and a half feet wide, seven feet long, and fully floored, so you don't need an extra tarp. And in spite of its light weight, it, too, has storm flaps, a rain fly, and netting. It costs about $70, but that's average for a good nylon backpacking tent.

If you don't mind carrying a slightly heavier model—six and a half pounds—one version of the Sears Hillary Go-Pack nylon tent costs less than $50 and is even roomier. It's another one with foot-high side walls, and the sloping roof has a center height of four feet nine inches while

Ted Williams Sportsman Tent (left) and four-man Pack Tent are in Sears, Roebuck line of backpacking gear.

Two-man Trailtent weighs under five pounds, yet is sufficiently large; its coated nylon is strong and very water repellent.

the waterproof flooring covers a full five by seven feet. The rather similar nylon Trailtent, made by Trailcraft, is not quite as high but is a tiny bit wider and longer. It sells for around $40 or so.

Naturally, Sears also has fancier models at higher prices, and they go clear up to cabin size. A couple that I like for their light weight, ease of pitching, protective features, spaciousness when erected, and compactness when taken down are the Ted Williams two-man Sportsman and four-man Hillary Pack Tent.

L. L. Bean has a two-man nylon tent that provides a five-by-eight floor, weighs less than five pounds, and costs about $40. I think it's safe to say that good hiking tents begin at about that price, and some of them—particularly insulated ones like the fine Camp Trails Thermal Storm Tent—cost about $100. A few cost still more.

A real hiking tent shouldn't weigh more than about ten pounds. Some of the nylon models, including the insulated ones, weigh less than six. The water-repellent nylon itself weighs less than the water-repellent cotton that was most popular until recently. Telescoping aluminum or fiberglass poles, very light (often plastic) pegs, and clever design save weight as well as space.

Orvis Out-Frame tent is much like author's roomy two-man cotton-twill tent but made of nylon and therefore lighter. This type of exterior-frame tent has no space-robbing center pole and can be moved about (to get in or out of sunlight, for instance) when erected.

When watertight nylon first gained wide acceptance, a frequently heard complaint was that breath condensed inside a tent made of this material and caused too much dampness. However, both design and fabric have now been improved, and most of the camping-supply manufacturers and outfitters I've named in this book—the same ones who market packs and sleeping bags—now feature nylon backpacking tents.

The styles and sizes seem almost infinite, and some are truly ingenious. Gerry's Lodgepole, for example, employs tent-within-a-tent construction, with an inner fabric that "breathes" and keeps condensation at a minimum. It weighs about three and a half pounds and has a four-by-seven-foot floor, which is about minimum for comfortable sleeping. It's another of those costing around $70, and a roomier version can be had for about $20 more. I singled out the Lodgepole because I happen to have examined one, but several other companies employ more or less similar and equally clever designs.

Among other firms that offer excellent light tents are Alpine Designs, Eddie Bauer, Coleman, Himalayan, Hirsch-Weis, Orvis, Trailblazer, etc.

At one time I'd have advised getting the kind of two-man cloth tent that takes down into two shelter halves. With two partners each carrying one of the halves, the packing weight was acceptably light. But the really light nylon backpacking models have made that unnecessary.

Among the interesting variations in design are the Thermos Pop-Tents which fold down into a fairly compact bag and virtually spring up for use. You link the rods, hold the structure erect, and then push down on the top joint until a lock clicks and the tent pops up. You can raise one of the smaller models in about a minute and a half. This type isn't as light as some of the more conventional tents but, like my old cotton Eureka, it's great when you don't have to lug a heavy pack very far.

Incidentally, if you have an old cotton tent and it has begun to leak a little, you can improve it by spraying it with Scotchgard (do this when it's up and taut), or you can stretch a nylon or plastic fly over it while camping.

For hiking purposes, I don't like a tent larger than the biggest two-man models—about six-by-

Thermos Pop-Tents pop up on ingenious frames and can be readied for use in less than two minutes. They offer plenty of headroom, even in small models.

eight. They get too heavy for backpacking, and if a number of people are hiking together it will be easier to carry enough small tents than fewer large ones. The big models are primarily designed for truly long sojourns at base camps—or for traveling by canoe, horse, or vehicle, not for foot travel. But I must add that some of the newer four-man models are surprisingly light for their size and are really fine base camps.

This brings to mind still another clever design, the "modular" concept exemplified by the Browning Wind River tents. These are constructed as "modules" which can be used by themselves or can be enlarged by combining a module with a poncho, an extension shelter, or a second module. Two such tents can be joined directly together or connected with one or more extension shelters between them.

What I've given here is a basic set of guidelines for choosing a tent (if you use a tent at all). With so many types available, there's no way to know which kind will best suit an individual or family. Since tents are relatively expensive, it's smart to visit several dealers and inspect a number of styles before selecting one. And before making a final decision, it's also wise to rent one that appeals to you and try it. This is one more reason for welcoming the rise of the rental business among camping-equipment dealers.

Flashlights and Lanterns

A candle and a two-cell flashlight are minimum lighting gear for every hiker. If you're going to be out longer than overnight, at least one member of the party ought to have a three- or four-cell flashlight or something still more powerful and with a long battery life or long-lasting fuel supply. It isn't just that you may want to read or make notes in the evening; you may need illumination for all sorts of practical purposes, from repairing a tent to finding the latrine trench.

In addition to lanterns that utilize standard D-cell batteries, there are many models that use

Because of weight, hikers are advised to use large tents only at base camps, not for backpacking, but "cutaway" view shows how roomy four-man tent can be. This one is Bean's 30-pound Draw-Tite Alpine, set up for use as base-camp dining tent.

a more powerful energy source. L. L. Bean's Waterproof Sportsman's Lantern, for instance, holds a six-volt battery that throws a strong beam. It's encased in plastic and has both a carrying handle and a removable web carrying strap. Like many such lanterns, it has a selector switch that changes the steady beam to a red emergency flasher. A lantern of this type costs about $7.00.

Teledyne Big Beam makes a variety of metal-cased hand lanterns using the same standard six-volt lantern batteries. They feature wide lamp heads that pivot up or down on the front corner of the carrying handle, and prices begin at about $9.00. A single-battery lamp of this type, with a sealed-beam bulb, is rated at 40,000 candlepower. Its beam is visible a mile

away. Some models, beginning at about $12, have a red flasher on a folding arm and some of them attach directly to a twin-pack battery that supplies twelve volts rather than six. For a few dollars more you can get one that operates on either one or two six-volt batteries and has an even higher candlepower rating. This and other firms have a wide variety to choose from, but the larger models are relatively heavy and bulky.

Some hikers prefer to pack a small flashlight and a folding or telescoping candle lantern, which is very compact and costs under $5.00. It's a good emergency light, but a candle won't last very long and I don't like the idea of using one inside a tent.

Carbide lamps seem to be making a comeback, and Justrite Manufacturing Company produces camping models. This type of lamp is operated by water dripping onto calcium carbide pellets inside a handled container (which is made of tough plastic these days), thus producing acetylene gas. Ignited by a built-in flint mechanism, the burning gas emits a brilliant

Bean's Waterproof Sportsman's Lantern (*above*) has red emergency flasher with standard light inside reflector housing. Teledyne Big Beam features optional flasher on folding arm.

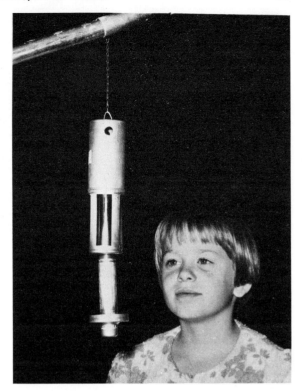

For traveling light, Gloy's telescoping candle lantern plus small flashlight may suffice.

white light from the reflector head. A typical hiking-camping model holds enough fuel for about seven hours, and when the light begins to dim you can add pellets from a waterproof pocket container and add a bit more water.

Many hikers who specialize in "spelunking"— cave exploration—favor the carbide lamp, partly for its brilliance and dependability, partly because a dimming of the flame may warn of the presence of carbon monoxide or marsh gas in a cave.

A carbide lamp has a hot enough flame to light damp tinder or warm your hands, but these advantages are offset by the possibility of starting a fire if you're not very careful. I wouldn't think of lighting such a lamp in a tent.

If you're going to be staying at one campsite for some time and are not concerned about packing bulk or weight, you may want a kerosene-, gasoline-, butane-, or propane-powered camp lantern. The gasoline and kerosene models that use mantles—which are safer, much brighter, less smoky, and more adjustable than the old-fashioned wick type—cost from about $15 to $23 and are made by most of the companies that produce camp heaters and stoves. I consider the wick type a fire hazard. Propane and butane lanterns utilize the mantle system and are probably even safer than mantled liquid-fuel types but are seldom quite as bright.

Justrite carbide lamp now comes in camping models.

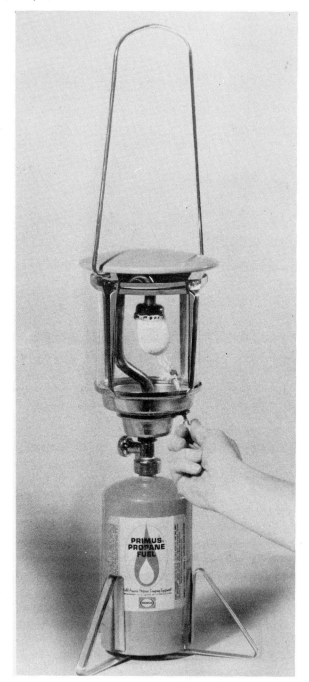

Ease of lighting propane lanterns is illustrated with Primus Model 300CP, which can be used with refillable cylinder.

The butane type isn't as powerful as the propane system, but is so light and compact that it's a good choice for backpacking. The Primus and Garcia Gaz butane lanterns give six or seven hours of light on a single, small, disposable cartridge and are adjustable up to about 75 or 80 watts of illumination. They cost around $11 or $12. It should be noted here that small butane heaters and compact, single-burner butane stoves are also available. If you use a butane stove, it makes sense to use a lantern fueled the same way; if you use a propane stove you'll probably want a propane lantern.

I have a Garcia Gaz lantern that works with a propane cylinder. It's adjustable and the mantle is shielded by a frosted cylindrical globe that makes for a soft light which can be brightened to about 150 watts. A cylinder provides about six hours of light if left on.

There are also models which can be hooked up either to a cylinder or a refillable bulk tank. Most of them give about a 100-watt light and are adjustable. There's a huge selection of styles and sizes, with prices ranging from less than $12 to around $60. For hiking use, I'd choose one of the smaller, less expensive models. Companies supplying good propane camp lanterns include BernzOmatic, Garcia, Coleman, Zebco/ Traveler, Thermos, Paulin, Primus, Trailblazer, and others.

One other and very unusual type of camp lantern has recently been produced by Coleman.

It's rectangular—4¾ inches wide, 13¼ inches high and just under nine inches from rear to front. The case is made of high-impact plastic, with a carrying handle at the top. The lamp itself is an eight-watt fluorescent tube—the type found in many desk and ceiling fixtures—shielded by a tough plastic lens. It gives a cool, soft light equivalent to the illumination of a standard 60-watt incandescent bulb. The light is nicely distributed by a white reflector. The power source is as unusual as the lamp; it's an eight-volt wet-cell battery that employs ordinary tap or spring water and has attached cords for up to 150 recharges from an automobile cigarette lighter or standard 110–115-volt electrical circuit. That means a battery will provide up to about 3,000 hours—125 days—of light. A dial on the side of the case can be switched to high or low illumination, or to an off or recharge position.

It's a big, heavy lantern, and not inexpensive—about $50—but has a lot of appeal for use around a base camp that's set up for long occupancy.

Coleman's Charger 3000, powered by long-lasting wet-cell battery, is well designed for use at hikers' base camps.

Knives, Axes, and Saws

Having already mentioned that a multibladed Boy Scout knife is a superb hiking implement, I must add here that some outdoorsmen prefer the so-called Swiss Army knife. It's a folding pocket model designed on the same principle and usually featuring a flat red or maroon plastic handle ornamented with a Swiss cross or some other little decoration. The real difference between this and the conventional Scout knife is that the Swiss form comes in several sizes and grades, with a startling choice of blade combinations. I can't convince myself that the nail file included on some models will get much use on the trail, and I'm not even intoxicated over the inclusion of a corkscrew—though it's hard to find a good hefty version without that. However, a sturdy outdoor model such as the $15 Woodsman marketed by Compass Instrument & Optical Company does combine an impressive array of tools: a large blade (almost 3½ inches long), a smaller blade, a can opener, bottle-cap lifter, screwdriver, reamer, scissors, double-cut saw blade . . . and the almost inevitable corkscrew.

The same company sells a single-bladed, five-inch, folding hunting knife for about $8.00. This general design, characterized by a lock-open safety blade, is becoming very popular among hikers as well as hunters. Bob Hinman markets one for about the same price with a snap-flapped leather belt sheath. Browning offers an extremely high-quality version for around $25. Other reliable brands include G-96, the Henckels knife imported by Eddie Bauer, the Precise Imports, Puma, and Buck knives. A couple of the Precise and Puma models have two blades, one of which is a sturdy little saw.

My own knife of this type is the Folding Hunter made by Buck Knives. With a heavy-duty, snap-flap leather belt sheath it's priced at about $16. It has a four-inch, high-carbon steel blade (you don't need anything longer than that), an ebony handle, and solid brass bolsters. With the honing oil and stones produced by Buck or Russell, a knife like this keeps a magnificent edge.

When you're going to be on the trail more than a couple of days, an item to keep in pocket or pack is a small sharpening stone. You may want to use it on your ax as well as on a knife blade. At home, you should have a

Standard Scout Knife (top) such as that made by Schrade-Walden and marketed by Gutmann Cutlery is excellent hiking implement, as is Swiss Army knife of type imported by Compass Instrument and others. Deerslayer folding knife distributed by Precise Imports comes with leather sheath and has saw as well as standard blade. Lock-open device prevents danger of accidental closing.

sharpening kit consisting of honing oil, a soft "Arkansas" stone, and a harder, fine-grit finishing stone which is usually small and is the kind to pack. Sharpening is easy, and the kits come with instructions that tell you all you need to know, right down to suggested angles at which to run a blade over a stone.

To digress for a moment, a camp ax must also be kept sharp, and not just to make your work easier. A dull one tends to glance or bounce, which is dangerous. The first stage of sharpening an ax is to get rid of any bad nicks or depressions with a file or grindstone. (Don't use a power-driven grindstone on a good ax useless you've had plenty of experience; if you do, you may roll the edge or even burn out the temper of the steel.) After the initial smoothing, proceed with a coarse stone and then a finer stone just as with a knife.

In addition to the single and double lock-open knives I've described, there are lots of other well-made folding models. Some of the good but moderately priced brands include Edgemark, Schrade-Walden, (my Scout knife is a Schrade-Walden), Puma, Gerber, Buck, Normark, Precise, and Browning.

These same companies and a number of others also make non-folding sheath knives of the type originally developed for hunters. The large ones are special-purpose knives and there's no need for a hiker to carry one. However, a sturdy sheath knife with a blade of four to five inches can be useful. It might almost be regarded as a spare, or emergency, trail ax. Get a well-balanced one with a sturdy handle, a small handguard, and a good steel blade. Don't get one that doesn't have a rugged belt sheath with a snap-flap or strap to keep the knife from falling out. I like the flap type best, as it prevents the blade from slipping even part-way out. The price range is about the same as for folding models.

In addition to your folding and/or belt knife, you may want a sharp, thin-bladed filleting knife in your cooking kit. Normark, Gloy's, and Ipco import good ones for about $4.00 to $6.00, depending on length and grade. The thin, tapered blade of such a knife is handy for many cooking chores besides filleting.

An ax is far from essential on most hikes. The Sierra Club's booklet on knapsacking equipment recommends no sharp-bladed instrument

Author's hiking-camping knife is Folding Hunter made by Buck Knives. It keeps magnificent edge and has lock-open feature.

other than a Scout-type pocketknife, pointing out that axes are not only an unnecessary burden but that "cutting standing snags or chopping on large down trees is frowned upon in high-country wilderness."

In theory I certainly agree, but some hiking situations are an exception to the rule. If you travel through a National Forest on horseback, or even on foot but leading pack stock, you're *required* to have an ax, and it must have a handle at least twenty-six inches long. There are several reasons. Most obviously, you're expected to be on an extended outing, and chopping wood may be a real necessity. When you're very far from civilization, an ax can become a sur-

In camping scene at Everglades National Park, family unlimbers tent poles while Dad demonstrates hammering advantage of author's favorite type of trail ax.

vival tool. And there are even times when axes are used in fire fighting. The reason for stipulating a large one is that really tough chopping jobs call for a two-handed swing of the ax.

Under other conditions there is no such requirement, but a government booklet on backpacking in National Forest wilderness and primitive areas (Booklet PA-585—an excellent guide) lists an ax or hatchet among needed equipment. "Hatchet" is just another term for a short-handled trail ax, also called a belt ax. I prefer this type for outings that call for any ax at all. A long one is too heavy and cumbersome. You won't need it for most expeditions.

I believe the very worst kind of ax for the average outdoor enthusiast is the double-bit "timber-cruiser's" design. You'll have absolutely no need for two sharp edges. An axhead that's sharp at one end and forms a hammer at the other is far more useful. Moreover, it takes long ax-wielding experience to use a double-bit ax safely.

A good belt model may be anywhere from about eleven to fifteen inches long and may weigh anything from less than a pound to about three pounds. I prefer a short to medium length and fairly light weight for the occasional chopping or splitting that might be called for at a typical campsite. Buck makes a good 10½-inch all-steel model with a phenolic handle for about $20, but most steel-hafted axes are neither as

well balanced nor as thickly hammerheaded as wood-hafted models. Good wood-hafted axes are priced from about $6.00 to $10. Edgemark, Forester, Kelly, Collins, Hinman, Gloy's, and a host of other companies supply them. The best handle is hickory, but maple and oak and even birch are satisfactory. Just don't buy one with sharply contrasting lines or layers of wood, as it may split. Otherwise, if it's made of good steel, feels well-balanced in your hand, and comes with a secure leather belt sheath, it will do. Edgemark, Hercules, and a few other brands offer an ax and a knife together, sold as a unit with a combination sheath or connected sheaths. Kelly and a few others offer odder combination purchases, such as an ax, camp spade, and bow saw that can be clamped together for packing.

If you're going to be doing a lot of work around a base camp, you may want to spend a few dollars on a folding saw, or a camping spade, or a wire saw, or all three. They cost very little but aren't needed by the average hiker. I prefer a garden trowel to a folding spade except for use at semipermanent campsites. A wire, or cable, saw has a finger ring at each end of a flexible cutting wire that can be rolled up so it takes no space. It will cut small logs if you're strong and patient. A folding saw will take care of bigger jobs, but it, too, is only needed at a permanent or semipermanent campsite.

Chapter 8

FIRES AND STOVES, FOOD AND COOKING

There was a time when I couldn't see much point in packing a portable stove, even a very small one, unless I planned to be at one campsite for a long spell. I considered the camp stove just one more encumbrance. It was (and is) more fun to cook over a fire. And I didn't carry a portable heater, either, because the cooking fire, with a good-sized reflector, also provided comforting warmth.

But nowadays many hiking clubs and conservation groups discourage fire-making, and at some campsites it's prohibited. For one thing, the current boom in outdoor recreation has sent so many people into certain camping areas that there is just not enough dead, dry wood to go around. For another thing, too many novices chop away at living trees, which generally make poor firewood, and the killing of trees is inexcusable now that we have gained a belated awareness of the need for conservation. For still another thing, carelessness (and not just among novices) has caused forest fires. Finally, even where there is enough firewood to go around, it must be used sparingly because nature doesn't replenish it all that quickly. Deadfalls, blowdowns, and the like add to the wild natural beauty of the forests even while decomposing to form compost that will renew the life of those forests.

On the other hand, there are obviously places where careful, responsible fire-making will add to hiking enjoyment without doing any harm. Also, a situation can arise that calls for a fire whether you want one or not. I'm not thinking only of getting lost or needing to signal for help. Suppose a stove were to break or a faulty fuel cylinder were to leak away your gas supply?

Not likely, but always possible. Fire-making is therefore a required skill of the proficient hiker.

Firewoods

Some hardwoods (generally speaking, the term refers to woods from deciduous trees) are poor burners or fail to make good coals, but most of them are the fundamental materials of a proper cooking fire. Many are called "sweet woods" because of the fine aroma and subtle flavor they impart. Speaking of aromas, the Indians sometimes attracted deer and other animals by putting dried bearberries or aster roots in their fires. Incense also works; occasionally it will attract various kinds of wildlife close enough for photography if you remain still and silent. This can be a poor idea where it might attract bears or skunks, but in some areas it's an enjoyable experiment for the hiking nature lover.

Unfortunately, it's difficult to get a fire started quickly with hardwoods. The easiest-starting, hottest materials are the fast-burning conifers, but I recommend using them only to get the blaze going. Then switch to hardwoods exclusively or very preponderantly, because the soft conifers are smoky, tend to pop, spark, and spit dangerously, burn away too quickly without leaving a sufficient bed of coals, and the resin in some species will taint food with an astringent or even turpentiny flavor.

Cedar is almost an exception. White cedar, although it does shoot sparks at first, is not only a top starting wood but useful in larger pieces and in combination with other woods for cooking. It splits easily, and I like its aroma.

Hiker-fishermen in Manitoba cook lunch over dry driftwood, which usually makes good, slow-burning embers. (Canadian Government Travel Bureau Photo)

Other coniferous species which are particularly good as starters include balsam and other firs, pine, spruce, and tamarack (if you skin it of its practically fireproof bark). I'm speaking only of dry, relatively seasoned wood. When green, most of these burn badly, as do certain deciduous types that start fast and make good kindling: alder, box elder, catalpa, cottonwood, cypress, and (if you hike in the Southwest) mesquite. Sometimes when mesquite is present, nothing else is; fortunately, it can be used both as kindling and as firewood. Small, dry pieces of the other woods I've mentioned are likely to

spark, but they burn fast and hot; their drawback for cooking is that they first blaze too much and are consumed too fast, and then leave hardly any coals.

Small dry twigs of hemlock will also start a fire, but big, knotty pieces are so fire-resistant that they make good andirons, or backlogs. Other woods that are especially good for this purpose are basswood (linden), buckeye, elm, willow, and pine (in the form of fairly sizable, round logs). Cypress is also good andiron material *if* it's still green. When seasoned, it burns fast.

More often than not, you won't be able to positively identify the species from a piece of dead dry wood. But you can frequently identify it or make a very educated guess from the live, standing trees around it, from its location and from its general appearance and bark. It is therefore helpful to pack a field guide.

Dried driftwood, which may be just about any species, is usually slow burning, makes good embers, and can also be used as backlogs. It's common along the coasts and on inland lake shores.

Anyone who has ever eaten smoked meat or fish must be aware that hickory imparts a delightful flavor. In burning characteristics, too, it's tops among firewoods for cooking. Others that are good when dry and seasoned are ash, beech, birch (though it tends to smoke up utensils), black haw, cherry and other fruitwoods, holly, ironwood, locust, maple (except for the soft swamp varieties), mulberry, Osage orange, persimmon, poplar (aspen), and walnut.

Some varieties of oak are so fire resistant that they can be grouped with the other species I recommended as backlogs. But half a dozen types of oak are excellent for cooking fires: white, chestnut, overcup, post, barren, and pin oak.

Whether you're using birch or any other wood, you can reduce the sooting of pot and pan bottoms—and make the soot easy to remove—by coating the utensils' undersides with a thin film of soap. Just rub a moist soap bar on them before cooking.

I consider charcoal briquettes far too heavy, cumbersome, and messy to pack, but some luxury lovers take a small bagful on short hikes. They're great when—eventually—they begin to

"Hobo stove" made from large juice or coffee can is excellent over small fire for making pancakes, frying eggs, boiling water, and so on. (*Courtesy Quaker Oats*)

glow. That takes a long time, even if you wet them down with a liquid fire starter. To speed the process, you can start them in a confined pile, held together in a large juice or coffee can with both ends cut out. When they're good and hot, use tongs or a thickly padded pot glove to lift the can away. Spread the coals and they'll be ready for cooking.

Building a Fire

I've also used a large can to make a "hobo stove." For this purpose only one end is removed. The open end is the bottom and the other end is a burner surface on which you can fry an egg, a flapjack, a small trout or perch, etc., or heat a metal cup of soup or stew—or plain water for tea, instant coffee, or whatever. On the circular wall of the can at the bottom, you cut a fair-sized opening, like an oven entrance or miniature fireplace, with tin snips or an old-fashioned bladed can opener. You'll feed the fire through the opening. Around the upper part of the can wall, near the top rim, punch several holes. The easiest way to do this is with a pry-up can opener of the type that punctures triangular holes. This gives you a draft so that the fire will burn well with the can on top of it.

Following the fire-making instructions given below, build a small stick or chip fire and place the can on top of it. After that, feed the fire through the bottom hole you've cut. If you use the can's top surface for frying, be sure to grease it lightly.

For more ambitious cooking, you may want a backpacker's grill, a folding reflector oven, or a frame-and-hanger arrangement to suspend pots over the heat. But first let's get the fire going.

An area of at least six feet on all sides of your fire should be cleared of all twigs, leaves, dry grasses, or humus. Your fireplace is the center of this clearing. If you use flat rocks to set utensils on and to retain and reflect heat and shield the fire from the wind, be sure the rocks are perfectly dry so they won't crack or explode. Place a shovel, trowel, or scoop near at hand, together with a collapsible water bucket, full canteen, or pot of water. Some hikers also use a small syringe-type water sprinkler, which can tame a fire (for example, if fat drops into it) without completely drowning it or drenching the food. Spread out your utensils and food conveniently near so that you can easily reach everything needed while tending the fire. I usually just line everything up, but you may prefer to hang some utensils from a nearby line or a clip-type fish stringer, or hang up a shoe bag and fill its pockets with small utensils, condiments, packets of flour and seasonings, etc.

Even if you don't carry your own tinder, paraffin-soaked paper rolls, kerosene-soaked sawdust in a small container, or some other type of starter, you'll probably have little trouble except in wet weather. Fine tinder is provided by nature in the form of dry grasses, evergreen needles, dead leaves, shredded cedar bark, curls of birch bark, tiny dry twigs, abandoned birds' nests, little balls of pine resin, and so on. If the tinder isn't thoroughly dry, find a few fairly small twigs and cut a series of loose bark curls along them—peelings, but with the curls still clinging to the twigs. These "fuzz sticks" go on top of the loose, sizable ball of tinder, which you can place in the center of the fireplace. Toss on a few very small twigs, chips, or shavings— the driest you can find—and have a pile of wood ready, in graduated sizes from pencil diameter to chunks or logs. Get down low, in position to fan the tinder or gently blow on it. Light it at the bottom in several places, leaving the burning wooden matches poking into the tinder fluff as additional fuel. As soon as it blazes up a little, begin loosely crisscrossing the tinder wood, the smallest pieces, on top of it. Keep fanning until it's going well, and then begin adding the larger wood.

From this point on, you can be leisurely about feeding the fire. You don't want a large, high flame. A low one, or just glowing embers, will be best for almost all kinds of cooking except deep-frying in very hot oil. If you do happen to be frying a fish, say, or home fries in hot oil, use the center of the fire for that purpose and heat everything else over the glowing coals at the edges. The same "fringe-benefit" principle applies to potatoes, corn, or anything else you want to roast by wrapping it in foil and burying it in the coals. To prevent scorching, it should be poked in among the outermost embers.

There are several basic types of fires. If you just want to boil water, do a quick bit of frying, warm up, or briefly provide some light, the simplest structure is the inverted-V, or tepee fire. Make it by piling sticks over the kindling in a tepee shape. It will soon collapse, forming a star which is hottest at the center. Push the sticks inward as they burn and add more until you have a hot, slow-burning bed of charcoal embers.

Building it against rocks, a backlog, or the rear of a fireplace, you can make a variation known as the "dinglestick" fire—piled up like half of a tepee against the rear support, which acts as an ovenlike heat reflector. If you wish, you can contain the fire and provide a support for a pot, skillet, or grill by adding two sidelogs, fanned out in a V shape. In addition, you can dangle a kettle, stew pot, tea pail, or coffeepot over the heat—hanging from long sticks propped and anchored by rocks or logs at an angle above the fire. The angle must be high enough so that a pot-holding stick won't burn.

To suspend several pots over a fire without benefit of a grill, you can build a stick frame. Sharpen the unforked ends of two long, forked sticks and drive one into the ground on each side of the fire. The forks should be high enough (say, two to four feet) so that the pots will be

Hiker scrapes knife on Metal Match to spark tinder for tepee-style fire.

Hiker combines rock fireplace with use of propped-up pole to dangle pot over dinglestick fire.

nicely elevated and the wooden frame and hangers won't burn. Lay a straight sapling pole (preferably a dead but still green one) across the forks. Now find two or three straight sticks with branches growing out at an angle so that they can be hooked over the sapling pole and will hang down fairly straight. Trim the angled branches short enough to leave a reliable overhanging hook without having branch ends get in your way. Cut several notches in the straight, longer leg of each such hanger-stick. Hoop-type pot handles can now be slipped onto whatever notch will dangle a pot at the desired elevation. Incidentally, hooked sticks can also be used

to lift a hot pot by the hoop handle when you've misplaced your padded potholder glove.

If you don't have many utensils, and you want a fast, hot fire on which you can directly place a pot or pan, start with a tepee fire and transform it into a crisscross fire—crisscrossing sticks around its rim like the walls of a log cabin. The diameter of this structure must decrease slightly as it climbs or it may collapse outward. In a short time, you'll have a hot ember fire, fairly level on top.

For cooking a real meal, a trapper fire is far better. It's built between two sidelogs—usually called "firedogs"—or flat-topped rocks. The rocks or firedogs are usually closer together at one end than at the other, almost forming a V. They're close at the tight end so you can place a small pot or saucepan across them, wide at the other end to accommodate your largest skillet or grill.

**New Jersey Scout combines pit fire with use of
wood spit-frame in case he wants to hang pots
over coals. (Leonard Lee Rue Photo)**

Between the firedogs, at about the center,
you build a tepee fire. As soon as it's going well,
enlarge it, spreading it toward both ends of the
semi-V that contains it so that you'll have a full-
length bed of coals.

A variation is the pit fire—more work, but
best of all for cooking. Instead of supporting
your grill or pots and skillets across a pair of
firedogs, you dig a shallow, oblong pit with your
trowel or spade. The sides of the pit reflect heat
and form a partial windscreen. They also con-
fine the fire and enable you to build up a thick
bed of coals which is excellent for all types of
cooking and superb for baking. Lay your grill
across the top of the pit and you can prepare
several dishes at once.

A Dutch oven is far too heavy to pack on
hikes, but I do recommend a reflector oven,
either made on the spot or the collapsible commercial kind. Aluminum foil is handy for many
camping purposes, including the fashioning of a
reflector. For use as a reflector, face a flat board,
or even a skillet or extra grill, with it. Prop it on
the ground at a steep angle about a foot and a
half from the fire, so it will reflect heat both for
cooking and to warm you. You can even prop or
pin a piece of meat or fish on it (with a trough
foil at the bottom to catch juices), and you will
have an excellent reflector oven. The commercial type of reflector has V or semi-V sides and a
sloping top and bottom which converge from the
wide open front. The top, bottom, and sides reflect heat onto a center shelf, where the food is
cooked. This provides a windshield and also
produces very uniform heat. It's good for cooking many things, especially for baking anything

Trapper fire uses sidelogs, or "firedogs," to support grill or utensils above fire. (Leonard Lee Rue Photo)

from potatoes to pies, cakes or biscuits. It's also excellent for warming up the cook.

You can improve the oven's reflecting quality and protect its metal by lining it with aluminum foil. Good reflector ovens are available from camping suppliers for about $8.00 to $16. Small, light steel-tubing grills, expressly designed for backpacking, cost less than $6.00. Such a grill comes in a carrying case and is narrow enough for use as an emergency splint. I've used a grill to prepare a full meal without using any pots or pans; the trick was simply to fashion small pots and pans (which subsequently served as cups and bowls) from double layers of heavy-duty aluminum foil. A larger, adjustable grill (nearly sixteen inches long) with its own collapsible legs

is offered by Sportsgear for about $8.00, and at about twice that price the manufacturer supplies an even larger, more sophisticated version with a collapsible spit. Another alternative is to remove and pack the grill from a larger, permanent-camp stove such as the Raemco.

In addition to reflectors and grills, there are sophisticated commercial versions of the hobo stove, which will also work beautifully as a charcoal lighter. A well-designed type is the Auto Fire model, about the size of a large coffeepot, with a carrying handle, made of aluminized steel and priced at around $5.00.

Cooking and Eating Implements

Accessories to consider are a protective plastic egg carrier, folding reflector-type bread toaster, knife-fork-spoon kit and "Sierra Club-style" wide

Combination leg and spit holds Sportsgear grill and reflecting foil over baking fire.

less than a dollar in aluminum. As a matter of fact, none of the items above costs more than about $4.00. Accessories of this general type are supplied by Edgemark, Gloy's, Bean, Gleason, and many others.

A good-sized but light aluminum ladle and/ or stirring spoon will come in handy, but such implements can usually be found around the house so there's no need to buy them just for hiking.

A nesting set of cooking ware, on the other hand, is an excellent $10 investment because the whole works will be so light and compact. L. L. Bean's cooking unit consists of two pots which can be used as a double boiler, deep lids that can be inverted to form excellent skillets, and a pot-lifter handle that can clamp onto the pots or skillets. The kit also includes a base and windscreen for the little Svea single-burner gasoline hiker's stove, which costs about $11 or $12 from Bean, Hinman, and other outfitters. The stove lid turns into a pot. Gleason's, Hinman, and other outfitters supply nesting cooking *and eating* sets—including cups and three-compartment mess plates—at prices ranging from about $8.00 to more than $20. The cups and plates should be either plastic or aluminum for durability and light weight. Disposable paper cups and plates are all right for short hikes, but only if they're burned or carried home after use.

aluminum cup with a wire handle (with which you can clip it to your belt). An alternative to that last item is a collapsible (telescoping) cup which will cost less than half a dollar in plastic,

Nesting sets of cooking and eating utensils, like these from Hinman, are useful on long hiking trips.

Stoves

Long ago when I was in the Army, my company was ordered to bivouac in 30° weather without fires, stoves, or heaters. We were, however, permitted to pack little cans of Sterno—"canned heat," as it's traditionally known—and we kept reasonably warm by huddling close over those cans of burning fuel. A seven-ounce can of the stuff still costs only about half a dollar and will burn for more than an hour before it's all consumed. The manufacturer now produces a little grill-topped aluminum folding stove that holds the can of fuel. It weighs less than eleven ounces, costs only a couple of dollars, and can be used for simple cooking jobs like scrambling eggs, frying hamburgers or fish, boiling coffee. It isn't the world's most efficient heat-producer but is fine for a single hiker who really wants to travel light, will cook no more than a couple of meals on the trail, and therefore won't have to pack more than a can or two of fuel.

For about the same price as this one-burner stove, the company also makes a two-burner, which holds two cans of fuel side by side and slightly separated. You may prefer it, but it weighs over a pound and I'd rather pack two of the single-burners.

The next step up in efficiency and sophistication is the single-burner alcohol or gasoline stove. Some hikers prefer models that burn white gasoline or kerosene. The Sierra Club knapsacking booklet rates these high for reliability in cold weather, lightness, clean burning, fuel capacity, and stability of the burner surface on which you place the pot or pan. For parties of one to four hikers, the booklet favorably mentions Primus and Svea white-gasoline stoves, which are indeed good. For larger parties, the booklet recommends kerosene models which have bigger fuel tanks and a more stable base for big pots or skillets. You'll have no problem keeping such a stove going at maximum heat for more than two hours.

Recently, the Svea and Primus have gained a competitor—the squatly compact Gerry #360 single-burner stove, which works well on any liquid fuel. It's less than three inches high, less than six inches in diameter, and though it looks heavy it weighs only one and a half pounds. It's reliable and will keep going on one filling just as long as the others.

In many areas, propane is replacing kerosene and gasoline (especially white gasoline, which isn't always available except in rural areas). About the only complaint I've heard regarding

(From left to right): Three fine single-burner backpacking stoves are Svea, Primus, and Gerry.

propane is that some types of this bottled gas will fail to function in very cold weather, but you can check with your dealer before buying any particular brand of propane unit. Among the suppliers of good, compact single-burner propane stoves are BernzOmatic, Coleman, Paulin, Primus, Trailblazer, and Zebco/Traveler. Look for a model that weighs no more than three pounds or so *including* the LP fuel cylinder.

I have a Primus propane Grasshopper, a single-burner model that's certainly as compact as the kerosene and gasoline stoves. It consists of nothing more than the burner platform itself and two thin but strong legs. When you attach the propane cylinder, that forms a third leg, making a stable little tripod on which to cook. It costs about $8.00. The same company offers an even more compact, lighter butane version for around $10 and Garcia has a small butane model on a squat, stable little stand. It costs about $8.00 and, with a fuel cartridge, weighs under a pound. Still smaller and lighter is a Gerry model priced at about $10.

Propane is more efficient and is used on most of the newer two-burner bottled-gas stoves. I prefer it to gasoline or kerosene, because it requires no pouring, pumping, priming. (Some of the conventional liquid-fuel single-burners need no pumping, either, but most of the larger stoves do.) Gloy's Cook-Pal two-burner is an alcohol stove that needs no priming or pumping. It weighs 12 pounds, folds to 18 by 10 by 3½ inches for carrying and costs about $60.

For most hiking families, I think it's a great idea to have two single-burners of whatever type you prefer. That way, your cooking equipment can be carried in two packs, with the least possible weight and bulk in each, and the stoves can be used together at mealtime. But if you do a lot of outdoor cooking, you may well want a two-burner plus (depending on the number of people in the family) one or two single-burners, each with its own propane or other fuel supply. My vote would go to propane in a situation of that kind. Several companies (Coleman, Paulin, Thermos, perhaps others) make good *three*-burner models, but they're relatively large and heavy; I'd recommend them only for permanent or semipermanent camps, not for hiking.

Excellent two-burner propane models are made by Paulin, Primus, Garcia, Coleman, Ther-

mos, Zebco/Traveler, BernzOmatic, Trailblazer, and others. The weight of such a stove varies from just over seven pounds with a windscreen to about fifteen, the average being eleven or twelve pounds. Be sure to get a model with a windscreen, whether detachable or permanent, which shields both the back and sides of the stove. On most models, the screen folds down for carrying or packing, so that the unit has a closed shape like that of an attaché case. Prices range all the way from less than $10 to about $50. The qualities to look for (all available at medium prices) are ease of operation, adjustability, durability, and portability.

Trail Menus and Cooking Tricks

I mentioned earlier that the average hiker consumes about a pound and a half of food per day. The figure does *not* include the between-meals trail snacks which I described as essential; it refers to actual meals. You may walk along munching a Jones Jiffy Meal (a famous fruit-nut-molasses bar with a high-energy yield and strong resistance to disintegration) and still want a full dinner at the end of the day's hike, having burned up that intake of energy. Moreover, the pound-and-a-half estimate is only a very rough average; some hikers require two-and-a-half pounds of food per day. A woman's or youngster's trail appetite may be just as large as a man's, and everyone's appetite invariably increases after a day or two of outdoor activity.

The human metabolism is remarkably variable. You'll have to calculate your own requirements on the basis of your normal appetite, adding a little to the calculations as a safety margin. And you'll have to calculate the needs of family members the same way—on the basis of what each person normally eats, plus a little extra. Then, if you're going to be in a wilderness area far from food sources, add two days' worth of rations per person, just in case.

Food requirements aren't just a matter of weight, of course. You must have a balanced diet, including sufficient carbohydrates, proteins, vitamins, and minerals. If you're not accustomed to planning family menus, there are two excellent sources of information. One is the Sierra Club book *Food for Knapsackers,* by Hasse Bun-

Hiker at Echo Lake, Colorado, proves Trailblazer propane stove functions properly in thin air of 10,600-foot elevation.

nelle ($1.95 from Sierra Club, 1050 Mills Tower, San Francisco, California 94104). It includes lists of recommended foods and cooking gear, excellent recipes, and up-to-date information on freeze-dried foods and their preparation. The other is a booklet called *Food Packing for Backpacking*, by Gerry Cunningham (free from Gerry Division, Outdoor Sports Industries, 5450 North Valley Highway, Denver, Colorado 80216). It includes advice about a balanced trail diet, supplementary foods and vitamins, cooking utensils, etc., plus three breakfast, lunch, and dinner suggestions.

One other qualification regarding the *amount* of food to pack: It's much easier than you might imagine to carry a pound and a half of food per day per person, because that weight refers to the actual intake, or "yield," not to the weight of freeze-dried and other dehydrated dishes in their packaged form. National Packaged Trail Foods, the firm that markets the excellent Seidel's Trail Packet foods, has printed a revealing list of packet weights, and a few examples will show what I mean. A 13-ounce packet of beef Stroganoff yields 52 *eating* ounces when heated up with water. That's four ample servings. You get 48 eating ounces from the 11¼-ounce packet of Seidel's Frontier Stew (a delicious concoction of ground beef, beans, corn, red and green peppers in a seasoned gravy). A 9½-ounce packet of chicken à la king yields 56 ounces. And so on. Wilson Campsite Foods, which are also delicious, furnish additional examples: A 2¾-ounce ham-and-scrambled-egg packet yields two good servings, as does a 7-ounce pork chop packet.

For anyone who isn't already acquainted with freeze-dried food packets, I must mention that they keep forever. One of these months I'll use the office hot plate to fix a lunch of Lipton's chicken noodle soup, but the packet is less than a year old and there's no hurry. These and other dehydrated foods have been vastly improved in recent years. Almost all of them are very tasty. They're invariably labeled (with surprising honesty) as to the number of servings yielded, and some also list the yield weight.

A development that's particularly appealing for family outings is the recent proliferation of single-serving packets of cereals and other foods. With these packets, you can have more variety in your menus, and can give family members several choices at a single eating session. For breakfast, as one example, you can offer each of the kids a selection of Quaker oatmeal plain or preflavored with apples and cinnamon, raisins and spice, maple and brown sugar, or chocolate. Mom or you might prefer the same company's instant grits. I'll have the pancakes or cornbread, thanks.

Other companies offer the same kind of wide selection. For lunch you might give family members a choice, say, of ground beef or wieners with a further choice of French's Chili-O Mix or Brown Gravy Mix. (You won't have to use anything like a full packet for just one serving.) Meanwhile, I might have mine with the same firm's mashed-potato flakes on the side, or maybe I'll have an Armour Swiss steak dinner. An envelope of those instant mashed potatoes, by the way, will thicken a stew superbly.

Many such foods, produced by these and other well-known companies, are now available in grocery stores and supermarkets. Other food packets, sold usually or exclusively through camping-supply dealers, have been developed expressly to provide backpackers with gourmet menus. Seidel's list totals about a hundred choices—including over twenty main dishes, most of which contain meat of one kind or another. Well over a hundred items—the Tea Kettle, Mountain House, and Rich-Moor brands —are on the food list distributed by Alpine Recreation (4B Henshaw Street, Woburn, Massachusetts 01801 and 455 Central Park Avenue, Scarsdale, New York 10583). Alpine, by the way, is among the dealers that rent as well as sell backpacks, stoves, and other equipment. Other companies that specialize in excellent backpacking food packets—entrees, juices, egg dishes, vegetables, even milk shakes—are Bernard and Dri-Lite.

To give you a more specific idea of what

Pit fire can be made even in snow, with wood lining fire hole. This party's menu includes hot chowder, chili, and muffins. Snowshoe and ski-tour hikers sometimes take turns pulling sled of provisions and gear, dispensing with packs. (Courtesy R. T. French Company)

and how much to pack, here's a three-day food list for two people, compiled by Sears:

1 packet each:
  cheese omelet
  hashed brown potatoes
  noodle soup mix
  onion soup mix
  chili bean mix
  dehydrated fruit cocktail
  peach slices
  chocolate pudding mix
  vanilla pudding mix
  lemonade mix
  Armour Ranch Style Breakfast
  Armour Chicken Stew Dinner
  Armour Pork Chop Dinner
  Armour Swiss Steak Dinner
1 can each:
  white bread
  deviled ham

2 packets each:
  raisins
  fruit-punch mix
  lemons
  Swiss Miss hot chocolate mix
other items:
  2 cups cornflakes
  dozen dried apricots
  dozen crackers
  4 candy bars
  4 teaspoons Tang orange juice mix
  24 teaspoons instant coffee
  24 teaspoons Pream
  48 teaspoons sugar
  1 tablespoon shortening
  2 tablespoons powdered milk (for puddings)
  salt and pepper

Personally, if I were hiking in some of my favorite areas, I'd add a small take-down fishing rod to my list of "provisions" and round out the suggested fare with pan-fried or foil-baked fish.

Based on foods and food sources of the kind discussed above, here are some sample trail menus I've garnered from Forest Service booklets, Gerry's food-packing booklet, tips from Quaker, French's, Seidel's—and my wife:

BREAKFAST ⅞1: orange juice, oatmeal with raisins and milk, cornbread, coffee, tea, milk, or cocoa.

BREAKFAST ⅞2: stewed fruit, pancakes with syrup (made from 1 packet of syrup crystals), coffee, tea, milk, or cocoa.

BREAKFAST ⅞3: grapefruit juice, hash, cheese, biscuits with jam, coffee, tea, milk, or cocoa.

BREAKFAST ⅞4: sliced peaches, bacon and eggs, buttered toast, coffee, tea, milk, or cocoa.

LUNCH ⅞1: spaghetti with tomato sauce, vegetable salad, gingerbread, fruit punch, or other beverage.

LUNCH ⅞2: Landjaeger sausage (or salami, pepperoni, or other luncheon meat), Pillsbury's Space Sticks, candy, choice of beverage.

LUNCH ⅞3: wieners, cornbread, cheese-and-bacon spread, fruit, choice of beverage.

LUNCH ⅞4: soup or chili or rarebit, meat-spread on crackers, biscuits or bread, choice of beverage.

DINNER ⅞1: chowder, vegetable salad, ham-and-noodles, butterscotch pudding, choice of beverage.

DINNER ⅞2: pork chops with applesauce, diced potatoes, choice of green vegetables, cherry cobbler, choice of beverage.

DINNER ⅞3: shrimp creole, vegetable salad, bread and butter, cheese and fruit or blueberry cobbler, choice of beverage.

DINNER ⅞4: French onion soup or fruit mix, beef and vegetable stew, biscuits, cocoanut pudding or Sierra coffeecake, choice of beverage.

All of the above menus can be prepared from trail-type packets. For that matter, so can beef steaks or burgers, chicken Romanoff or meatballs and spaghetti, turkey supreme or a Mexican taco dinner. There are many more choices, and the vegetables, breads, salads, and desserts are similarly diversified.

Anyone who does much outdoor living learns many little laborsaving tricks with food and drink. For instance, it's smart to fold and save the foil packets in which some beverage crystals are sold. An emptied packet makes a good measure and a better drinking cup. Another example: If bread goes stale, use it with powdered eggs to make great French toast. Another: Pre-mix some seasoned flour, and mark this and all other plastic bagfuls of food with an exact description of the contents. Another: To speed up cooking in high country (where it takes longer because water boils at lower temperatures), keep a tight lid on the pot. If it won't go on tight, pack a couple of small alligator clips (the clips used with electrical wiring) and clamp the lid on.

Here's one from Aladdin Industries, which makes vacuum bottles as well as handwarmers. If your youngsters wake up so hungry they can hardly wait for breakfast, have some oatmeal ready and waiting when you roll out of the sack. To do this, boil the water in the evening, stir in the oatmeal (or cracked wheat, whole rice, millet, or other cereal) and reheat to an active boil. While doing this, preheat a plastic-lined, wide-mouthed vacuum bottle with boiling water. Pour out the water as soon as the cereal is ready, and pour in the cereal. Cap it and lay it on its side overnight. In the morning, just stir it and serve.

Your spouse may be as impatient as the kids, and this can make for frayed nerves if you're trying to fix several dishes fast over a small fire or single-burner camp stove. The way to solve that is to line a deep saucepan (again on the previous evening) with aluminum foil, folding the foil into ridges that partition the pan into two or three sections. Then you can cook several different items simultaneously in one pan without having one kind of food run into another.

You've probably collected tricks and techniques of your own, and anyone who cooks outdoors learns many more by experience. With modern camp-cooking utensils and trail foods, preparing meals in the open is no more of a chore than at home. Of course, washing pots and dishes is still a chore, but it can be made easier if everyone takes a turn and if you put soapy water in each pot as soon as it's emptied and place it on the fire again to heat.

Photo taken from inside tent shows Montana camp-out that combined hiking with two special interests: fly fishing and photography. (Bill Browning/Montana Chamber of Commerce Photo)

Chapter 9

SPECIAL-ACTIVITY HIKES AND CLUBS

The fact that hiking for its own sake is an ex- hilarating experience certainly doesn't argue against combining it with other pet activities or special interests. Apart from nature study, which has really become an integral aspect of hiking, amateur photography is probably the most common activity associated with back-country rambles. There are photography handbooks (some of them emphasizing wildlife and scenic pictures) as well as magazines, clubs, and even schools. However, the average camera buff merely packs his equipment—which, if he's smart, includes nearly twice as much film as he thinks he'll need—and takes off for the woods. After a few outings, he will have acquired any number of techniques and little tricks to protect his gear and get the best possible results.

Just as a course in photography is beyond the scope of this book, so too is a course in fishing or hunting. These activities need only be men- tioned as reminders that a hike can be tailored to your special interests. Other such interests include spelunking (the exploration of caves and caverns), mountaineering, and rock climbing. Scrambling down into the earth has not yet attained the popularity of climbing its heights, and spelunking can be hazardous if you're im- properly equipped or don't know how to go about it. Caves should never be explored alone. Fortunately, there are a few clubs devoted to the hobby, but before joining one, how do you find out whether spelunking is for you? A good beginning is to write to state tourism depart- ments for information on the big, spectacular (and quite safe) caverns through which there are guided tours. At the sites of such tourist attractions you can usually pick up some litera- ture on cave formations. Then do a bit of re- search to find local spelunking clubs. This can sometimes be done through chambers of com- merce, educational institutions, outdoor-supply dealers, and sportsmen's or civic groups. (Some hiking and mountaineering clubs include spe- lunking among their activities and among the topics in the literature they provide.) You might also make inquiries at the geology department of the nearest university. There's almost always at least one faculty member or student who takes an active interest in mineral hunting (an allied but separate and fascinating pastime), cave exploration, or mountaineering.

Rock Climbing

To some people, mountaineering is simply an advanced form of high-country hiking, but it can be much more challenging, especially if it involves rock climbing. For those who are un- acquainted with this sport, rock climbing is the scaling of sheer cliffs and other really difficult heights, using special ropes and a variety of sophisticated hardware. I know of dealers in the vicinity of Mount Washington (highest of New Hampshire's White Mountains) and Mount Mansfield (highest of Vermont's Green Moun- tains) who not only sell the equipment but give rock-climbing lessons. You can rent or buy cram- pons, pitons, ice axes, and related hardware from such dealers as Alpine Recreation, pre- viously mentioned in connection with trail foods and camping gear. There are mountain-climbing schools and clubs in all the major ranges, from the Cascades and Sierras of the Pacific coast to the Rockies and Tetons of the West and the Appalachians and Adirondacks of the East.

If you're interested in the more demanding forms of mountaineering, you should read *Fundamentals of Rock Climbing*, prepared by specialists at MIT and available for $1.00 (plus $.50 postage) from the Appalachian Mountain Club, 5 Joy Street, Boston, Massachusetts 02108. This is the country's oldest hiking club and the largest in the eastern United States. It's one of those that conduct instruction and practice sessions in all kinds of mountaineering.

Instead of just ordering that single publication, you might write to the club and request the publications list, which includes many books on mountain hiking and climbing, ski touring, canoeing, etc., plus maps. From the same source you can also get guides to climbing in several other regions of the continent. Instruction can also be obtained from groups located in the West, such as the Colorado Mountain Club and the Seattle Mountaineers. (See appendix for addresses.)

Strange stalactites and stalagmites in "Throne Room" of Idaho's Minnetonka Cave intrigue many hikers with prospect of specializing in cave exploration.

Snowshoeing and Ski Touring

A fine way to introduce yourself to mountain climbing as well as to cross-country skiing and snowshoeing is to take advantage of Yosemite National Park's Mountaineering School and Guide Service. First you take a brief but thorough course which includes the use of skis and snowshoes and even survival techniques like the building of snow shelters. Then you go on an overnight snow-camping trip.

Anyone who does much winter camping in isolated areas of deep snow should pack a pair of snowshoes. There seems to be a prevalent notion that snowshoeing is difficult and very tiring. It isn't—if you don't walk stiff-legged or try to lift one showshoe high over the other. Relax and you'll have little trouble even with deep drifts. Keep your toes pointing straight ahead and bend your knees but don't try to lift the snowshoes high. Let the tail of each shoe drag, and develop a steady, gliding rhythm.

There are three basic types of snowshoes: the very short, wide bearpaw, the equally wide but longer type often called the beavertail, or Maine, snowshoe; and the long, narrow type variously known as the Alaskan, Cree, or pickerel style. A modified pickerel, often designated as a "cross-country" style, has a nicely upturned front and slightly greater width—almost as if it were a pickerel-bearpaw hybrid. Each type comes in more than one size, and the dealer will recommend a good size for a person of your weight.

The bearpaw has no rear extension, or tail. It's excellent for walking through thick timber or brushy areas and is strongly favored by many northwoodsmen, though novices find it more awkward than the narrower, tailed styles. The pickerel is for fast walking over open terrain. The cross-country or (in wooded and deeply drifted areas) the beavertail will probably serve best for most winter hikers.

Good snowshoes usually have frames and crosspieces of white ash or hickory, and webbing of cured cowhide, horsehide, or moosehide. The binding is a leather harness, or "sandal," which goes over your boot—snug but not tight—and leaves your heel free so that it can rise with each step. Carry a couple of extra lengths of rawhide for repair, and don't wear boots with

Mountain-climbing hikers scale peak above
Agnes Lake in Banff National Park, Alberta.
(*Canadian Government Travel Bureau Photo*)

hard, sharp heels and soles that might damage
the snowshoes. Some of the newer models,
though traditional in design, replace leather with
durable, supple plastic.

Having described the traditional, and still
most common, snowshoes, I must mention a recent introduction—framed with rattan wood
and employing wide, belted rubber-nylon webbing and nylon bindings. Imported from Europe,
where they're used by some of the NATO
troops, they're distributed in the United States
by Ipco. Very small and weighing only one
and a half pounds each, they're of the basic
bearpaw configuration but seem to work well

over a variety of terrain and are not difficult to
master. At about $18 (including the bindings)
they're less expensive than good conventional
snowshoes.

Cross-country skiing, or ski touring, is another
form of winter hiking that has a false reputation
for difficulty. If you can manage an "intermediate" slope at a typical ski resort, you can
easily ski cross-country in many areas. Naturally,
the kind of terrain you plan to cross will have
to be determined by your degree of proficiency,
and "suicide" slopes can be circumvented. I
know of a ski-tourer who almost fell 500 feet
down a narrow rock chute near Alta, Utah—he
saved himself by grabbing a protruding moun-
tain-cedar root. Yet most cross-country skiing is
done over fairly level ground or gentle hills, not
across high and treacherous traverses.

Ski touring on fairly level or gently rolling terrain is an exhilarating but not very difficult form of winter hiking. (Courtesy R. T. French Company)

If you use your regular skis (with standard attachments rather than the cross-country, heel-freeing type) slip the cable bindings off the rear hitches that normally clamp your heels down. Those are designed for downhill running. Use only the forward hitch, so that your heels can rise as you ski-walk or ski-climb just as they do when you're snowshoeing. Speaking of climbing, some skiers fasten a sealskin covering along the bottoms of their skis. This is especially popular in Europe for Alpine touring. The grain of the fur slants rearward, with the result that the skis slide forward, but the stiff fur catches to prevent slipping backward during a difficult climb. Of course, if you're out of condition for anything more strenuous than a chair lift, you'll want to limit your ski touring to slopes of gentle enough incline to make sealskin coverings mildly absurd.

Another point to remember is that in ski

touring you use your poles less than in conventional skiing. A lot of pushing and flailing with the poles, even when walking uphill, will do more to tire than to propel you.

There are those aforementioned special bindings—with a forward attachment only—for cross-country skiing, and there are also special "barrel-stave" skis for the purpose. They're easier to walk with, shorter and lighter for packing, and they can be bought for only about $30 or so.

Again, the Appalachian Mountain Club's list of publications will guide you to literature on the subject—*The Cross Country Ski Book,* by Johnny Caldwell, for example, as well as the *Adirondack Winter Mountaineering Manual* and *Ski Touring in the Northeastern U.S.*

Survival Hikes

The idea of packing the absolute minimum of equipment and little or no food seems to hold great appeal for some hikers who want to feel very close to nature and at the same time test their wilderness survival skills. Generally speaking, I don't favor winter survival hikes; they can become unpleasant and even dangerous unless you're extremely experienced and do your hiking near enough to civilization so you can get out fast if things get too rough.

The best season for a survival hike is late summer or autumn, when the weather is dry and warm, fishing is legal (and perhaps some kinds of hunting, too, in a given area), and many edible fruits, nuts, and other wild plants are ripe. Another rule is not to go off on a survival hike by yourself. For safety and maximum enjoyment, plan and start your hike with a group; with a club or family, this sort of venture can be most instructive and pleasant. Hike together to a rendezvous point and then you can split up into pairs. The approximate camping location of each pair should be known to the others, and everyone should return to the rendezvous at an appointed time. Planning must be thorough, and "roughing it" must not be overdone.

Minimum gear, in my opinion, includes water-purifying tablets, a first-aid kit, canteen, knife, sleeping bag, poncho, one change of socks, compass and map, waterproof matches in a waterproof case, soap, a few small fishhooks, and a few feet of monofilament fishing line. If it's legal to take small game, some hikers add a powerful slingshot to the list. (A .22 rifle would be more effective, but the idea is to get along with the most primitive gear possible.) If you think you'll need more than your poncho or an improvised lean-to for shelter, you can add a tarp or light backpacking tent. Since I don't claim to be an expert on edible plants, I consider a field guide essential.

You may feel you're breaking the "rules" if you pack any food at all. Personally, I would take along at least a couple of high-energy candy or food bars and a few slices of bread on a survival weekend. The bread is not just for eating. Bits of it rolled into tight doughballs can also be used as fish bait in the unlikely but calamitous event that you can't find any worms or catch any insects, crayfish, frogs, or lizards. The first fish you catch, incidentally, furnishes additional bait in the form of entrails as well as small chunks of flesh.

Except for such wonderful fare as wild raspberries, the color red is more often than not a danger signal in wild plants, and another class of foods to avoid is the fungus family. But there are many other edible and delicious plants: wild onions, wild young asparagus, watercress, dandelions, purslane, fiddlehead ferns, nuts, berries, and so on. In addition to a field guide, you'll do well to pack one of the wonderful books on edible plants by Euell Gibbons, and perhaps a manual such as *Bushcraft,* by Robert Graves.

I wouldn't attempt a survival weekend without knowing and being able to identify the region's common edible plants, nor would I attempt it in a place where I couldn't catch fish.

Horses, Canoes, and Bikes

Perhaps you don't think that the use of horses —a pack train—qualifies as hiking. Sometimes it doesn't, but there are two uses of mounts that also involve plenty of travel by shanks' mare. One is a horseback trip to a wilderness campsite from which you strike out on foot to explore or climb to spectacular vantage points or just roam the trails. The other is a long hike on which you walk but lead pack stock instead of carrying all the gear and supplies on your back.

Guided horseback trips can be arranged at a number of national parks (including my favorite, Yellowstone), and throughout the West there are outfitters and livery stables or horse ranches —as well as dude ranches—that offer such excursions. In most cases, you pack the same personal equipment, bedding, and clothing that you would take on an ordinary outing. However, tents and/or food may be provided; you'll have to inquire, and then plan accordingly.

Some of the same places offer foot trips on which you lead pack stock, and the same guidelines apply. Naturally, it isn't necessary to travel as light with a pack train—whether you ride or walk—as when you serve as your own beast of burden.

National Parks have lately been promoting pack-train camping excursions in order to reduce the crowding at the more accessible campsites. You see a great deal more of a National Park's really wild and beautiful portions this way than when you camp near a road and make only short exploratory hikes.

The Wilderness Society conducts horseback trips for its members, and there were group journeys into a dozen different wild regions of America in 1972 alone. The Sierra Club also stages mounted excursions. Both of these organizations conduct walking trips with pack stock—horses, mules, or burros—and both offer canoe and raft trips.

The same observation applies to canoeing as to horseback riding—it's an activity that often includes plenty of foot hiking. I'm not speaking of portaging, an acquired taste that I've never acquired—but of setting out from an encampment at the water's edge to explore overland.

Canoeing, like riding, involves special skills and yet can be enjoyed thoroughly by a novice under the guidance of an experienced group leader. In my opinion, the only indispensable skill demanded of a novice is the ability to swim. There are white-water trips requiring great boat-handling and paddling dexterity, but there are even more float trips and easy-paddling excursions that call for little exertion and less proficiency. Your choice of canoe trips should be determined in part by the region you'd most

like to penetrate and in part by your degree of ability.

One vital item of equipment is a life vest or flotation jacket. This, as well as the canoe, raft, or other river craft, is usually provided by the Sierra Club or Wilderness Society, a policy followed by many guide-outfitters as well as canoeing and general-outing clubs. You'll automatically check into this beforehand when you obtain information on what to pack. As a rule, you need a warm sleeping bag, outdoor clothing, and personal items. You may also need a ground cloth or tarp. Food is usually provided by the organization and included in the cost of the trip.

A Sierra Club booklet describing outings notes that on all river trips "there is ample time to enjoy off-river activities; traveling usually ends in the early afternoon, leaving time to explore side canyons, or to fish and swim. There are trips to fit almost any combination of ages. . . . A great variety of scenery and climate is available to river runners—from the warm, colorful desert country of Utah and Arizona to the dense forests and cool lakes of Idaho and British Columbia."

Similarly, the Wilderness Society's water excursions are widely varied geographically. The listings for a single year (1972) include the Yukon River, Missouri River, Grand Canyon, Everglades, Okefenokee Swamp, Voyageurs National Park, and a number of others.

Canoe trips are also scheduled and equipped by a number of other organizations, ranging from the American Canoe Association to the Boy Scouts, Girl Scouts, and American Youth Hostels. Moreover, private operators conduct many float trips, some lasting a couple of hours, others lasting days or weeks. I recall walking down the main street of Jackson Hole, Wyoming, just south of Grand Teton National Park, and reading store-window advertisements for at least a dozen different float trips on the Snake River.

Bike hikes could qualify for inclusion in this book on the basis that pedal power is leg power, but there's more to it than that. As a boy, I did a great deal of bike hiking with a couple of friends, and we almost invariably designated some geographic point as our "semidestination." The idea was to reach that point by midafternoon at the latest—just as we did when canoeing

Scout group loads up for canoe trip after hike to initial launch site. (*Leonard Lee Rue Photo*)

or horseback riding—and from there we hiked farther on foot. Usually our semidestination was within reasonable walking distance of a good fishing hole. We'd catch our dinner and then roam the local woods and hills. Sometimes we camped overnight. When we left the bikes unattended, we chained and padlocked them together, because even then petty theft and vandalism had become a problem in the country as well as in urban centers.

The best kind of bicycle for long-distance riding is the light "roadster," or "tourist," type which weighs about thirty to forty pounds, has relatively thin tires (with inner tubes) and is equipped with a variable speed gear and double hand brakes. Choose whatever handlebar style

is most comfortable for you, but bear in mind that dropped handlebars are no big advantage except for racing; most people tire less quickly with slightly upturned bars.

Many companies now make pack bags for bikes. A saddlebag design that drapes over the rear fender is most popular. It's commodious and doesn't get in your way. Such packs are offered in a wide price range, and there are even lightweight bike trailers to haul larger loads on long-distance excursions. An alternative is two sets of saddlebags, one pair over each wheel. If you use the saddlebag style, be careful to load the two compartments about equally in terms of weight. If the two sides are unbalanced you'll tire fast, and the bike may tend to tip or sideslip.

By the way, some people use the same type of saddlebag to harness a small amount of gear on a dog's back, and there are also packs and harnesses specifically designed for carrying by a large dog. If your dog is strong, big, and of a cheerful disposition, he won't mind carrying a light pack with his own food in it (tightly sealed so the aroma doesn't drive him to distraction). In areas where there isn't much wildlife, it's all right to take a well-trained dog on a hike, and a pet's companionship can increase your pleasure.

But if your dog has any tendency at all to wander, keep the animal on a lead. And don't take a dog where there will be any temptation to run after deer or rabbits. You may think your dog won't do such a thing; you may even be

able to make the honest claim that your dog doesn't know what a deer is. Nevertheless, the dog hasn't yet been born that isn't tempted by a whiff of deer or other wildlife scent. We've needlessly killed off great numbers of wild predatory species, while unleashing two far more destructive predators in the nation's woods. The second most destructive predator in this country today (if you don't count the automobile) is the free-running dog. In case you're wondering, the *most* destructive predator is the ordinary house cat, whose toll in birds, ground squirrels, and the like is beyond belief. I'm fond of both dogs and cats, but statistics compiled by wildlife biologists prove that pets must not be permitted to wander uncontrolled.

With that off my chest, I'll get back to bike hiking. In America as well as in Europe, this

Well-balanced saddlebags draped over front and rear wheels are ample for most bike hikes. Girl's bike is equipped with Alpine-brand gears to ease uphill pedaling.

method of roaming the country has become so popular that special bicycling trails—usually called "bikeways"—have been established, as have bike hostels. The Department of the Interior has helped to fund some of the bikeways (usually supported by state, county, or municipality), one of the most recent being a 19-mile scenic waterfront trail along the Pacific coast from Santa Monica to Torrance, California.

If, instead of camping out on a long bike trip, you occasionally stay at one of the hostels maintained by American Youth Hostels, a cot, mattress, and blanket will be provided, but you'll be required to provide a "sheet sleeping sack": sewn-together top and bottom sheets with attached pillow case. For further details, you can write to American Youth Hostels, 20 West Seventeenth Street, New York, New York 10011. For general information on bike touring, you can contact any of the cycling organizations listed in this book's appendix of association addresses.

Both public and commercial campgrounds are available throughout United States. Some are for tenting only, but many now accommodate trailers. Hiking family shown here has parked its mobile base camp in secluded Alaskan woodland.

Camping Vehicles and Campgrounds

I don't advocate the building of any more highways or trailer parks than already blanket this continent, but I must concede that America's favorite method of reaching a take-off point for hiking is to travel by camping vehicle to commercial campgrounds. Privately operated campgrounds now outnumber the public ones maintained by the states and the federal government. Some of the commercial sites are just for tenting, but most can accommodate anything from a small mountain tent to a huge trailer.

Much can be said in favor of both public and private campgrounds. If you use the public sites, some of which are attractively isolated—even remote—you can make a vacation tour in the United States or Canada for about a third of the money you'd have to spend on a conventional motel-and-restaurant tour. For example, in my own state of New York, there are forty-four scenic campsite locations in the Adirondacks and Catskills, and the fee for overnight use of a site at most locations is $2.50. You can stay a full week for $17.50. Each site is limited to occupancy by a single family or a group of no more than six persons at a time.

As a rule, you get an ample site for tent or trailer, with a parking area, fireplace, picnic table, garbage can, and access to drinking water and toilet facilities. Some sites even have boat-launching ramps or docks, and there are dumping stations for the holding tanks of trailers. Pretty much the same description can be applied to state sites all over the country and to many sites in national parks. I've camped for about the same fee and with the same facilities in Yellowstone.

The Bureau of Land Management maintains public campsites at various points on federally owned lands from Arizona to Alaska. Generally, these sites are more primitive (also less crowded and more fun), and the fees range from $1.00 to $2.00 per night. A descriptive list—Information Bulletin No. 3, *Camping on the Public Lands*—is available for $.05 from the U. S. Government Printing Office. It includes over 160 locations in a total of twelve states: Alaska, Arizona, California, Colorado, Idaho, Montana, Nevada, New Mexico, Oregon, South Dakota, Utah and Wyoming. These are *in addition* to the sites at state parks, National Parks and National Forests. Futhermore, in designated Wilderness and Primitive Areas of National Forests, there are places where you can camp for no fee at all aside from the charge for an entry permit.

More than 2,500 federal recreation areas are open to you with the purchase of a single $10 Federal Recreation Permit—the wallet-sized card known as a Golden Passport that's sold at access points to National Parks and other recreation areas, or can be obtained from the regional offices of the federal agencies which maintain these areas.

The fees at commercial campgrounds are, of course, higher, and they vary quite a bit, but they're still much lower than the cost of motel accommodations. Such campground facilities are often quite lavish. To use my own state as an example again, a commercial association known as the Campground Owners of New York (R.D. #2, Box 421, Endicott, New York 13760) distributes a free list locating and describing the facilities of fully ninety-three member operators plus a small batch of associate-member campgrounds. Many of them feature such attractions as nature hikes, fishing, boating, archery, and swimming—plus water, sewer and electric hookups, propane gas, self-service laundry, showers, supply and food stores, etc.

Most states and Canadian provinces supply descriptive brochures listing campsites—often the privately operated as well as public ones. The big trailer-oriented franchise operations like Safari Camps of America (with eighty-one campgrounds at this writing) and Kampgrounds of America (with about seven hundred sites in the United States, Canada, and Mexico) offer free directories so you can plan a tour. Literally thousands of campgrounds are located, described, and rated in the larger directories prepared by such publishers as Woodall's and Rand McNally for sale in bookstores, camping-supply stores, and by mail order.

The kind of camping vehicle you buy or rent should depend not just on the number of persons it must accommodate, but also on the kind of camping you plan to use it for. Only a compact, four-wheel-drive vehicle can penetrate to some of the free campsites on public lands or some privately owned timberlands where you'll be welcome. (For that matter, no vehicle at all can reach some of these spots.) But a roomy, luxurious trailer or pick-up camper can take you to many public campgrounds and to all of the trailer-park-type commercial sites.

The latter approach is not necessarily as unadventurous as you might suppose. A couple of years ago, I rented a pick-up camper at Salt Lake City and toured several states with my wife and two children. We camped one night on the shore of Great Salt Lake, spent another night in an isolated Utah canyon where a rancher gave us permission to camp and fish for trout, later stopped at the Caribou National Forest in Idaho, and then, on our way up to a campsite in Yellowstone National Park, stayed overnight at the KOA (Kampgrounds of America) outside Jackson, Wyoming, at the edge of the Teton Range and near the big elk refuge.

Setting out on foot from that trailer park, which provided all sorts of home comforts, we hiked up into the hills above Jackson Hole to hunt for mineral specimens, wildflowers, and fossils. In addition to those finds, we discovered bones and tracks of several species of wildlife. The single arrowhead obtained on that tour was found at a far-distant location, but a longer hike —far from the roadside areas that have been combed by previous visitors—might well turn up Indian and pioneer artifacts in this part of the country.

Historic Site-Seeing

In addition to hunting for artifacts, you can visit historic sites and monuments to combine hiking with a glimpse into the country's past. City, state, and federal agencies supply lists and descriptive brochures for people wishing to visit such sites. Some museums, civic organizations, and schools conduct guided walks through historic areas. Civil War "round-table" clubs and other history buffs still find occasional relics as they hike over old battlefields. And tours are sometimes sponsored by commercial groups, local and national clubs, and public institutions ranging from a town library or genealogical society to the Smithsonian Institution.

Nature Hikes

The New York Department of Conservation

has lately been supplying exhibits and literature on the establishment and maintenance of nature trails (including trails for handicapped persons), and similar programs are being adopted by other states. A number of museums, clubs, and civic groups have been conducting nature walks for many years, and similar excursions are now conducted by almost every environmentally concerned group. Local affiliates of such organizations as the Isaac Walton League and Trout Unlimited are actively promoting such activities.

One of the most important conservation groups is, of course, the National Audubon Society, whose local chapters organize informal outings for ecological study, and sometimes also to inspect the proposed site of some new power plant, dam, or other project of environmental concern. In addition, many members (and nonmembers) attend the society's one- or two-week ecological camp sessions which include field trips by water and on foot.

There is an Audubon Ecology Workshop at Greenwich, Connecticut, where campers stay in twin-bedded rooms, each with a private shower; one situated on Hog Island, at Medomak, Maine, with large rooms in comfortable frame buildings, and a similar one at Hunt Hill Sanctuary, Sarona, Wisconsin; and the Audubon Camp of the West is at Trail Lake Ranch, Dubois, Wyoming, where single campers share cabins and married couples occupy private rooms. The enrollment fees at the various camps are reasonable and, of course, help to maintain the facilities and environmental programs at these sites.

While it isn't necessary to become an Audubon member in order to enroll at an ecology-workshop camp, I think that anyone who does so will hardly begrudge the $12 annual membership dues ($6.00 for students). The reason for joining any of the conservation groups is not merely to be informed of opportunities for ecological studies or nature walks; it's a commitment to the protection of our endangered natural resources.

And since it is a commitment, usually involving financial support, beware of joining groups whose views may turn out to oppose your own. Noble-sounding names, slogans, even literature can be deceptive, but you can write to a group's headquarters and ask about its stand on conservation matters that you consider important.

Outdoor Clubs

In addition to the National Audubon Society, there are several other national organizations that merit attention here. I happen to be among the 70,000 or so members of The Wilderness Society. A student membership entails annual dues of only $4.00. Regular members pay annual dues of $7.50; contributing members $12.50; sustaining members $25; and those who can afford higher dues and wish to support an extremely worthy movement may pay more. Like the Audubon Society, the Sierra Club, and other such groups, the Wilderness Society has helped to lead the legislative and legal battle against despoilers of the country's beauty and dwindling natural resources.

The objectives are: to aid in securing the preservation of wilderness; to conduct an educational program concerning the value of wilderness and how it may best be used in the public interest; to make and encourage scientific studies concerning wilderness as a part of the essential conservation of soil, water, forest, and wildlife; and to play an active role and co-operate with others in the protection of wilderness values.

It is not claiming too much to say that without such groups, the current ecological awareness (which is largely attributable to their efforts) would be too little too late.

In addition to this tremendously important program, the Wilderness Society sponsors a great variety of wilderness outings—ninety-three of them in thirteen states and Canada in 1972 alone. These are non-profit five- to twelve-day trips, with six to eighteen people per party (depending on the type of trip), led by highly qualified outfitters and trip directors. The major equipment is provided and participation does not require membership in the organization. The costs are lower and the adventure higher than you could obtain on your own, working directly with commercial guide-outfitters. To cite just one typical example, $230 was the 1972 price for a week-long guided walking trip—with pack stock to carry the gear—in a 49,000-acre Colorado wilderness straddling the Continental Divide. The outfitter provided the food and everything else except personal clothing, boots, and sleeping bags. The country was breath-taking, and its rich wildlife population included fish, birds, deer, elk, and bighorn sheep.

In addition to horseback trips and hikes with pack stock, there are backpacking expeditions, canoe and rubber-raft trips, ski and snowshoe tours. Occasionally a backpacking trip is offered for as little as $100; the longest raft trips may cost more than four times as much.

Naturally, you should be in good health when you sign on for an outing, and not inclined to suffer adverse effects from remaining at high altitudes, but you don't have to be adept at the activities involved since you'll get expert guidance and help. The Society supplies a free

booklet describing all the trips, accompanied by an application form.

In terms of membership, the Sierra Club is even larger than the Wilderness Society. Founded by John Muir in 1892, the Sierra Club has forged a very honorable history of accomplishments, including its help in establishing the National Park Service, the Forest Service, a number of individual National Parks, the Wilderness Preservation System, and the Wild and Scenic Rivers System. Its objectives are fundamentally the same as those of the other, previously mentioned conservation forces, all of which frequently co-operate in fighting for the natural

Hiking with pack stock is highly recommended for extended trips through wilderness country. This party is in Flathead area south of Montana's Glacier National Park, near top end of Conti- **nental Divide Trail. Wilderness Society and other clubs have organized walking trips with pack stock on many trails, including Continental Divide. (*Clif Merritt Photo*)**

environment. Regular dues are $15 a year; dues for a member's spouse are $7.50; student and junior memberships are $5.00; and, again, there are supporting, contributing, and life memberships at higher rates. A $5.00 admission fee (waived for students) is charged to defray processing costs, and it covers all members of an immediate family joining at one time.

At present, the Sierra Club averages more than a hundred major outings a year (not counting hikes by local chapters). The outings are open to members, applicants for membership, and members of outdoor clubs that grant reciprocal privileges. Some of these excursions take place as far off as Nepal, Africa, Yugoslavia, or Ecuador. The 1972 list also included a skin-diving expedition, exploring the waters of Grand Cayman in the West Indies. There are outings in Alaska and Hawaii as well as in the contiguous states and Canada. Aside from some of the necessarily expensive exotic trips, most Sierra Club outings cost between $5.00 and $40 per person per day. The expenses depend on distance, mode of travel, the need for a professional boatman on raft trips, and so on.

The hikers share the chores and the burden on some outings, while on others there's a commissary staff or work crew. There are trips—particularly high-country backpacking expeditions—that are strenuous enough so that every participant should be in top condition. There are even trips that include rock climbing and other advanced types of mountaineering; if you haven't acquired these skills, you won't be able to participate fully in all the activities, and you should select an easier trip. There are outings, either with knapsack or pack burros, geared for entire families, including young children. Some of the canoe, raft, and saddle trips are also easy enough for youngsters.

It was the Sierra Club that pioneered "service trips"—service meaning trail clean-up and/or maintenance. These hikes appeal especially to college students and other young people. Many, though not all, are backpacking expeditions, and some are strenuous. In a dozen years, Sierra Club service hikers cleaned out nearly one hundred tons of debris left by less conscientious campers. As a rule, work days and free days alternate on these trips. Such outings are partly subsidized with club funds, but a ten-day service

trip may still cost a participant $45 or $50. Environmentally concerned young people pay this amount eagerly for the fun of the hike and the privilege of serving. Anyone who has taken part is entitled to feel a special kind of pride.

There are also commercial clubs—profit-making ventures—which can only compete successfully by putting a strong emphasis on fun and a huge variety of services and imaginative excursions in return for somewhat higher costs. An excellent example is the Chalet Club, headquartered in New York, which stresses environmental awareness and offers a tremendous array of activities ranging from local hikes to river trips, mounted pack trips, ski tours, scuba diving—even balloon ascensions and African safaris. People residing near the club are happy to pay about $12 per person for a day's hike on which they are provided with refreshments, a woodland guide, and transportation between the city and the starting point. People from all over the country make reservations for weekend river trips costing about $60 and for longer vacation excursions varying from less than a couple of hundred dollars to more than a couple of thousand. You need not be a member to participate, but for a $10 initiation fee and annual dues of $15 you're entitled to price reductions. Instruction is included in the fees, and on the big trips all food and gear are provided, as are little refinements like cocktails and wine. For those who like to do their wilderness living in high style, with the cooking and chores done for them, the Chalet Club adds very attractive frills to conventional hiking.

In addition to such commercial services and the non-profit conservation groups, there are numerous local and national hikers' and campers' clubs, trail associations, and trail conferences. Major organizations are listed in an appendix, and some of those associated with specific trails or trail systems will be mentioned in Chapter 10. But three national groups should be included right here.

One is the National Campers and Hikers Association (7172 Transit Road, Buffalo, New York 14221), which is composed of more than 1,700 self-governing local chapters throughout the United States and in Canada. The NCHA recommends and promotes improvements in hiking and camping facilities maintained by local, state (or province), and national agencies; establishes regional centers where members can get up-to-date reports on local trails, campsites, etc.; cooperates with other groups to promote conservation; provides membership identification (cards, car decals, buttons, and so on) which will be recognized by other members encountered in unfamiliar areas, thereby assuring a welcome and an introduction to fellow-hikers; and provides an interchange of information and ideas, not only by word of mouth but through the association's bulletin *Tent and Trail* and by means of a subscription to *Camping Guide* magazine, which is included in the dues. Membership for the first year costs $6.00. Thereafter, it's only $4.00 a year.

This is a very active, enthusiastic group. The local chapters hold camp-outs and group hikes, dinners and other events—though you can receive all the membership benefits without belonging to a particular chapter. There are six regional directors, whose headquarters can supply specific information pertaining to their regions. There are state-wide gatherings and national "campventions." These national meetings are held in a different state each year, and they draw thousands of hikers from all over the United States and Canada.

A second nationwide group of particular interest is the North American Family Campers Association (Box 552, 76 State Street, Newburyport, Massachusetts 01950), which has over 80,000 members in the United States and Canada. Its basic purposes are pretty much like those of the National Campers and Hikers As-

sociation. There's an emphasis on encouraging the development of camping areas and on providing information regarding camping equipment and facilities.

The group holds annual spring and fall outings, and publishes its own magazine, *Campfire Chatter*. A subscription is included in the $6.00 annual dues.

The third group I alluded to is the Family Camping Federation, a unit of the American Camping Association (Bradford Woods, Martinsville, Indiana 46151). In essence this is an industry association representing campground owners, camping-equipment manufacturers, and so on. However, the membership also includes camping clubs, thus providing a voice for the camping public—the consumer as well as the industry. Membership for clubs numbering less than one hundred members is $25; there are graduated rates for larger clubs. If you belong to a club, your secretary or other representative can request details from the Federation, which may be of value to your group as a clearing house for information, particularly regarding commercial campgrounds.

There are scores of other clubs and organizations, some of them specializing in a particular activity. For $.35 you can get a 68-page booklet listing them from the U. S. Government Printing Office. It's entitled *Private Assistance in Outdoor Recreation: A Directory of Organizations Providing Aid to Individuals and Public Groups.* It has separate listings for hiking, boating and canoeing, bicycling, horseback riding, nature study, and other special interests.

Chapter 10

TRAILS TO EVERYWHERE

America has 154 National Forests in thirty-nine states and Puerto Rico—182 million acres without even counting National and State Parks, officially designated Wild and Scenic Rivers, and other protected havens of nature. Those 182 million acres are all open to the hiker with a backpack; according to a recent estimate, the Forest Service's domain alone contains over 165,000 miles of trails. I suspect that the estimate was conservative. After all, there are about 200,000 trails, either well defined or at least blazed, in the National Forests and National Parks of the West.

In addition, there are thousands of miles of trails which meander *out* of these forests and parks and connect many of them. Most of the land crossed by these footways is federally or state owned, but not all of it. For example, the greatest portion of the Pacific Crest Trail—winding 2,313 miles from the Mexican border up through California, Oregon, and Washington to the Canadian border—lies within 25 National Forests and six National Parks, but includes 444 miles over private property. (The states own but 27 miles and the federal government owns 1,842.)

Of the famous 2,000-mile Appalachian Trail, from Maine's Mount Katahdin to Georgia's Springer Mountain, 866 miles are in private ownership, 452 are owned by the states and 682 are owned by the federal government.

In some areas, private ownership of land has been an obstacle in the opening of trails to the public, yet it has not deterred their spread. In certain ways, perhaps it has been a blessing. Privately owned land is usually bordered or crossed by roads, thus giving easier access to

National Scenic Trails are marked with signs, or in some cases paint blazes, and signs also mark short Recreation Trails.

trails, and it's often situated reasonably near habitations, supplies, and facilities of various kinds. Moreover, it's possible that hikers on these trails are more considerate of the environment than they might otherwise be, knowing that at any time they may be crossing a stretch of private property.

At any rate, private ownership did not hinder the establishment in 1968 of the National Scenic and Recreation Trails System, which continues to grow as rights-of-way are obtained and trails opened or built.

The rather impressive figures I've been giving here don't even include millions of acres of public property administered by the Bureau of Land Management or more millions owned by timber companies which permit hiking and camping on their holdings.

No book can provide a complete survey of trails because new ones are continually opened, old ones often extended. However, I can describe the longest ones as well as some of the particularly interesting shorter trails, and I can tell you where to get up-to-date information on hiking trails throughout the United States and Canada.

Major Lists of Regional Guides

In my opinion, the first and probably most important source book to obtain is a 116-page publication compiled by the Bureau of Outdoor Recreation, Department of the Interior, entitled *Guides to Outdoor Recreation Areas and Facilities*. Available from the U. S. Government Printing Office for $.55, it lists trail and area maps, campground directories, guidebooks, and other sources of information covering the United States and Canada. Addresses of the sources are listed, together with prices where applicable. There are separate sections listing national, regional, and state guides—with the states listed in alphabetical order for quick reference—plus a cross reference covering hiking, camping, and other outdoor activities. In essence, it's a comprehensive bibliography, an index of other publications that you can obtain to find any needed information about any specific area.

A more specialized book listing published reference materials is *Hiking and Hiking Trails, A Trails and Trail-Based Activities Bibliography*. This is a compilation of five hundred references —writings appearing in books, periodicals, and public documents from 1900 through 1969, plus some that were published in 1970. It includes just about everything from hiking and trail guides to congressional hearings. Designated as Bibliography Series No. 20, it can be consulted at all Interior Department libraries or you can purchase a copy for $3.00 from the National Technical Information Service, Springfield, Virginia 22151.

National Trails System

The National Trails System now encompasses twenty-nine relatively short footways (ranging from less than a mile to about thirty miles) designated as National Recreation Trails, plus the tremendous ones (most of them extending over a thousand miles) designated as National Scenic Trails.

Only two of the Scenic Trails are officially open under federal management as of this writing—the previously mentioned Appalachian and Pacific Crest—but fifteen more are being studied or are already under development.

For practical hiking purposes, *at least parts of all fifteen already exist.* The Bureau of Outdoor Recreation considers routes on the basis that they pass through areas of historic, scenic, natural, or cultural interest and have access points near urban centers. In general, they follow important historic routes—post roads, canals, rivers, pioneer trails, and the like. Along all of them, therefore, stretches exist where people already can and do hike. As a rule, what remains to be done is to survey blank stretches, obtain rights-of-way where a trail is interrupted, and mark or build connecting footways where needed. I think it's safe to say that all fifteen will be completed within the next few years, though several trails may not follow the precise routes now shown on the Bureau's study maps; some may be lengthened, shortened, or slightly detoured.

The fifteen (listed here geographically, from the West Coast to the East Coast) are: the Gold Rush Trails (a short network in Alaska), the Oregon Trail, Lewis and Clark Trail, Mormon Battalion Trail, Mormon Trail (not to be confused with the more southerly Mormon Battalion), Continental Divide Trail, Santa Fe Trail, North Country Trail, Chisholm Trail, Old Cattle Trails (actually two connected routes which merge and then run into the Chisholm), Natchez Trace Trail, Kittanning Trail, El Camino Real Trail, Potomac Heritage Trail, and Long Trail.

Map (on facing page) prepared by Bureau of Outdoor Recreation shows two existing Scenic Trails (Pacific Crest and Appalachian) plus 15 others being studied, planned, or built for National Trails System.

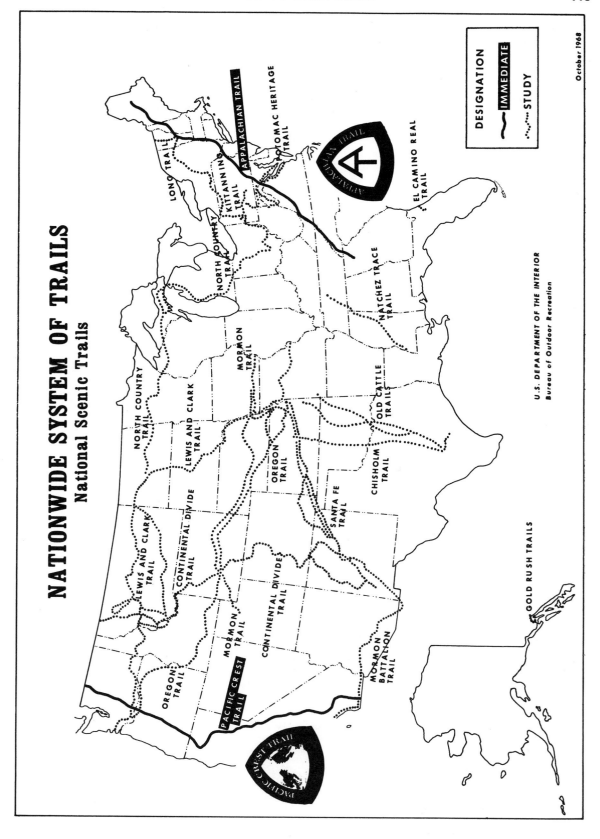

NATIONWIDE SYSTEM OF TRAILS
National Scenic Trails

DESIGNATION
IMMEDIATE
STUDY

October 1968

U.S. DEPARTMENT OF THE INTERIOR
Bureau of Outdoor Recreation

LONG TRAIL

POTOMAC HERITAGE TRAIL

APPALACHIAN TRAIL

KITTANNING TRAIL

NORTH COUNTRY TRAIL

EL CAMINO REAL TRAIL

NATCHEZ TRACE TRAIL

NORTH COUNTRY TRAIL

LEWIS AND CLARK TRAIL

MORMON TRAIL

OLD CATTLE TRAIL

OREGON TRAIL

CHISHOLM TRAIL

CONTINENTAL DIVIDE TRAIL

LEWIS AND CLARK TRAIL

SANTA FE TRAIL

MORMON TRAIL

CONTINENTAL DIVIDE TRAIL

OREGON TRAIL

PACIFIC CREST TRAIL

MORMON BATTALION TRAIL

GOLD RUSH TRAILS

APPALACHIAN TRAIL

PACIFIC CREST TRAIL

At this writing there are 29 short National Recreation Trails, as numbered on map (on *facing page*). Key below explains them:

Legend: B-bicycle; F-foot; H-horse; M-motorized, general; SM-snowmobile; WC-wheelchair

INDEX
NO.   STATE: NAME OF TRAIL (LENGTH) TYPE OF TRAIL, ADMINISTRATING AGENCY

1.	Alaska: PINNELL MOUNTAIN TRAIL (24 miles) F, Bureau of Land Management, USDI
2.	Washington: LAKE WASHINGTON BICYCLE PATH (2.5 miles) B-F, City of Seattle Department of Parks and Recreation
3.	Washington: LAKE WASHINGTON SHIP CANAL WATERSIDE TRAIL (1,200 feet) F, U. S. Army Corps of Engineers
4.	Washington: FRED CLEATOR INTERPRETIVE TRAIL (1.3 miles) F, Washington State Parks and Recreation Commission
5.	Oregon: TILLAMOOK HEAD TRAIL (6 miles) F, Oregon State Highway Division, State Parks and Recreation Section
6.	California: KING RANGE TRAIL (10 miles in 2 segments) F-H, M, Bureau of Land Management, USDI
7.	California: SOUTH YUBA TRAIL (6 miles) F-H, Bureau of Land Management, USDI
8.	California: EAST BAY SKYLINE TRAIL (14 miles) F-H, East Bay Regional Park District
9.	California: GABRIELINO TRAIL (28 miles) F-H, Forest Service, USDA
10.	Arizona: SOUTH MOUNTAIN PARK TRAIL (14 miles) B-F-H, Phoenix Parks and Recreation Department
11.	Colorado: HIGHLINE CANAL TRAIL (18 miles) B-F-H, South Suburban Metropolitan Recreation and Park District, Denver
12.	New Mexico: ORGAN MOUNTAIN TRAIL (8.7 miles) F-H, Bureau of Land Management, USDI
13.	South Dakota: BEAR BUTTE TRAIL (3.5 miles) F, South Dakota Department of Game, Fish and Parks, Division of Parks and Recreation
14.	South Dakota: SUNDAY GULCH TRAIL (4 miles) F, South Dakota Department of Game, Fish and Parks, Division of Parks and Recreation
15.	South Dakota: TRAIL OF SPIRITS (0.5 mile) F, South Dakota Department of Game, Fish and Parks, Division of Parks and Recreation
16.	Nebraska: FONTENELLE FOREST TRAIL (3.9 miles) F, Fontenelle Forest Association
17.	Texas: GREER ISLAND NATURE TRAIL (3 miles) F, City of Fort Worth Park and Recreation Department
18.	Arkansas: SUGAR LOAF MOUNTAIN NATURE TRAIL (1 mile) F, U. S. Army Corps of Engineers
19.	Wisconsin: ELROY-SPARTA TRAIL (30 miles) B-F-SM, Wisconsin Department of Natural Resources, Bureau of Parks and Recreation
20.	Wisconsin: ICE AGE GLACIAL TRAIL (25 miles) F-SM, Wisconsin Department of Natural Resources, Bureau of Parks and Recreation

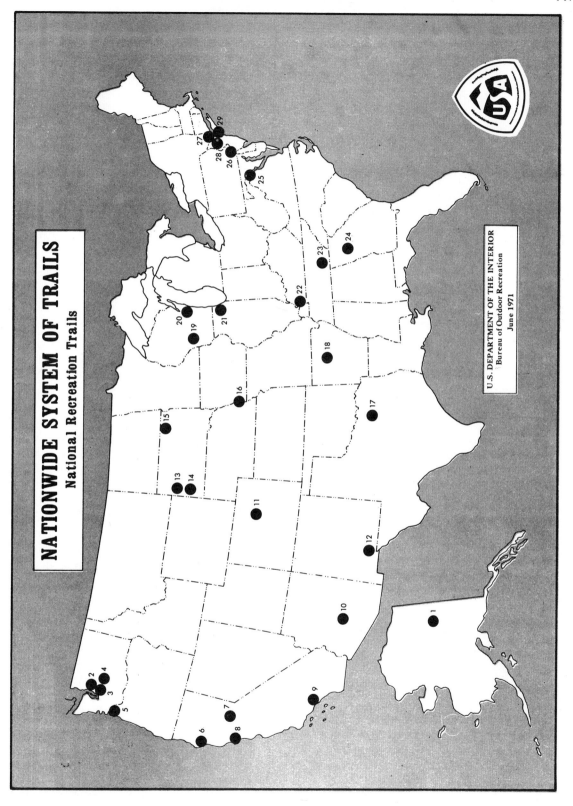

NATIONWIDE SYSTEM OF TRAILS
National Recreation Trails

U.S. DEPARTMENT OF THE INTERIOR
Bureau of Outdoor Recreation
June 1971

21.   Illinois: ILLINOIS PRAIRIE PATH (12.5 miles) B-F-H, The Illinois Prairie Path, Inc.

22.   Kentucky: LONG CREEK TRAIL (0.25 mile) F-WC, Tennessee Valley Authority

23.   Tennessee: LAUREL-SNOW TRAIL (8 miles) F, Bowaters Southern Paper Corporation

24.   Georgia: STONE MOUNTAIN TRAIL (6.51 miles) F, Stone Mountain Memorial Park Association

25.   District of Columbia: FORT CIRCLE PARKS TRAIL (7.9 miles in 2 segments) B-F, National Park Service, USDI

26.   Pennsylvania: FAIRMOUNT PARK BIKEWAY (8.25 miles) B-F, City of Philadelphia, Fairmount Park Commission

27.   New Jersey: PALISADES LONG PATH (11 miles) F, Palisades Interstate Park Commission

28.   New Jersey: PALISADES SHORE TRAIL (11.25 miles) F, Palisades Interstate Park Commission

29.   New York: HARRIMAN LONG PATH (16 miles) F, Palisades Interstate Park Commission

Of the entire group, only Florida's El Camino Real is less than a hundred miles long. But a hike of any desired length can be made on the longest of them. You simply choose a convenient access point and proceed from there to another access point or for a desired distance and then back to the trail head where you entered.

The accompanying maps show the seventeen Scenic Trails (two marked and opened plus the fifteen just listed) and the twenty-nine Recreation Trails.

Note that some of the Recreation Trails are for other uses as well as walking—some are designated for bicycling, horseback riding, snowmobiling, wheelchair use, motoring, or general use.

It isn't possible to describe in detail the entire length of all seventeen of the sprawling Scenic Trails, but here's a more or less brief account of each.

Gold Rush Trails: These form a short circuit across part of Alaska's narrow southeastern leg in the vicinity of Skagway and Glacier Bay, the spectacularly scenic area made famous by the Klondike gold strikes of 1897. At the western extremity of this route is Glacier Bay National Monument with twelve miles of trails and a shelter. The Monument is known for its massive icebergs and glaciers, lush coniferous forests, and richly varied wildlife.

Oregon Trail: About as long as the Appalachian, it stretches from Independence, Missouri, some 2,000 miles to the coast of Washington, near Fort Vancouver. Many a wagon train traveled west by this route, across the prairies and mountains to the Pacific. It crosses the Continental Divide and wends over Wyoming's majestic Rockies and on into the tall northwestern timber.

Lewis and Clark Trail: This one forms a sprawling loop along part of the way because it follows both the outbound and inbound routes of the renowned Lewis and Clark Expedition, from Wood River, Illinois, just above the confluence of the Missouri and Mississippi, all the way across the Bitterroot Mountains to the Fort Clatsop National Monument, commemorating the fort built by the expedition on the shores of the Pacific. It was there that Lewis and Clark spent the winter of 1805–6, before heading back to St. Louis. Parts of the trail follow wild stretches of the Snake, Columbia, and Yellowstone rivers.

Mormon Battalion Trail: The route winds southwestward from Mount Pisgah, Iowa, 2,000 miles through Kansas, Colorado, New Mexico, Arizona, and up the California coast to Los Angeles. It retraces the path of a Mormon expedition that was sent forth to fight in the War with Mexico and helped to prepare the way for California statehood.

Mormon Trail: It retraces the great Mormon

migration under the leadership of Brigham Young, following the murder of Joseph Smith in 1846, from Nauvoo, Illinois, to the Great Salt Lake. It passes through Iowa, Nebraska, and Wyoming to the new home where the Mormons settled in 1847 and where Brigham Young was appointed governor of the Utah Territory three years later.

Continental Divide Trail: This is one of the very long routes, a trail extending over 3,100 miles from southwestern New Mexico, near the Mexican border, north and slightly westward to the boundary of Montana and Canada in Glacier National Park. Beginning outside Silver City in New Mexico's Gila National Forest, it roughly follows the Continental Divide—the great ridge of the Rockies separating westward- and eastward-flowing streams. It goes through, next to, or near a whole string of National Forests and Parks. In addition to Glacier, there's Rocky Mountain National Park in Colorado and Yellowstone in Wyoming. The National Forests (and wilderness areas within them) are many.

Perhaps for no better reason than familiarity, I've always particularly liked the northern stretch that runs up through Montana. Coming out of Yellowstone, you go through portions of Beaverhead and Gallatin National Forests. Part of the 157,000-acre Anaconda-Pintlar Wilderness is in the Beaverhead; the Absaroka, Spanish Peaks, and Beartooth Primitive areas are in the Gallatin. To the north, in the Helena National Forest, is the Gates of the Mountains Wilderness. Spilling over onto the west side of the Divide are the Bitterroots. Just below Glacier National Park are the Lewis and Clark National Forest and the Flathead National Forest. The famous and wildly beautiful 950,000-acre Bob Marshall Wilderness is in the Lewis and Clark Forest. Up in the Flathead are 35 miles of trails in the Jewel Basin Hiking Area, which contains nearly thirty alpine lakes.

Short side trips from the main route of the Continental Divide will unfold not just the panoramas of the places listed but many others. In Montana alone, a 657-mile portion of the trail passes through seven National Forests, and a 106-mile stretch is in Glacier National Park.

Santa Fe Trail: Independence, Missouri, is the northern terminus of this trail, on which the caravans of a single year, 1860, comprised 3,033 wagons, 9,084 men, 6,147 mules and 27,920 oxen, all plying the 800-mile trade road to Santa Fe. As early as the period of Spanish rule, isolated trapping parties used the trail, but American imports were not welcome at Santa Fe until Mexico was freed in 1821. Thereafter, trade increased every year until the Civil War disrupted it. By then, a monthly stagecoach had been using the trail for a decade, and traffic resumed along the old frontier path after the war, but the road became a ghost trail after 1880, when the Atchison, Topeka & Santa Fe Railroad finally reached Sante Fe. Hikers now follow the hoof and wheel ruts where once the mules and oxen trod.

North Country Trail: Here's another long one, some 3,200 miles from its conjunction with the Appalachian Trail in Vermont through New York, Pennsylvania, Ohio, Michigan, Wisconsin, Minnesota, and North Dakota, where it meets the Lewis and Clark Trail. It seems hardly necessary to recount the history of a trail that was walked by Indians, by westward-faring settlers, traders, and trappers, by soldiers during the French and Indian War and again during the War of 1812, and thereafter by pioneers, mountain men, and French-Canadian voyageurs. Along this trail there are magnificent views of Lake Michigan, Lake Superior, the Straits of Mackinac, and the giant timber country of the mythical Minnesota lumberjack, Paul Bunyan.

Chisholm Trail and Old Cattle Trails: The lower end of the Chisholm Trail is in southern Texas, in the vicinity of San Antonio and Cuero. It sweeps northward, following the old course of the great cattle drives—up through the Indian Territory that's now Oklahoma to Abilene, Kansas. Hundreds of thousands of longhorns stirred immense dust clouds along this way after 1866, when a half-breed Cherokee trader named Jesse Chisholm drove a heavy wagonload of buffalo hides up through the Indian Territory to his trading post at Wichita.

The wheels cut deep ruts in the prairie, just as today's oil-prospecting vehicles rip lasting scars in the Alaskan tundra. Thus Chisholm marked the route for the cattle drives of the next two decades. With the development of railroads and the introduction of wire fencing, the trail fell into disuse, though it lived in cowboy ballads, and traces of it have always been visible along the line of the Santa Fe Railroad.

Hiker on high promontory gazes out over Cibola National Forest in New Mexico, just above Gila National Forest at lower end of Continental Divide Trail. (*Forest Service Photo by Ray Manley*)

The two connecting trails are not mere spurs but alternate routes that brought the cattle to other railheads. One branches out from the Chisholm near its southern end and takes a more easterly direction through Oklahoma and lower Kansas, passing through Chetopa to Fort Scott. The other branches from this second one in Texas, after going some distance north toward Fort Worth, then swings slightly northwestward and loops back northeastward, crossing the second one near Lake Texoma on the Red River, and veering farther east through Oklahoma to Baxter Springs, Kansas, and the Missouri border near Joplin.

Natchez Trace Trail: Of great military and commercial importance from the 1780s to the 1830s, this route was developed from a series of Choctaw and Chickasaw trails. At first it was used only on northward trips, from Natchez, Mississippi, on the river above New Orleans, up to Nashville, Tennessee, about 600 miles to the northeast. The frontiersmen used flatboats to float their goods south. But with America's southwestward expansion, the trail came into use for travel in both directions. It became a post road in 1800. At the end of the War of 1812, Andrew Jackson marched his men down it on the way to the Battle of New Orleans, and he used it again in his Indian campaigns. Though the trail declined with the rise of steamboat transportation, stretches of it have always remained popular for hiking and sight-seeing.

Kittanning Trail: This is one of the shorter

In Jewel Basin area, northeast of Montana's Bob Marshall Wilderness, hikers look down on little alpine lake near upper end of Continental Divide Trail. (Bob Cooney Photo)

trails, branching from the great North Country Trail near the Allegheny River in the region of Kittanning, Pennsylvania, eastward to Shirleysburg, Pennsylvania, on the Aughwick. But this simple description may be misleading. Since the Kittanning cuts across the North Country in the western part of the state and the upper reaches of the Potomac Heritage Trail in the south-central area, it can be considered a scenic extension or a connecting trail for both of these longer routes. Moreover, Pennsylvania now has over 6,000 miles of trails (about 2,000 of which have been opened just between 1966 and 1972). Many trails connect, so that there is a vast network of footpaths through the mountains and

forests. You can leave the Kittanning, for example, and hike over to the well-known Baker Trail, which will be described in the section on shorter trails.

It should also be remembered that the hiking paths described here are not complete or final. The Continental Divide Trail, for example, will not be finished for several years. The North Country Trail, as presently proposed, swings northward through Pennsylvania and New York to connect with the Appalachian in Vermont, but perhaps in its final version it will have additional spurs.

El Camino Real Trail: This is the shortest of the currently planned trails, covering only about thirty miles from St. Augustine, on Florida's upper eastern coast, to the Fort Caroline National Memorial on the St. Johns River. Though short, it has a special subtropical beauty unmatched on

Minnesota hiker arrives at white-water flow from Moose Lake into Basswood Lake, near North Country Trail.

other trails under study, and is in an area of high urban concentration and tourist use.

Potomac Heritage Trail: Originating in Pennsylvania, west of the Kittanning Trail's terminus at Shirleysburg, this route traces the sources of the Potomac River in that state and West Virginia and more or less follows the main course of the river (on both sides along its lower reaches) through parts of Maryland and Virginia to where it empties into Chesapeake Bay. It passes right through the nation's capital on the way from Harpers Ferry to Westmoreland State Park in Virginia and to Cedarville State Forest in Maryland. Its 825 miles include the 170-mile towpath of the old Chesapeake and Ohio Canal.

Long Trail: Descending through the mountains of Vermont from the Canadian border near. Lake Memphremagog, the Long Trail winds 255 miles to the Massachusetts border at the southwestern corner of Vermont. Along its lower reaches, it has now become part of the great Ap-

palachian Trail. It's among the oldest of state trails and certainly merits inclusion in the federal system, for it's also one of the most beautiful. A hike along any segment of this trail when the autumn foliage is at the height of color can never be forgotten.

Appalachian Trail: The first of the National Scenic Trails to reach completion, this trail begins at Mount Katahdin, in Maine's Baxter State Park, and meanders south through New Hampshire's White Mountain National Forest and Vermont's Green Mountain National Forest, past Mount Greylock and through the Berkshires in Massachusetts, past Schaghticoke Mountain in Connecticut, Clarence Fahnestock Memorial State Park in New York, Palisades Interstate Park in that state and New Jersey, along the Jersey side of the Delaware River in sight of the Kittitinny peaks, across the Susquehanna River in Pennsylvania, through western Maryland to the Chesapeake and Ohio Canal National Monument, down the Shenandoah to Virginia's George Washington National Forest and Jefferson National Forest, into North Carolina's Cherokee National Forest and Nantahala Gorge in the Nantahala National Forest, which blends into Chattahoochee National Forest in Georgia, where the trail finally terminates at Springer Mountain, eighty miles north of Atlanta.

The history of this great trail is closely associated with a network of regional footpaths built and maintained by volunteer hiking associations. The Appalachian Mountain Club managed trails in New Hampshire dating from 1876, and the Dartmouth Outing Club also operated a trail system in this region. These paths were gradually lengthened, with one segment forming the famous Long Trail in Vermont. Down in New York, a trail system through the Palisades Interstate Park also served outdoor enthusiasts for many years before the national program was initiated. In 1921, Benton MacKaye proposed the construction of the Appalachian Trail in an article appearing in the *Journal of the American Institute of Architects.* His idea was to establish a

Map (on facing page) shows proposed route of 3,200-mile North Country Trail, from junction with Lewis and Clark Trail in North Dakota to junction with Appalachian Trail in Vermont.

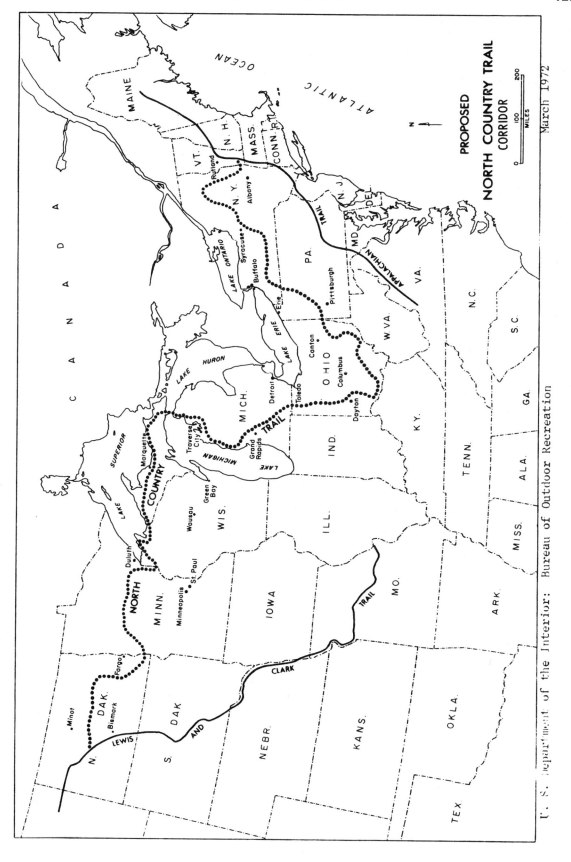

PROPOSED
NORTH COUNTRY TRAIL
CORRIDOR

March 1972

U. S. Department of the Interior: Bureau of Outdoor Recreation

Hiker pauses along towpath of Chesapeake and Ohio Canal, on Potomac Heritage Trail between Cumberland and Washington, D.C. (*George F. Blackburn Photo*)

trail for hikers living in metropolitan centers along the Atlantic seaboard. The following year, the first mile of the trail was cut and marked in Palisades Interstate Park, and the entire length was completed in 1937 by private organizations working with the Forest Service and other agencies.

The private groups had formed a federation, the Appalachian Trail Conference, in 1925 to coordinate efforts. The Conference has promoted improvements ever since and has the gratitude of all hikers who have set foot anywhere on the Appalachian.

This route has been described by the writer Harold Allen as "remote for detachment, narrow for chosen company, winding for leisure, lonely for contemplation." He observed that "the Trail

leads not merely north and south but upward to the body, mind and soul of man."

Pacific Crest Trail: Second of the great walking routes to be officially designated as a National Scenic Trail, the Pacific Crest is actually not quite complete at this writing, but a well-equipped, intrepid hiking party, checking the route with map and compass, could traverse the entire 2,313 miles of it. In fact, though a border-to-border walk is not the purpose of the trail, it has been done. Not just by Indians, explorers, pioneers, trappers, and prospectors, but by modern outdoorsmen. One of them, Mike Edwards, contributed an account of the feat to the June 1971 issue of *National Geographic* magazine. His party set out in May, twenty miles southeast of San Diego, traveled 1,450 miles in California, 406 in Oregon, and 457 in Washington to reach the terminus at the Canadian border in September.

He estimated that a brisk hiker would require more than four months for the trip, averaging twenty miles a day. Such an undertaking

This is trail shelter at White Oak Bottoms Recreation area in Nantahala National Forest, North Carolina, along lower reaches of Appalachian Trail. (Forest Service Photo by J. L. Rich and Daniel O. Todd)

Short detour from Pacific Crest Trail has taken these hikers to beautiful Broken Top Mountain in Three Sisters Wilderness of Oregon's Deschutes National Forest. (*Forest Service Photo by Jim Hughes*)

could at times become a hardship, especially in view of unpredictable weather conditions. The Forest Service advises that snow normally falls in the higher elevations of the Cascade and Sierra Nevada ranges through May, and winter storms can occur as late as mid-June. From mid-July until about Labor Day, there are frequent afternoon or evening thunder showers in the high country, and in southern California's lower elevations, where rainfall is minimal, the temperature may soar well above 100.

At least 80 per cent of the trail is through federal lands—twenty-five National Forests and

half a dozen National Parks. Looking at a map, it almost seems that you never leave the National Forests, but as Mike Edwards pointed out, you also cross "a lot of ranches and some bouldery badlands."

Tracing the trail from the top, as I did with the Appalachian, here are some of the outstanding areas traversed. It starts at the British Columbia-Washington border near Ross Lake, in the North Cascades Primitive Area, and progresses southward through a vast chain of National Forests and past Mount Rainier National Park and the Yakima Indian Reservation, across the Columbia River, into Oregon, along the edge of the Warm Springs Indian Reservation, through the Mount Washington Wilderness and other wild Cascade areas into Crater Lake National Park, over the Rogue River and into California for the remainder of the route: across the Klamath and the upper fingers of Shasta Lake, the Thousand Lakes Wilderness, Lassen Volcanic National Park and down the National Forests of the Sierra Nevadas into Yosemite National Park, then Kings Canyon and Sequoia National Parks, and out of public lands for a short way above Los Angeles, then back into National Forests for most of the remaining journey to the Mexican border.

The trail consists mainly of very old paths, some of which were surveyed by the Forest Service as early as 1920. A Pasadena conservationist named Clinton C. Clark proposed the idea for a border-to-border foot and horseback route in 1932, and soon afterward helped to organize the Pacific Crest Trail Conference. Surveying and construction have been proceeding intermittently ever since. Marked temporary routes bypass most of the relatively short sections on which work is still needed.

Because existing trails (some of them state maintained) were incorporated into the Pacific Crest, some segments are generally known by their individual names: in Washington, the Cascade Trail; in Oregon, the Skyline Trail; in California, the Lava Crest; the Tahoe-Yosemite; the John Muir Trail along one of the most beautiful portions; the Sierra Trail; and the Desert Crest Trail.

Additional Future Possibilities

The Bureau of Outdoor Recreation and other co-operating federal agencies have not ended their planning work. Additional scattered and scenically diversified routes qualify for possible future consideration: a Pacific Coast Trail along the seacoast, west of the present Crest Trail; Upper Colorado River Trail, from the Flaming Gorge Recreation Area in Utah and Wyoming down the Green and Colorado rivers to the Glen Canyon Recreation Area in Utah and Arizona—with branches into spectacular side canyons; Rio Grande International Trail along the U.S.-Mexican boundary; Mississippi River Trail paralleling a proposed Great River Road; Great Lakes International Trail circling the most scenic portions of the United States and Canadian shorelines; Ozarks Trail through the pic-turesque Missouri and Arkansas plateaus, ridges, and river valleys; Gulf Seacoast Trail, from Florida's southern tip along the coastlines of Alabama, Mississippi, and Louisiana to the southern tip of Texas; Atlantic Coast Trail, east of the Appalachian, along the coast from Maine to Florida; Daniel Boone Trail, from Kentucky's Cumberland Gap to Nashville, Tennessee; Trail of Tears, tracing the way of the exiled Cherokees from the southeast into Oklahoma; DeSoto Trail, from Tampa Bay, Florida, through Georgia, South Carolina, North Carolina, Tennessee, Alabama, Mississippi, and Arkansas to the Mississippi River; and California Trail, branching from the Oregon Trail in Wyoming and rolling through Idaho, Utah, and Nevada to California's Sacramento Valley.

It's impossible to say which of these trails will materialize, but some surely will, and sections of all of them do exist, either in *de facto* form or as state, local, park, forest, or metropolitan trails.

Some Outstanding Shorter Trails

There are thousands of relatively short trails maintained by local, state, and federal agencies, often in co-operation with private groups. I'll describe a few with which I'm acquainted or which are earning the acclaim of hikers. Then I'll list total trail mileages and sources of trail information for each state.

On the Kentucky-Tennessee border is a 40-mile peninsula between two man-made lakes—Kentucky Lake on the Tennessee River and Lake Barkley on the Cumberland River. This peninsula contains 177,000 acres of woods, ridges, marshes, meadows, and waters teeming with birds and other wildlife, all administered by the Tennessee Valley Authority. It's not only a TVA showplace but an experiment in environmental education. A well-staffed Conservation Education Center, on a point jutting into Lake Barkley, is near the main visitor center and within 500 miles of one third of this nation's population. Every year, thousands of people study the plant and animal life along well-planned nature trails. One of these, the 2½-mile Hematite Trail, winds around 100-acre Hematite Lake and employs a boardwalk over a marshy woodland.

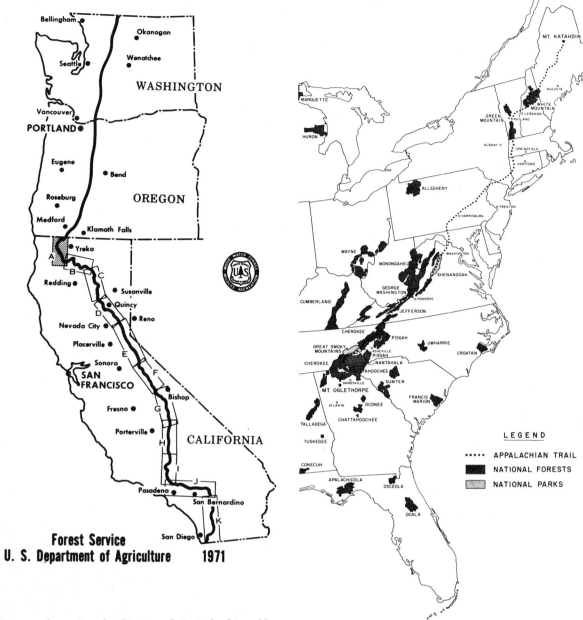

Forest Service
U. S. Department of Agriculture   1971

Maps show Pacific Crest and Appalachian National Scenic Trails. On Pacific Crest map, lettered rectangles in California portion show size of sections depicted on small-scale maps available from Forest Service. On Appalachian map, shaded areas indicate National Forests and National Parks.

Teachers often bring their classes here on group hikes to study the varied wildlife, including a small herd of bison and a resident flock of wild Canada geese.

The staff loans out gear such as binoculars, telescopes, and even waders for field study. In addition to daytime activities, there are nighttime "animal watches" and observations of the stars. There are family campsites for tent or trailer, with electricity, showers, toilets, drinking water, boat-launching ramps, swimming areas, and playgrounds. Actually, this is a recreational as well as educational facility.

A very famous foot and horse path is Ohio's Buckeye Trail, at least part of which will eventually become a link in the 3,200-mile North Country Trail and will thus be included in the National Scenic Trails System. It was originally conceived as a single diagonal route from the Ohio River, at Cincinnati in the southwestern corner of the state, northeastward to Lake Erie, but now a western branch is being developed by the Ohio Department of Natural Resources and the energetic Buckeye Trail Association. This branch will reach north from Cincinnati to Toledo and points west. The extension is only partly completed, but there are already over 600 miles of hiking trail and there will be about 900. The trail is well marked in both directions with blue paint blazes. There are some public camping areas, with more of them needed and planned.

John Bay, President of the Buckeye Trail Association, has furnished this vivid description of the main route, which retraces old Indian trails, towpaths, and roads:

Hikers on Buckeye Trail make their way across Ohio Power Recreation Area in Morgan County. (John Bay Photo)

"The trail begins at Eden Park in Cincinnati and crosses relatively flat country until it reaches Pike State Forest. Between Pike State Forest and Tar Hollow State Forest near Chillicothe it follows ridgetops along woods trails and quiet country roads. In Hocking County it goes through deep sandstone gorges and caves, and the popular Hocking Hills State Parks. (At the annual hike between Old Man's Cave and Ash Cave State Parks in January 1972, over 1,400 people made the six-mile trek via the trail, some in both directions.) In Morgan and Noble Counties, the Buckeye Trail crosses 22 miles of the Ohio Power Recreation Area. Here hikers can see reclamation in action, as well as a radio-operated electric railway for hauling coal from mine to tipple, 'Big Muskie'—the world's largest dragline coal shovel—and many lakes stocked with gamefish. The trail links the Muskingum Watershed Conservancy District reservoir lakes across eastern Ohio. It follows the Ohio and Erie Canal from Zoar, a restored historic settlement with an inn and craftshops, across Stark County, through Akron, and along the Cuyahoga River past Blossom Center, summer home of the Cleve-

land Symphony Orchestra, and Deep Lock Quarry, where rock was quarried to build the canal. It follows the Cleveland Metropolitan Parks System and links several Lake County parks before reaching Lake Erie at Mentor Headlands State Park. An alternate branch links Akron's reservoir lakes and several Geauga County parks.

"In western Ohio, the completed part of the second branch follows the scenic Little Miami River north from Cincinnati to Yellow Springs, then swings west past the Wright Brothers Memorial and flight-trial field, and the National Air Force Museum, then follows an abandoned interurban railway into Dayton. From Dayton it follows the Miami-Erie Canal and Great Miami River northward to Lockington."

A couple of Pennsylvania trails merit description. One is the Horse-Shoe Trail, beginning just across Valley Creek from General Washington's Headquarters in Valley Forge Park (near Philadelphia) and running westward over 120 miles until it intercepts the Appalachian Trail in the Rattling Run area of Stony Mountain, 12 miles north of Hershey (near Harrisburg). A large part of the trail runs through private property and is used with permission of the owners, who allow both walking and horseback riding. No motorized vehicles of any kind are permitted. The entire length of the trail is well marked with yellow blazes, while side trails and horse run-arounds are marked with white blazes.

The Horse-Shoe Trail Club schedules half a dozen 10-mile loop walks on or touching the trail in spring and fall for its two hundred or so members. Others, too, can use the route, as it's a free public trail. I'm informed by Trails Chairman John A. Goff that Second-Sunday Work Hikes are becoming better and better attended. This and other clubs that combine hiking with trail maintenance are doing a commendable job.

The second Pennsylvania trail I want to mention is the Baker, in the western part of the state, running 108 miles from Freeport up into the Cook Forest State Park. (It used to extend to Aspinwall, below Freeport, but urban development in the Pittsburgh area forced the abandonment of the southernmost section.) This trail was established in 1950 by the Pittsburgh Council of American Youth Hostels, and was named after Horace Forbes Baker, who was president

of the Council before World War II and worked untiringly to build the organization and further its work.

Actually, the trail had its origin on a 1948 A.Y.H. canoe trip down the Allegheny River. Several members of the group so admired the bluffs above the river that they suggested building a bluff-top trail from which the great river valley could be viewed. Today there are eight open-front shelters along the trail—spaced from eight to sixteen miles apart—and, as of this writing, two more are planned. There are fireplaces, and most shelters have nearby springs; some have latrines as well, and some have streams or lakes for swimming. The trail is marked with yellow blazes and wooden signs.

One section, from Route 66 to Cochran's Mills, is exceptionally well marked and maintained, so novices are encouraged to take their first hikes along this portion. Among its features is a covered bridge over Horney Camp Run.

The trail is shown on the official state highway map and on Exxon's Pennsylvania map. You should, however, get the topographical maps covering the trail sections. They're available at local stores or from the Distribution Section, Geological Survey, 1200 South Eads Street, Arlington, Virginia 22202, for $.50 to $.80 each. Better still, get a copy of the *Baker Trail Guide*, which is available for only $.75 from the Pittsburgh Council of A.Y.H. (See appendix for the address of this and other hiking organizations.) The guide includes eleven topographical maps, and a map showing road access points, shelter

Between Cochran's Mills and Crooked Creek State Park, Pennsylvania's Baker Trail crosses covered bridge. (Don Woodland Photo)

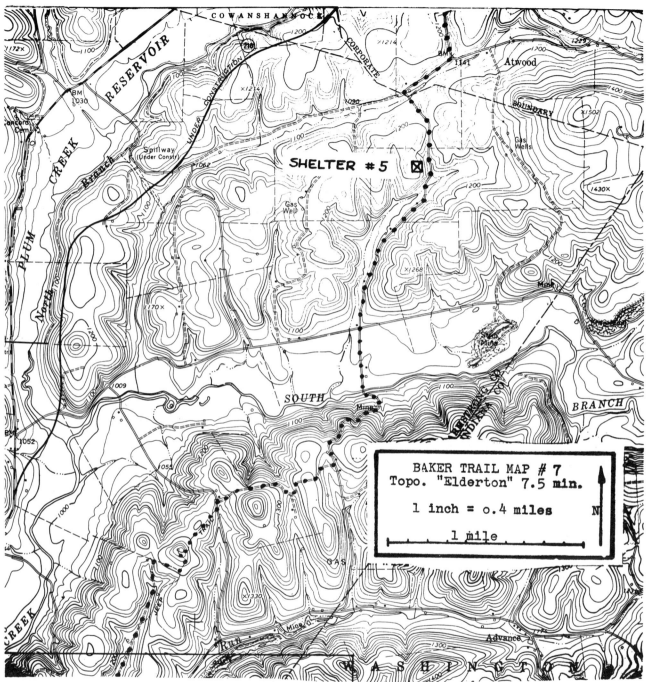

SHELTER #5

BAKER TRAIL MAP # 7
Topo. "Elderton" 7.5 min.

1 inch = o.4 miles

1 mile

This is one of eleven section maps in Baker Trail Guide distributed by Pittsburgh Council of American Youth Hostels.

locations, and so on. It also contains excellent descriptive information, and will be sent with a list of other publications covering a number of trails in Pennsylvania and West Virginia.

There are times, of course, when a trail of this kind may be "snowed in," and for winter hiking without winter weather I can't think of a more beautiful pathway than the Florida Trail. When it's finished, it will run the length of the state, from Everglades National Park in the South clear up past Jacksonville in the North and then west across the upper panhandle to Panama City. That's about 700 miles. At this writing,

Near Lake Okeechobee, Florida Trail winds among cypresses and beneath Spanish moss. (Florida Trail Association Photo)

over 200 miles are cleared, marked, and maintained, thanks to the Florida Trail Association, which was formed to construct the path and to stimulate interest in Florida's wilderness. Permission to cross private property has been obtained on the basis that the trail may be used only by Association members, but an annual individual membership for $3.00, or family membership for $5.00, certainly can't be called an obstacle.

Currently open sections of the trail include stretches north from the Tamiami Trail, from Ocala National Forest to Goldhead Branch State Park and from Osceola National Forest along the banks of the Suwannee to Suwannee River State Park. This is a flatland trail through pine woods, cypress stands, and sloughs of strange beauty. Maps and brochures are available from the Association.

You may have some favorite of your own— perhaps New York's 133-mile Northville-Lake Placid Trail, laid out through the forests by the Adirondack Mountain Club in 1922 and 1923; or Michigan's 210-mile foot and horseback trails across the peninsula from Lake Huron to Lake Michigan; or the 100-mile Lone Star Trail and connected self-guiding nature trails blazed by Sierra Club members through the heart of the Sam Houston National Forest in the Big Thicket country of Texas; or the Big or Little Cottonwood Canyon camping areas outside Salt Lake; or the trails through the Haleakala and Hawaii Volcanoes National Parks. Vermont has more than 7,000 miles of trails and Michigan has more than 10,000; of the other states, the most trail-conscious ones are in the West, where half a dozen of them have more than 7,000 miles apiece. It's impossible to describe or even list all the trails individually, but here's a state-by-state list of roughly approximate trail mileages and sources at the state capitals that can be contacted for information:

STATE	APPROXIMATE MILES OF EXISTING TRAILS	SOURCES OF INFORMATION
Alabama	456	Director, Dept. of Conservation (Montgomery)
Alaska	1,200	Theodore G. Smith, Director, Div. of Parks (Juneau)
Arizona	3,104	Roger Gruenewald, Outdoor Recreation Coordinating Commission (Phoenix)
Arkansas	45	Frank A. Patalano, Exec. Director, Arkansas Planning Commission (Little Rock)
California	12,234	William Penn Mott, Jr., Director, Dept. of Parks and Recreation (Sacramento)
Colorado	7,126	Harry K. Woodward, Director, Div. of Game, Fish & Parks (Denver)
Connecticut	390	Joseph N. Gill, Commissioner, Dept. of Agriculture & Natural Resources (Hartford)
Delaware	48	David R. Keifer, Director, State Planning Office (Dover)
Florida	247	Ney C. Landrum, Director, Div. of Recreation & Parks (Tallahassee)
Georgia	226	Tom Linder, Bureau of State Planning & Community Affairs (Atlanta)
Hawaii	471	Shelly M. Mark, Director, Dept. of Planning & Economic Development (Honolulu)
Idaho	10,817	Wilhelm M. Beckert, Director, Idaho Dept. of Parks (Boise)
Illinois	700	Henry N. Barkhausen, Director, Dept. of Conservation (Springfield)
Indiana	928	John R. Lloyd, Director, Dept. of Natural Resources (Indianapolis)
Iowa	182	E. B. Speaker, State Conservation Commission (Des Moines)
Kansas	33	Lynn Burris, Jr., Director, State Park & Resources Authority (Topeka)
Kentucky	717	Frank J. Groschelle, Special Assistant to the Governor (Frankfort)
Louisiana	214	Lamar Gibson, Director, State Parks & Recreation Commission (Baton Rouge)

Maine	2,935	Lawrence Stuart, Director, State Parks & Recreation Commission (Augusta)
Maryland	818	Spencer P. Ellis, Director, Dept. of Forests & Parks (Annapolis)
Massachusetts	2,513	Arthur Brownell, Commissioner, Dept. of Natural Resources (Boston)
Michigan	10,526	Ralph A. MacMullan, Director, Dept. of Natural Resources (Lansing)
Minnesota	2,673	Robert Herbst, Commissioner, Dept. of Conservation (St. Paul)
Mississippi	50	Spencer E. Medlin, Comptroller, Mississippi Park System (Jackson)
Missouri	1,818	Robert L. Dunkeson, Exec. Secretary, Inter-Agency Council for Outdoor Recreation (Jefferson City)
Montana	9,496	Robert F. Cooney, Recreation & Parks Div. (Helena)
Nebraska	70	Willard R. Barbee, Director, Game & Parks Commission (Lincoln)
Nevada	503	Elmo J. De Ricco, Director, Dept. of Conservation & Natural Resources (Carson City)
New Hampshire	1,262	George Gilman, Commissioner, Dept. of Resources & Economic Development (Concord)
New Jersey	3,772	Richard J. Sullivan, Commissioner, Dept. of Environmental Protection (Trenton)
New Mexico	3,648	State Planning Office (Santa Fe)
New York	4,548	Sal J. Prezioso, Commissioner, Office of Parks & Recreation (Albany)
North Carolina	1,884	William L. Turner, Director, Dept. of Administration (Raleigh)
North Dakota	590	John Greenslit, Coordinator, State Outdoor Recreation Agency (Bismarck)
Ohio	2,331	William B. Nye, Director, Dept. of Natural Resources (Columbus)
Oklahoma	307	Industrial Development & Park Dept. (Oklahoma City)
Oregon	8,963	R. L. Porter, State Highway Dept. (Salem)
Pennsylvania	6,172	Irving Hand, Exec. Director, State Planning Board (Harrisburg)
Rhode Island	60	John L. Rego, Director, Dept. of Natural Resources (Providence)

South Carolina	70	Bob Hickman, Director, Dept. of Parks, Recreation & Tourism (Columbia)
South Dakota	1,252	Robert Hodgins, Director, Dept. of Game, Fish & Parks (Pierre)
Tennessee	708	William L. Jenkins, Commissioner, Dept. of Conservation (Nashville)
Texas	750	Paul Schlimper, Dept. of Parks & Wildlife (Austin)
Utah	5,348	Gordon E. Harmston, Exec. Director, Dept. of Natural Resources (Salt Lake City)
Vermont	7,438	Forrest E. Orr, Planning Director, Agency of Environmental Conservation (Montpelier)
Virginia	913	Ben Bolen, Commissioner of Parks (Richmond)
Washington	8,356	Lewis A. Bell, Chairman, Inter-Agency Committee for Outdoor Recreation (Olympia)
West Virginia	776	William H. Loy, Acting Director, Federal-State Relations (Charleston)
Wisconsin	433	John A. Beale, Deputy Secretary, Dept. of Natural Resources (Madison)
Wyoming	6,400	Paul H. Westedt, Director, Wyoming Recreation Commission (Cheyenne)

The above figures represent recent surveys and estimates. Some states are now in the process of planning increases, of obtaining land or rights-of-way, or of building new trails. But even if the miles of trails have already grown beyond the figures given for a few states, the listing will provide you with a good idea of the extent of hiking paths in your state and others.

Canadian Highlights

A bit more ought to be said here about hiking in Canada. After all, some of the world's most spectacular forests, mountains, and alpine lakes are in Canada and are threaded with well-marked trails and good campsites. The country has 24 National Parks, 33 Historic Parks—and literally thousands of provincial, municipal, and private campgrounds.

Camping fees are agreeably low. Charges in National Parks range from $1.50 a day for an unserviced site to $2.00 for one with electricity or $2.50 for one with water, electricity, and sewage connections. For organized groups with a qualified camping leader, there are special National Park campsites where the fee is $.25 per person. The fees at provincial, municipal, and private campgrounds vary but are always quite reasonable.

Even some of the relatively short trails in many of the parks—the nine-mile hike to the summit for which British Columbia's Mount Revelstoke National Park is named, for instance —offer breath-taking experiences. Many seasoned backpackers feel that Alberta is the best province for the hiker, and the best spots in Alberta are the National Parks situated in the Rockies: Waterton Lakes, Banff, Jasper. Banff is generally considered to be the acme in terms of trail networks, but Jasper is also wonderful. And what about Waterton Lakes, with its 100 miles of wide trails crisscrossing the park and leading into those of the adjoining Glacier National Park?

Tourism is important to Canada's economy, and the various agencies of the Canadian government (and the individual provinces as well) are therefore most courteous and helpful in furnishing information to resident and visitor alike. Before setting out on a hiking or camping trip north of the border, I'd advise you to request *Campers' Tour Kit No. 9* from the Canadian Government Travel Bureau in Ottawa. The literature and maps will give you some splendid leads. Those interested in horseback trips will also be well advised to request a brochure from the Trail Riders of the Canadian Rockies, Box 6742, Station D, Calgary 2, Alberta.

No account of Canadian hiking would be complete without a description of the Bruce Trail and the Bruce Trail Association. You can take an hour's walk, a day's hike, or a long camping trip on this route, marked with white blazes and extending some 430 miles up the Niagara escarpment of southern Ontario. Access points are marked with diamond-shaped signs much like those that mark a number of American trail heads, and side trails are blazed in blue. There's a string of three-sided shelters along the route, maintained by the voluntary workers of the Bruce Trail Association, but some of the way is rough and remote, so hikers are urged not to travel alone.

The trail begins near Niagara Falls, below Hamilton and between lakes Erie and Ontario. It extends north across the Niagara Peninsula, through the city of Hamilton and on to Nottawasaga Bay, which is the bottom of Georgian Bay, which in turn is really an eastern arm of Lake Huron. The trail then meanders northwest up the Bruce Peninsula, which separates Georgian Bay from Lake Huron, to the very tip of the land at Tobermory. If you were to trek the entire distance, you'd pass through the Caledon Hills, the valleys of the Pretty and Mad rivers, along the high country of the Blue Mountains, then northwest across beautiful Beaver Valley to Owen Sound, Wiarton, Lions Head, Cabot Head, and finally to the tip of the Bruce.

There's a footpath cleared to a width of five feet, but no attempt has been made to level or smooth it; the idea, after all, is to see this wilderness in its magnificent natural state. There are sectors, particularly toward the northern end, where the trail may be overgrown or precipitous. This most remote part of the trail is not for novices, as it can be hazardous. This, incidentally, is one of the hiking areas where you must take care where you step and must carry a snakebite kit, as there's a healthy population of rattlers.

But I don't want to frighten anyone off; there are parts of the trail on the lower sector that are appropriate for a family outing. I spent a summer month of my boyhood on an island in Georgian Bay, picking wild blueberries, catching fish, swimming the cold waters, watching mink and eagles and other intriguing fauna, and I don't know of a more beautiful region.

Within the Bruce Trail Association there are a number of Bruce Trail Clubs, each of them located in and responsible for a particular portion of the trail. Their service is commendable. Membership costs very little. Whether or not you wish to join, if you would like to consider an outdoor excursion in that area I strongly advise you to request literature from the Bruce Trail Association at the address listed in the appendix.

Tips on Private Timber and Mining Lands

There's no denying that lumbermen and miners have committed a number of atrocities against the environment during the last century and a half. And this is not the place to enter the dispute as to whether they're beginning to reform or are only becoming more adept at polishing their public image. There's no doubt, though, that at least some of them are making an effort toward conservation and at the same time trying to improve their relations with the public. It's hardly surprising that a portion of the Continental Divide Trail crosses property owned by the Anaconda Company. Big landowners—particularly timber and mining companies and railroads, but including others as well—are now showing an absolute eagerness to have people travel and camp on their land. Hospitality is good business, and it's also smart to let people see that vast, privately owned tracts are not being raped. (There's no point in commenting here on other tracts which *are* being raped.)

If you reside or vacation in the vicinity of timber or mining holdings, ask the management about hiking on the property. Chances are, you'll be welcomed. I can't speak from personal experience about most of them, but I do know something about the policies of two big timber outfits—Weyerhaeuser Company, in the Pacific Northwest and in the South; and Bowaters Southern Paper Corporation, in Tennessee, Georgia, Alabama, and Mississippi. Weyerhaeuser owns about 5½ million acres, and I've been on a little of the Douglas fir land in Oregon and Washington, as well as among the Ponderosa pines in Oregon. The company maintains fourteen free camping and picnicking areas in those two states.

In recent years, Weyerhaeuser has co-operated with backpacking clubs which have printed guides to some of its lands and have prepared trail maps. Since 1967 it has been engaged in a joint venture with Washington's Department of Natural Resources to develop the Capital Forest Recreation Area near Olympia. You can contact that agency or the company for information on hiking these lands.

Recently, while toying with the idea of walking down the Appalachian Trail and camping in the Southeast, I contacted the Bowaters Southern Paper Corporation. The company sent me a free booklet of topographical maps showing hiking trails, picnic areas, campsites, and "Pocket Wildernesses."

Bowaters maintains about 1,100 acres of small pocket-wilderness areas (none larger than 700 acres but quite ample for a retreat back to nature) on several of its holdings. The idea of these pocket wildernesses is simply to leave them as they are—without timbering them, without "improving" them for sight-seeing tourists who don't want their surroundings wild.

But there are signs of human use: beautiful loop trails, ranging up to eight miles in length and winding through virgin forests and along the banks of fast waters. Fine idea. In addition to the brochure, the company will supply copies of Geological Survey maps of its management units, and these are provided at cost. It's worth while to get in touch with companies like this, and also with the American Forestry Association.

Tips on National Parks and Forests

An important tip on finding the best—most peaceful and natural—park hiking is to think about the under-used National Parks. Those which are most renowned among hikers (Sequoia, Yosemite, Glacier, Yellowstone, etc.) are spectacular, but so are Crater Lake National Park in Oregon, Isle Royale National Park (absolutely laced with 160 miles of fine trails) in Minnesota, the new Voyageurs National Park in the same state, and Cumberland Gap National Historic Park, 80 miles north of Great Smoky Mountains National Park, where Kentucky, Tennessee, and Virginia meet.

The Cumberland Gap still shows traces of the Wilderness Road hacked out by Daniel Boone's men in 1775, as well as many other intriguing historic features. It's seldom crowded, has beautiful hiking trails through its 18,000 acres, and provides 165 campsites. The other parks mentioned—and numerous additional ones throughout the country—have similarly attractive features. To get a better notion of what's available to the hiker, get the booklet *Back-Country Travel in the National Park System* ($.35 from the U. S. Government Printing Office). The booklet will also give you tips on safety and trail use, plus a list of regulations you'd better know about. For example, there are areas where no dogs or cats are permitted, even on a leash, and no hunting is permitted in the parks.

Other valuable publications from the same source include:
Camping in the National Park System, $.25
National Parks and Landmarks, $.55
Living History in the National Park System, $.30
Winter Activities in the National Park System, $.35
National Parks of the United States (series of eight maps), $1.50

Another publication you should have is the previously mentioned *Camping on the Public Lands* ($.05, same source), regarding property administered by the Bureau of Land Management. Here again, you'll find a lot of material on where and how to hike in real wilderness country.

In addition, there are some publications you can get from the U. S. Government Printing Office before setting out on any ambitious hiking trips through National Forests. Anyone who has camped in the Bridger Wilderness (in the Wind River Range of Wyoming) or in Idaho's Sawtooth Primitive Area knows the tremendous thrill of exploring these Forest Service Lands—and I could give almost endless additional examples. The publications:

Search for Solitude, $.65

National Forest Vacations, $.45

Wilderness (booklet PA-459), $.20

Camping (booklet PA-502), $.25

National Forest Wildernesses and Primitive Areas (pamphlet with map), $.15

Backpacking in the National Forest Wilderness, $.25

One more, straightforwardly entitled *Regulations Governing the Occupancy and Use of National Forest Recreation Sites and Areas,* will be supplied by a Ranger or other officer at any of the Forests, or by the regional office or the supervisor of the forest you wish to visit.

National Trails Council

I've had occasion to mention several trail conferences, or associations, in this book, as well as numerous hiking clubs either independent or affiliated with larger associations. These groups are of tremendous value, whether as clearing houses of information, or as enjoyable social gatherings, or as teaching units, or as planners, builders, and maintainers of trails and facilities, or as powerful forces for all sorts of goals, from conservation to the acquisition of abandoned railroad rights-of-way for new trails. I will therefore list a number of them, with their addresses, in an appendix. But I will do so with the knowledge that a profusion of such groups, while much to be desired, can lead to bewilderment for hikers who aren't members. The names and addresses of some hiking clubs fail to give any real indication of the regions in which they're active. There are others that specialize in some particular type of activity, but whose names aren't clearly indicative of that activity. There are new ones, continually being formed, whose names won't appear on the list. And there are members and non-members who have no way of knowing what some of the other groups are doing and how they can work together.

To discuss these and other problems, a national trails symposium was held in 1971. The result was the formation in 1972 of the National Trails Council, representing a diversified group of trail users. There are individual members ($10 annual dues), student members ($5.00), club and association memberships ($25), and commercial members ($100), as well as industrial and foundation members who qualify through gifts.

The Council functions as a clearing house for all types of hiking information. It also publishes a quarterly newsletter, promotes trails locally and nationally, and fosters the co-ordination of efforts by various conferences and associations. For further details you can write to Gunnar A. Peterson, Executive Director, National Trails Council, Open Lands Project, 53 W. Jackson Blvd., Chicago, Ill. 60604.

As you have seen, America now has trails to just about everywhere and hikers' associations to help you find and enjoy them. We've come a long way since the small New England hiking clubs began blazing trails over the wooded mountains in the 1870s.

Appendix 1

ORGANIZATIONS

Hiking Clubs, Trail Associations, Campers' Associations, and Related Groups

NOTE: For information on trail organizations or trail development in any area, or if your own group needs assistance in planning and development, write to NATIONAL TRAILS COUNCIL, OPEN LANDS PROJECT, 53 W. JACKSON BLVD., CHICAGO, ILL. 60604. When asking for information, also request details about joining the Council; membership includes both individuals and groups.

When writing to any of the groups included here, ask if the group can furnish a descriptive price list or catalogue of brochures, trail guides, maps, books, and other helpful literature. Most of them do.

Adirondack Mountain Club, R.D. 1, Ridge Road, Glens Falls, N.Y. 12801.

Alpine Club, P. O. Box 2885, Idaho Falls, Idaho 83401.

American Alpine Club, 113 E. Ninetieth St., New York, N.Y. 10028.

American Youth Hostels National Headquarters, 20 W. Seventeenth St., New York, N.Y. 10011.

Appalachian Mountain Club, 5 Joy Street, Boston, Mass. 02108.

Appalachian Trail Conference, 1718 N St., N.W., Washington, D.C. 20036.

Baker Trail Chairman, Pittsburgh Council, A.Y.H., 6300 Fifth Ave., Pittsburgh, Pa. 15232

Boy Scouts of America, New Brunswick, N.J. 08903.

Bruce Trail Association, 33 Hardale Crescent, Hamilton, Ontario, Canada.

Buckeye Trail Association, P. O. Box 8746, Columbus, Ohio 43215.

Camp Fire Girls, Inc., 1740 Broadway, New York, N.Y. 10019.

Chalet Club, 135 E. Fifty-fifth St., New York, N.Y. 10022.

Chicago Mountaineering Club, 8 S. Michigan Ave., Chicago, Ill. 60603.

Colorado Mountain Club, 1400 Josephine St., Denver, Colo. 80206.

East Bay Trails and North American Trails Ride Council, George H. Cardinet, Jr., P. O. Box 5277, Concord, Calif. 94524.

Family Camping Federation of the American Camping Association, Bradford Woods, Martinsville, Ind. 46151.

Federation of Western Outdoor Clubs, P. O. Box 2067, Carmel, Calif. 93921.

Florida Trail Association, 33 S.W. Eighteenth Terrace, Miami, Fla. 33129.

Girl Scouts of the U.S.A., 830 Third Ave., New York, N.Y. 10022.

Green Mountain Club, 108 Merchants Row, Rutland, Vt. 05701.

Hawaiian Trail and Mountain Club, P. O. Box 2238, Honolulu, Hawaii 96813.

Horse-Shoe Trail Club, 623 Righters Mill Rd., Narberth, Pa. 19072.

Illinois Prairie Path, William Nemec, P. O. Box 5, Wayne, Ill. 60184.

Iowa Mountaineers, P. O. Box 163, Iowa City, Ia. 52240.

Kachina Mountain Club, 2217 Encanto Dr., N.W., Phoenix, Ariz. 85026.

Lewis & Clark Trail Heritage Foundation, Mr. F. Edward Budde, 3745 Yaeger Rd., St. Louis, Mo. 63129.

Mazamas, 909 N.W. Nineteenth Ave., Portland, Ore. 97208.

Mountain Club of Maryland, 5300 Holder Ave., Baltimore, Md. 21214.

Mountaineering Club of Alaska, 700 Fifth Ave., Anchorage, Alaska 99502.

The Mountaineers, 719 Pike Street, Seattle, Wash. 98101.

National Campers and Hikers Association, 7172 Transit Road, Buffalo, N.Y. 14221.

New England Family Campers Association, P. O. Box 308, Newburyport, Mass. 01951.

New England Trail Conference, P. O. Box 241, Princeton, Mass. 01541.

New York-New Jersey Trail Conference, G. P. O. Box 2250, New York, N.Y. 10001.

North American Family Campers Association, P. O.

Box 552, 76 State St., Newburyport, Mass. 01950.

Potomac Appalachian Trail Club, 1718 N St., N.W., Washington, D.C. 20036.

Rocky Mountaineer Club, 2100 S Ave., W., Missoula, Mont. 59801.

Santa Barbara County Trails Council, Mrs. Vivian Obern, 4140 Marina Dr., Santa Barbara, Calif. 93110.

Sierra Club, 1050 Mills Tower, San Francisco, Calif. 94104.

Wilderness Society, 729 Fifteenth St., N.W., Washington, D.C. 20005.

Appendix 2

GOVERNMENTAL AND REGIONAL INFORMATION SOURCES

Government Sources of Maps and Information

Denver Distribution Section, Geological Survey, Federal Center, Denver, Colo. 80225. (Topographical maps and state indexes of maps for the United States west of Mississippi River.)

Washington Distribution Section, Geological Survey, Washington, D.C. 20242. (Topographical maps and state indexes of maps for the United States east of Mississippi River.)

Bureau of Land Management, Department of the Interior, Washington, D.C. 20240.

National Park Service, Department of the Interior, Washington, D.C. 20240.

U. S. Forest Service, Department of Agriculture, Washington, D.C. 20250.

Bureau of Sport Fisheries and Wildlife (for wilderness lands within National Wildlife Refuges and Ranges), Washington, D.C. 20240.

NOTE: All government-agency booklets about hiking and camping on public lands can be ordered from:

U. S. GOVERNMENT PRINTING OFFICE, WASHINGTON, D.C. 20402. See text for recommended booklets and their prices.

Sources of Information on National Scenic and Recreation Trails

For a free 30-page booklet—*National Scenic and Recreation Trails*—write to Bureau of Outdoor Recreation, Department of the Interior, Washington, D.C. 20240.

For information on Scenic and Recreation Trails in specific regions, write to:

Northeastern Regional Director, Bureau of Outdoor Recreation, Federal Building, Seventh Floor, 1421 Cherry St., Philadelphia, Pa. 19102.

Southeastern Regional Director, Bureau of Outdoor Recreation, 810 New Walton Building, Atlanta, Ga. 30303.

Lake Central Regional Director, Bureau of Outdoor Recreation, 3853 Research Park Dr., Ann Arbor, Mich. 48104.

Mid-Continent Regional Director, Bureau of Outdoor Recreation, Building 41, Federal Center, Denver, Colo. 80225.

Pacific Southwestern Regional Director, Bureau of Outdoor Recreation, Box 36062, 450 Golden Gate Ave., San Francisco, Calif. 94102.

Pacific Northwestern Regional Director, Bureau of Outdoor Recreation, 1000 Second Ave., Seattle, Wash. 98104.

Sources of Canadian Hiking Information

For literature and maps:
Canadian Government Travel Bureau, Ottawa, Ontario, Canada.

For maps only:
Map Distribution Office, Department of Mines and Technical Surveys, Ottawa, Ontario, Canada.

For information on Bruce Trail and on hiking clubs:
Bruce Trail Association, 33 Hardale Crescent, Hamilton, Ontario, Canada.

For information on horseback trips:
Trail Riders of the Canadian Rockies, P. O. Box 6742, Station D, Calgary 2, Alberta, Canada.

For information on canoe trips:
Canadian Waters, Inc., Ely, Minn. 55731. (Send

$.35 and request brochure, *Canoe Camping with Canadian Waters.*)

Sources of Information About Hiking and Camping on Privately Held Timberland

American Forest Institute, 1619 Massachusetts Ave., N.W., Washington, D.C. 20006.

American Forestry Association, 919 Seventeenth St., N.W., Washington, D.C. 20006.

Bowaters Southern Paper Corp., Public Relations Dept., Calhoun, Tenn. 37303.

Hudson Pulp & Paper Corp., Palatka, Fla. 32077

Open Lands Project, 53 W. Jackson Blvd., Chicago, Ill. 60604.

Westvaco, Timberlands Div., Box 699, Summerville, S.C. 29483.

Weyerhaeuser Co., Public Affairs Dept., Tacoma, Wash. 98401.

Appendix 3

INFORMATION ON SPECIAL ACTIVITIES

Sources of Bike-Hiking Information

American Youth Hostels, National Headquarters, 20 W. Seventeenth St., New York, N.Y. 10011.

Bicycle Touring League of America, 260 W. Twenty-sixth St., New York, N.Y. 10001.

Bicycling Magazine, H. M. Leete Company, 256 Sutter St., San Francisco, Calif. 94108.

Canadian Wheelmen's Association, 4000 Beaubien St. E., Montreal, Quebec, Canada.

International Bicycle Touring Society, 846 Prospect St., La Jolla, Calif. 92037.

League of American Wheelmen, 5118 Foster Ave., Chicago, Ill. 60630.

Sources of Canoe-Trip Information

Adirondack Mountain Club, R.D. 1, Ridge Rd., Glens Falls, N.Y. 12801.

American Canoe Association, 4260 E. Evans Ave., Denver, Colo. 80222.

American Youth Hostels, 20 W. Seventeenth St., New York, N.Y. 10011.

Appalachian Mountain Club, 5 Joy St., Boston, Mass. 02108.

Boy Scouts of America, New Brunswick, N.J. 08903.

Canadian Waters, Inc., Ely, Minn. 55731.

Girl Scouts of the U.S.A., 830 Third Ave., New York, N.Y. 10022.

Izaak Walton League of America, 1800 N. Kent St., Arlington, Va. 22209.

Sierra Club, 1050 Mills Tower, San Francisco, Calif. 94104.

Wilderness Society, Trips Director, 4260 E. Evans Ave., Denver, Colo. 80222.

YMCA, 1308 Oak Brook Rd., Box 1000, Oak Brook, Ill. 60521.

YWCA, 600 Lexington Ave., New York, N.Y. 10022.

Sources of Horseback-Trip Information

American Association of Health, Physical Education, and Recreation, 1201 Sixteenth St., N.W., Washington, D.C. 20036.

Equestrian Trails, Inc., 10506 E. Washington Blvd., Whittier, Calif. 90606.

North American Trails Ride Council, George H. Cardinet, Jr., P. O. Box 5277, Concord, Calif. 94524.

Sierra Club, 1050 Mills Tower, San Francisco, Calif. 94104.

Trail Riders of the Canadian Rockies, P. O. Box 6742, Station D, Calgary 2, Alberta, Canada.

Wilderness Society, Trips Director, 4260 E. Evans Ave., Denver, Colo. 80222.

Sources of Mountaineering Information

Adirondack Mountain Club, R.D. 1, Ridge Road, Glens Falls, N.Y. 12801.

Alpine Club, P. O. Box 2885, Idaho Falls, Idaho 83401.

American Alpine Club, 113 E. Ninetieth St., New York, N.Y. 10028.

Appalachian Mountain Club, 5 Joy St., Boston, Mass. 02109.

Chicago Mountaineering Club, 8 S. Michigan Ave.. Chicago, Ill. 60603.

Colorado Mountain Club, 1400 Josephine St., Denver, Colo. 80206.

Hawaiian Trail and Mountain Club, P. O. Box 2238, Honolulu, Hawaii 96813.

Iowa Mountaineers, P. O. Box 163, Iowa City, Iowa 52240.

Kachina Mountain Club, 2217 Encanto Dr., N.W., Phoenix, Ariz. 85026.

Mazamas, 909 N.W. Nineteenth Ave., Portland, Ore. 97208.

Mountain Club of Maryland, 5300 Holder Ave., Baltimore, Md. 21214.

Mountaineering Club of Alaska, 700 Fifth Ave., Anchorage, Alaska 99502.

The Mountaineers, 719 Pike Street, Seattle, Wash. 98101.

Potomac Appalachian Trail Club, 1718 N St., N.W., Washington, D.C. 20036.

Rocky Mountaineer Club, 2100 S Ave., W., Missoula, Mont. 59801.

Sierra Club, 1050 Mills Tower, San Francisco, Calif. 94104.

Wasatch Mountain Club, 425 S. Eighth St., W., Salt Lake City, Utah 84101.

Wilderness Society, Trips Director, 4260 E. Evans Ave., Denver, Colo. 80222.

Yosemite Mountaineering School and Guide Service, Yosemite National Park, Box 577, Yosemite, Calif. 95389.

Sources of Information Emphasizing Nature and Conservation

American Association of Health, Physical Education, and Recreation, 1201 Sixteenth St., N.W., Washington, D.C. 20036.

American Forestry Association, 1319 Eighteenth St., N.W., Washington, D.C. 20036.

Association of Interpretive Naturalists, 6700 Needwood Rd., Derwood, Md. 20855.

Conservation Education Association, Mr. Clarence Billings, Missouri Department of Conservation, P. O. Box 180, Jefferson City, Mo. 65101.

The Mountaineers, 719 Pike Street, Seattle, Wash. 98101.

National Audubon Society, Nature Centers Div., 950 Third Ave., New York, N.Y. 10022.

Sierra Club, 1050 Mills Tower, San Francisco, Calif. 94104.

Wilderness Society, 729 Fifteenth Street, N.W., Washington, D.C. 20005.

Sources of Ski-Touring and Winter-Camping Information*

Rudolf Mattesich, President, Ski Touring Council, West Hill Rd., Troy, Vt. 05868.

American Association of Health, Physical Education, and Recreation, 1201 Sixteenth St., N.W., Washington, D.C. 20036.

Adirondack Mountain Club, R.D. 1, Ridge Road, Glens Falls, N.Y. 12801.

Alpine Club, P. O. Box 2885, Idaho Falls, Idaho 83401.

American Alpine Club, 113 E. Ninetieth St., New York, N.Y. 10028.

Colorado Mountain Club, 1400 Josephine St., Denver, Colo. 80206.

Mazamas, 909 N.W. Nineteenth Ave., Portland, Ore. 97208.

The Mountaineers, 719 Pike St., Seattle, Wash. 98101.

Sierra Club, 1050 Mills Tower, San Francisco, Calif. 94104.

Wilderness Society, Trips Director, 4260 E. Evans Ave., Denver, Colo. 80222.

Yosemite Mountaineering School and Guide Service, Yosemite National Park, Box 577, Yosemite, Calif. 95389.

Appendix 4

CAMPSITES

To Request Campsite Locations in the United States, Canada, and Mexico, Write to Appropriate Sources Listed Below (reprinted from *Better Camping Magazine*):

Alabama: Bureau of Publicity & Information, State Highway Department Building, Montgomery, Ala. 36104.

* (Most of the sources of mountaineering information can usually supply information on ski touring and winter camping as well. Even if they are not listed again under this heading, it may be worth while to send inquiries to them.)

Alaska: Department of Economic Development, Alaska Travel Division, Pouch E, Juneau, Alaska 99801.

Arizona: Travel Information Section, Arizona Department of Economic Planning & Development, Suite 1704, 3003 N. Central Avenue, Phoenix, Ariz. 85012.

Arkansas: State Parks, Recreational & Travel Commission, 149 State Capitol, Little Rock, Ark. 72201.

California: Office of Tourism & Visitor Services, 1400 Tenth Street, Sacramento, Calif. 95814.

Colorado: Colorado Travel Development, 602 State Capitol Annex, Denver, Colo. 80203.

Connecticut: State Park & Forest Commission, 165 Capitol Avenue, Hartford, Conn. 06115.

Delaware: Department of Natural Resources & Environmental Control, Division of Parks, Recreation & Forestry, P. O. Box F, Dover, Del. 19901.

District of Columbia: National Capital Region, National Park Service, 1100 Ohio Drive S.W., Washington, D.C. 20242.

Florida: Florida Department of Natural Resources, Education & Information, J. Edwin Larson Building, Tallahassee, Fla. 32304.

Georgia: Department of State Parks, 270 Washington Street S.W., Atlanta, Ga. 30334.

Hawaii: Hawaii Visitors Bureau, 2285 Kalakaua Avenue, Honolulu, Hawaii 96815. Also: State of Hawaii, Department of Land and Natural Resources, Division of State Parks, P. O. Box 621, Honolulu, Hawaii 96809.

Idaho: Department of Commerce & Development, Room 108, State Capitol Building, Boise, Idaho 83707.

Illinois: Tourism Division, Department of Business & Economic Development, 222 S. College Street, Springfield, Ill. 62706.

Indiana: Department of Natural Resources, Division of State Parks, 616 State Office Building, Indianapolis, Ind. 46204. Also: Indiana Tourist Division, 336 Statehouse, Indianapolis, Ind. 46204.

Iowa: Public Relations, State Conservation Commission, 300 4th Street, Des Moines, Ia. 50319.

Kansas: Department of Economic Development, State Office Building, Topeka, Kans. 66612. Also: State Park & Resources Authority, 801 Harrison, Topeka, Kans. 66612.

Kentucky: Department of Public Information, Travel Division, Capitol Annex Building, Frankfort, Ky. 40601.

Louisiana: State Parks & Recreation Commission, P. O. Drawer 1111, Baton Rouge, La. 70821.

Maine: Maine Department of Economic Development, Gateway Circle, Portland, Me. 04102. Also: State Park & Recreation Commission, State House, Augusta, Me. 04330.

Maryland: Department of Forests and Parks, State Office Building, Annapolis, Md. 21404.

Massachusetts: Department of Natural Resources, Division of Forests & Parks, Box 1775, Boston, Mass. 02105.

Michigan: Michigan Tourist Council, Stevens T. Mason Building, Lansing, Mich. 48926.

Minnesota: Division of Parks & Recreation, Centennial Office Building, St. Paul, Minn. 55101. Also: Minnesota Vacations, 51 E. 8th Street, St. Paul, Minn. 55101.

Mississippi: Mississippi Park System, 717 Robert E. Lee Building, Jackson, Miss. 39201.

Missouri: Missouri State Park Board, Box 176, Jefferson City, Mo. 65101. Also: Missouri Tourism Commission, P. O. Box 1055, Jefferson City, Mo. 65101.

Montana: Advertising Department, Montana Highway Commission, Helena, Mont. 59601.

Nebraska: Nebraskaland, State Capitol, Lincoln, Neb. 68509.

Nevada: Nevada State Park System, Room 221, Nye Building, 201 S. Fall Street, Carson City, Nev. 89701.

New Hampshire: Division of Economic Development, P. O. Box 856, Concord, N.H. 03301.

New Jersey: State Promotion Section, P. O. Box 400, Trenton, N.J. 08625. Also: Department of Environmental Protection, Division of Parks, Forestry & Recreation, P. O. Box 1889, Trenton, N.J. 08625.

New Mexico: State Park & Recreation Commission, Box 1147, Santa Fe, N.M. 87501. Also: Tourist Division, Department of Development, 113 Washington Avenue, Santa Fe, N.M. 87501.

New York: New York State Department of Environmental Conservation, Division of Lands & Forests, Albany, N.Y. 12201. Also: Park Information, Parks & Recreation, Building 2, State Campus, Albany, N.Y. 12226.

North Carolina: Travel & Promotion Division, Department of Conservation & Development, Raleigh, N.C. 27611.

North Dakota: Travel Division, North Dakota State Highway Building, Capitol Grounds, Bismarck, N.D. 58501.

Ohio: Ohio Department of Natural Resources, Division of Parks & Recreation, 913 Ohio Departments Building, Columbus, Ohio 43215. Also: Ohio Development Department, Information Central, Box 1001, Columbus, Ohio 43216.

Oklahoma: Oklahoma Tourism Division, 500 Will Rogers Building, Oklahoma City, Okla. 73105.

Oregon: Travel Information Section, State Highway Division, Salem, Ore. 97310.

Pennsylvania: Bureau of State Parks, Room 601, Feller Building, 301 Market Street, Harrisburg, Pa. 17101. Also: Travel Development Bureau, 402 South Office Building, Harrisburg, Pa. 17120.

Rhode Island: Rhode Island Development Council, Tourist Promotion Division, Roger Williams Building, 49 Hayes Street, Providence, R.I. 02908.

South Carolina: Department of Parks, Recreation & Tourism, Box 1358, Columbia, S.C. 29202.

South Dakota: Travel Division, Department of Highways, Pierre, S.D. 57501.

Tennessee: Division of State Parks, Department of Conservation, 2611 West End Avenue, Nashville, Tenn. 37203.

Texas: Parks & Wildlife Department, John H. Reagan Building, Austin, Tex. 78701. Also: Texas Highway Department, P. O. Box 5064, Austin, Tex. 78703.

Utah: Utah Travel Council, Council Hall, Capitol Hill, Salt Lake City, Utah 84114.

Vermont: Department of Forests & Parks, Montpelier, Vt. 05602.

Virginia: Division of Parks, State Office Building, Richmond, Va. 23219. Also: Virginia State Travel Service, 911 E. Broad Street, Richmond, Va. 23219.

Virgin Islands: Virgin Islands National Park, Box 806, Charlotte Amalie, V.I. 00801.

Washington: Visitor Information Bureau, General Administration Building, Olympia, Wash. 98501.

West Virginia: Division of Parks & Recreation, Department of Natural Resources, State Office Building, Charleston, W.Va. 25305.

Wisconsin: Vacation & Travel Service, Department of Natural Resources, Box 450, Madison, Wis. 53701.

Wyoming: Wyoming Travel Commission, 2320 Capitol Avenue, Cheyenne, Wyo. 82001.

CANADA

Canadian Government Travel Bureau, 150 Kent Street, Ottawa 4, Ontario, Canada.

Alberta: Alberta Government Travel Bureau, 1629 Centennial Building, Edmonton, Alberta, Canada.

British Columbia: Tourist Accommodation, Department of Travel Industry, Parliament Buildings, Victoria, British Columbia, Canada.

Manitoba: Tourist Branch, Department of Tourism & Recreation, 408 Norquay Building, 401 York Avenue, Winnipeg 1, Manitoba, Canada.

New Brunswick: Travel Bureau, Box 1030, Fredericton, New Brunswick, Canada.

Newfoundland & Labrador: Newfoundland & Labrador Tourist Development Office, Confederation Building, St. John's, Newfoundland, Canada.

Nova Scotia: Nova Scotia Travel Bureau, Box 130, Halifax, Nova Scotia, Canada.

Ontario: Ontario Department of Tourism & Information, 185 Bloor Street E., Toronto 5, Ontario, Canada.

Prince Edward Island: Prince Edward Island Travel Bureau, Box 940, Charlottetown, Prince Edward Island, Canada.

Quebec: Department of Tourism, Fish & Game, 12 Ste. Anne Street, Quebec, Quebec, Canada.

Saskatchewan: Saskatchewan Industry Department, Tourist Development Branch, Power Building, Regina, Saskatchewan, Canada.

Yukon: Yukon Department of Travel & Information, Box 2703, Whitehorse, Yukon, Canada.

Northwest Territories: Travel Arctic, Yellowknife, Northwest Territories, Canada.

MEXICO

Mexican Government Tourist Department, 625 N. Michigan Avenue, 12th Floor, Chicago, Ill. 60611.

CAMPGROUND OWNERS ASSOCIATIONS

National Campground Owners Association—USA (NCOA-USA). 3520 N. Western Avenue, Highland Park, Ill. 60035.

Atlantic County Private Campground Association, P. O. Box 61, Mays Landing, N.J. 08330.

California Campground Owners Association, 628 N Street, Sacramento, Calif. 95814.

Cape May County Camp Ground Association, Albert Thornborough, Secretary, P. O. Box 608, Ocean View, N.J. 08230.

Colorado Campground Association, Inc. P. O. Box 104, Lytle Star Route, Colorado Springs, Colo. 80903.

Connecticut Campground Owners Association, Inc. (CCOA), Mrs. Ann Daly, Secretary, Route 2, Danielson, Conn. 06239.

Delaware Recreational Park Owners Association, 212 S. Shore Drive, Dover, Del. 19901.

Florida Association of Camping & Trailering Parks (FACTP), Lynn Morey, President, P. O. Box 15365, Sarasota, Fla. 33579.

Association of Illinois Rural Recreation Enterprises (AIRRE), Route 1, Box 178, Troy, Ill. 62294.

Hoosier Outdoor Recreation Association, Cecil Nichols, President, Route 5, Greencastle, Ind. 46135.

Iowa Association Private Campground Owners (IAPCO), Marcheta Cooey, Secretary, Delhi, Ia. 52223.

Maine Cooperative Camping Areas (MECCA), Robbie Doughty, Secretary-Treasurer, Norway, Me. 04268.

Massachusetts Association of Campground Owners (MACO), Hank Wilgus, President, 200 Hillside Road, Westfield, Mass. 01085.

Michigan Association of Private Campground Owners (MAPCO), Herb Reeves, Secretary-Treasurer, P. O. Box 125, Jones, Mich. 49061.

Minnesota Association of Campground Owners, Inc. (MACO), Donald Eichen, President, Route 1, Box 13, Savage, Minn. 55378.

Missouri Campground Owners Association, Jean McCoy, Secretary, 1209 Parkside Drive, St. Charles, Mo. 63301.

New Hampshire Campground Owners Association (NeHaCa), Roy B. Heise, Executive Director, R.F.D. 3, Richmond, Winchester, N.H. 03470.

New Jersey Private Campground Association, West Kandle, Jr., President, Route 1, Box 208, Andover, N.J. 07821.

Campground Owners of New York (CONY), Route 2, Box 421, Endicott, N.Y. 13760.

Campground Owners' Association of Eastern North Carolina, R. C. "Tim" Malone, Secretary-Treasurer, Route 2, Box 468, Williamston, N.C. 27892.

Ohio Campground Owners Association, P. O. Box 376, Worthington, Ohio 43085.

Campground Association of Pennsylvania (CAP), Bald Eagle Campsite, Route 3, Box 230, Tyrone, Pa. 16686.

Rhode Island Campground Owners Association (RICOA), Mrs. John W. Moroney, Secretary, Moroney Road, Pascoag, R.I. 02859.

South Carolina Private Campground Owners Association, J. Rut Connor, President, Rocks Pond Campground, Eutawville, S.C. 29048.

South Dakota Campground Owners Association, K. F. Olsen, Executive Secretary, 1035 Lawrence Street, Belle Fourche, S.D. 57717.

Southeastern Campground Owners Association, Wayne Morrow, President, Cherokee Campground, Jekyll Island, Ga. 31520.

Vermont Association of Private Campground Owners & Operators, Shirley Hale, Secretary, Horseshoe Acres, Andover, Chester, Vt. 05143.

Virginia Campground Association, Route 2, Box 385, Blacksburg, Va. 24060.

Wisconsin Association of Campground Owners, Box 191, Wisconsin Dells, Wis. 53965.

Wyoming Campground Owners Association, William Parish, Hyland Trailer Park, Cheyenne, Wyo. 82001.

Quebec Camping & Caravaning Grounds Association (ATCCQ), Pierre-Paul Chalifoux, Executive Secretary, 8775 Lacordaire Boulevard, St. Leonard (Montreal), Quebec, Canada.

Directories Offered by Commercial Chain or Franchise Campground Operators with Trailer Accommodations

Kampgrounds of America, Inc., P. O. Box 1138, Billings, Mont. 59103.

Outside Inns of America, Inc., P. O. Box 182, 13085 Patterson Road, Canal Fulton, Ohio 44614.

Safari Camps of America, Inc., Eastgate Plaza, Columbia, Mo. 65201.

Directories Available in Bookstores

Rand McNally *Guidebook to Campgrounds.*
Woodall's *Trailering Parks and Campgrounds.*

Appendix 5

FOOD

Sources of Trail-Packet Foods

Alpine Recreation, 455 Central Park Ave., Scarsdale, N.Y. 10583.

Bernard's Food Industries, 217 N. Jefferson St., Chicago, Ill. 60606 or (if you're west of the Rockies) 222 S. Twenty-fourth St., P. O. Box 487, San Jose, Calif. 95103 or (in Canada) 120 Sunrise Ave., Toronto, Ontario, Canada.

Dri-Lite Foods, 11333 Atlantic Ave., Lynwood, Calif. 90262.

E-Z Food Products Co., 1420 S. Western Ave., Gardena, Calif. 90247.

Freeze-Dri & Dehydrated Foods, Cohasset, Mass. 02025.

National Packaged Trail Foods, 632 E. 185 St., Cleveland, Ohio 44119.

Ad Seidel Trail Packets, 1245 W. Dickens Ave., Chicago, Ill. 60014.

Trail Meals, J. B. Kisky, 1829 N. E. Alberta St., Portland, Ore. 97211.

Trailwise Ski Hut, 1615 University Ave., Berkeley, Calif. 94702.

Brochures, Tips, and Books on Outdoor Eating

Cooking Outdoors (recipe brochure), R. T. French Co., 1 Mustard St., Rochester, N.Y. 14609.

Food for Knapsackers, by Hasse Bunnelle ($1.95), Sierra Club, 1050 Mills Tower, San Francisco, Calif. 94104.

Food News tips (brief pages of suggestions), Quaker Oats Co., Merchandise Mart Plaza, Chicago, Ill. 60654.

Gerry Cunningham's *Food Packing for Backpacking,* Gerry Div., Outdoor Sports Industries, 5450 N. Valley Highway, Denver, Colo. 80216.

Appendix 6

OUTFITTING

Equipment Checklists, Suggestions, Books and Booklets

Backpacking booklets (free), Gerry Div., Outdoor Sports Industries, 5450 N. Valley Highway, Denver, Colo.

Backpacking ($.25), Himalayan Customer Service Dept., 2912 W. Second St., Pine Bluff, Ark. 71601.

The Complete Walker, by Colin Fletcher (353 pages, hardcover, $7.95), at bookstores or from Alfred A. Knopf, Inc., 201 E. 50th St., New York, N.Y. 10022.

The Hiker's & Backpacker's Handbook, by Bill Merrill (320 pages, hardcover, $5.95) at bookstores or from Winchester Press, 460 Park Ave., New York, N.Y. 10022.

Knapsacking Equipment ($.75) and *Sierra Club Wilderness Handbook* ($.95), Sierra Club, 1050 Mills Tower, San Francisco, Calif. 94120.

Lightweight Outing Equipment, Edited by Robert K. Cutter, M.D. (brochure and checklist, $.25), from Sierra Club or Cutter Laboratories, Inc., Fourth & Parker Sts., Berkeley, Calif. 94710.

The Ontario Outdoorsman's Manual, by J. A. Macfie (72-page booklet, $.25), Ontario Department of Lands and Forests, Ottawa, Ontario. Canada.

Outfitters and Manufacturers of Clothing and Gear

NOTE: Included here are manufacturers and suppliers who are known to the author or who replied in detail to inquiries in connection with this book. Those known to rent equipment are marked with an asterisk. There are others in all regions of the country. Many of these companies will supply a catalogue either free or at a small charge to defray cost.

Abercrombie & Fitch, 220 Post St., San Francisco, Calif. 94108, and Madison Ave. at Forty-fifth St., New York, N.Y. 10017.
(clothing and equipment)

Alaska Sleeping Bag Co., 13150 S. W. Dawson Way, Beaverton, Ore. 97005.
(down-filled sleeping bags, clothing, arctic and light backpacking equipment)

Alpine Designs, P. O. Box 1081, Boulder, Colo. 80302.
(clothing, packs, and frames, down sleeping bags, tents)

Alpine Hut, P. O. Box 1456, Wenatchee, Wash. 98801.
(clothing and equipment)

*Alpine Recreation, 455 Central Park Ave., Scarsdale, N.Y. 10583.
(clothing and equipment)

Auto-Fire Corp. P. O. Box 487, Fulton Dr., Corinth, Miss. 38834.
(wood or charcoal camp stove-heater)

Eddie Bauer Expedition Outfitter, 1737 Airport Way, S., Box 3700, Seattle, Wash. 98124.
(clothing and equipment, including extensive down-filled line)

L. L. Bean, Inc., Freeport, Maine 04032.
(clothing and wide range of equipment)

BernzOmatic Corp., 740 Driving Park Ave., Rochester, N.Y. 14613.
(camp lanterns, stoves, heaters, propane accessories)

Binneweg's, 2519 Telegraph Ave., Oakland, Calif. 94612.
(boots)

Thomas Black & Sons, Ogdensburg, N.Y. 13669.
(sleeping bags, camping and mountaineering gear)

Browning Arms Co., Rte. 1, Morgan, Utah 84050.
(clothing, boots, knives, tents)

*Camp & Trail Outfitters, 21 Park Place, New York, N.Y. 10007.
(clothing and equipment)

Camp Trails, 4111 W. Clarendon Ave., Phoenix, Ariz. 85019.
(packs and frames, pack accessories, tents, rainwear)

Codding & Wetzel Ski Center, 8 Pine St., Reno, Nev. 89101.
(ski and mountain gear)

Coleman Co., 250 N. St. Francis, Wichita, Kansas 67201.
(camp lanterns, heaters and stoves, sleeping bags, packs)

Comfy-Seattle Quilt Div., Olin, 310 First Ave., S., Seattle, Wash. 98104.
(sleeping bags, insulated clothing)

Cutter Laboratories, Inc., Fourth & Parker Sts., Berkeley, Calif. 94710.
(first-aid kits, snake-bite kits, insect repellents)

Dunham's Footwear, Brattleboro, Vt. 05301.
(boots and shoes)

Game Winner, Inc., 700 Wharton Dr., S.W., Atlanta, Ga. 30336.
(clothing)

Garcia Corp., 329 Alfred Ave., Teaneck, N.J. 07666.
(camp stoves, lanterns, heaters, knives)

Gerry Div., Outdoor Sports Industries, Inc., 5450 N. Valley Highway, Denver, Colo. 80216.
(packs and frames, tents, rainwear, insulated clothing, light backpacking equipment)

*Gerry Mountaineering, Ward, Colo. 80481, and 228 Grant St., San Francisco, Calif. 94108.
(light backpacking equipment and clothing)

Don Gleason's Campers' Supply, Inc., 9 Pearl St., Northampton, Mass. 01060.
(clothing and wide range of hiking and camping equipment)

Gloy's Division, Amdis Corporation, 12 E. Twenty-second St., New York, N.Y. 10010.
(Heat-Pal heater-stoves, alcohol backpacking and camp stoves, rucksacks, light backpacking equipment)

Gokey Company, 21 W. Fifth St., St. Paul, Minn. 55102.
(clothing and equipment)

*Leon R. Greenman, Inc., 132 Spring St., New York, N.Y. 10012.
(clothing and equipment)

Gutmann Cutlery Company, Inc., 3956 Broadway, New York, N.Y. 10032.
(tents, packs and frames, light backpacking gear and accessories, knives)

*Harberts Brothers, 2338 Shattuck Ave., Berkeley, Calif. 94704.
(clothing and equipment)

Herman's Sporting Goods, 135 W. Forty-second St., New York, N.Y. 10036.
(clothing and equipment)

Himalayan Industries, P. O. Box 950, Monterey, Calif. 93940.
(packs and frames, tents, sleeping bags)

Bob Hinman, 1217 W. Glen, Peoria, Ill. 61614.
(clothing and equipment)

Hirsch-Weis Div., White Stag, 5203 S. E. Johnson Creek Blvd., Portland, Ore. 97206.
(tents, sleeping bags, packs and frames, accessories)

Holubar Mountaineering, Ltd., 1215 Grandview, Boulder, Colo. 80302.
(packs and frames, tents, boots, down-insulated sleeping bags and clothing)

Kelty Pack, Inc., P. O. Box 3453, Glendale, Calif. 91201.
(packs and frames)

*Kreeger & Son, Ltd., 30 W. Forty-sixth St., New York, N.Y. 10036.
(clothing and equipment)

*Mountain Shop, 228 Grant Ave., San Francisco, Calif. 94108.
(clothing and equipment)

*North Face, 2804 Telegraph Ave., Berkeley, Calif. 94705.
(clothing and equipment)

Orvis Co., Inc., Manchester, Vt. 05254.
(clothing and equipment)

Paulin Products Co., 30520 Lakeland Blvd., Willowick, Ohio 44094.
(camp stoves, lanterns, heaters, propane accessories)

Primus-Sievert, 354 Sackett Point Rd., North Haven, Conn. 06473.
(backpacking stoves, camp stoves, lanterns, heaters, propane accessories)

Raichle-Molitor USA, Inc., 3 Erie Dr., East Natick Industrial Park, Natick, Mass. 01760.
(boots)

*Recreational Equipment, 523 Pike St., Seattle, Wash. 98101.
(clothing and equipment)

Refrigiwear, Inc., 71 Inip Dr., Inwood, L.I., N.Y. 11696.
(insulated clothing)

Sears, Roebuck & Co., 303 E. Ohio St., Chicago, Ill. 60611, and branch stores throughout country.
(clothing and equipment)

*Ski Hut (Trailwise Packs), 1615 University Ave., Berkeley, Calif. 94703.
(clothing and equipment)

*Swiss Ski Sports, 559 Clay St., San Francisco, Calif. 94111.
(clothing and equipment)

Ten-X Mfg. Co., 100 S. W. Third St., Des Moines, Iowa 50309.
(pants, light jackets, insulated clothing)

Thermos Div., King-Seeley Thermos Co., Norwich, Conn. 06360.
(camp lanterns, stoves and heaters, Space Blankets, sleeping bags, tents)

Norm Thompson, Inc., 1805 N.W. Thurman, Portland, Ore. 97209.
(clothing and equipment)

Trailblazer, Taylorsville Rd., Statesville, N.C. 28677.
(camp lanterns, heaters, stoves, tents, sleeping bags)

Utica Duxbak Corp., Utica, N.Y. 13502.
(insulated and standard outdoor clothing, rainwear, sleeping bags)

Vasque Div., Red Wing Shoe Co., 419 Bush St., Red Wing, Minn. 55066.
(boots)

Wisconsin Shoe Co., 1039 S. Second St., Milwaukee, Wis. 53204.
(boots)

Wolverine World Wide, Inc., Rockford, Mich. 49341.
(boots, cross-country ski equipment)

Woods Bag & Canvas Co., Ltd., 16 Lake St., Ogdensburg, N.Y. 13669.
(down-insulated sleeping bags and clothing)

Zebco/Traveler Div., Brunswick International, 69 W. Washington St., Chicago, Ill. 60602.
(camp stoves, lanterns, heaters, propane accessories)

INDEX